AFLOAT AT LAST

JOHN CONROY HUTCHESON

1st WORLD
LIBRARY
Literary Society

Afloat at Last

John Conroy Hutcheson

© 1st World Library, 2007
PO Box 2211
Fairfield, IA 52556
www.1stworldlibrary.com
First Edition

LCCN: 2007930800

Softcover ISBN: 978-1-4218-4843-3
Hardcover ISBN: 978-1-4218-4746-7
eBook ISBN: 978-1-4218-4940-9

Purchase *"Afloat at Last"*
as a traditional bound book at:
www.1stWorldLibrary.com/purchase.asp?ISBN=978-1-4218-4843-3

1st World Library is a literary, educational organization
dedicated to:

- Creating a free internet library of downloadable ebooks

- Hosting writing competitions and offering book publishing
scholarships.

Interested in more 1st World Library books? contact:
literacy@1stworldlibrary.com
Check us out at: www.1stworldlibrary.com

1St World Library Literary Society

Giving Back to the World

"If you want to work on the core problem, it's early school literacy."

- James Barksdale, former CEO of Netscape

"No skill is more crucial to the future of a child, or to a democratic and prosperous society, than literacy."

- Los Angeles Times

"Literacy... means far more than learning how to read and write... The aim is to transmit... knowledge and promote social participation."

- UNESCO

"Literacy is not a luxury, it is a right and a responsibility. If our world is to meet the challenges of the twenty-first century we must harness the energy and creativity of all our citizens."

- President Bill Clinton

"Parents should be encouraged to read to their children, and teachers should be equipped with all available techniques for teaching literacy, so the varying needs and capacities of individual kids can be taken into account."

- Hugh Mackay

CHAPTER ONE

IN THE RECTORY GARDEN

"And so, Allan, you wish to go to sea?"

"Yes, father," I replied.

"But, is there no other profession you would prefer—the law, for instance? It seems a prosperous trade enough, judging from the fact that solicitors generally appear well to do, with plenty of money—possibly that of other people—in their possession; so, considering the matter from a worldly point of view, you might do worse, Allan, than join their ranks."

I shook my head, however, as a sign of dissent to this proposition.

"Well then, my boy," went on father in his logical way, anxious that I should clearly understand all the bearings of the case, and have the advantages and disadvantages of each calling succinctly set before me, "there is medicine now, if you dislike the study of Themis, as your gesture would imply. It is a noble profession, that of healing the sick and soothing those bodily ills which this feeble flesh of ours is heir to, both the young and old alike—an easier task, by the way, than that of ministering to 'the mind diseased,' as

Shakespeare has it; although, mind you, I must confess that a country physician, such as you could only hope to be, for I have not the means of buying you a London practice, has generally a hard life of it, and worse pay. However, this is beside the question; and I want to avoid biassing your decision in any way. Tell me, would you like to be a doctor—eh?"

But to this second proposal of my father as to my future career, I again signified my disapproval by shaking my head; for I did not wish to interrupt his argument by speaking until he had finished all he had to say on the subject, and I could see he had not yet quite done.

"H'm, the wise man's dictum as to speech being silvern and silence gold evidently holdeth good with the boy, albeit such discretion in youth is somewhat rare," he murmured softly to himself, as if unconsciously putting his thoughts in words, adding as he addressed me more directly: "You ought to get on in life, Allan; for 'a still tongue,' says the proverb, 'shows a wise head.' But now, my son, I've nearly come to the end of the trio of learned professions, without, I see, prepossessing you in favour of the two I have mentioned. You are averse to the law, and do not care about doctoring; well then, there's the church, last though by no means least—what say you to following my footsteps in that sacred calling, as your brother Tom purposes doing when he leaves Oxford after taking his degree?"

I did not say anything, but father appeared to guess my thoughts.

"Too many of the family in orders already—eh? True; still, recollect there is room enough and work enough, God knows, amid all the sin and suffering there is in the world, for you also to devote your life to the same good cause in

John Conroy Hutcheson

which, my son, I, your father, and your brother have already enlisted, and you may, I trust, yet prove yourself a doughtier soldier of the cross than either of us. What say you, Allan, I repeat, to being a clergyman—the noblest profession under the sun?"

"No, father dear," I at length answered on his pausing for my reply, looking up into his kind thoughtful gray eyes, that were fixed on my face with a sort of wistful expression in them; and which always seemed to read my inmost mind, and rebuke me with their consciousness, if at any time I hesitated to tell the truth for a moment, in fear of punishment, when, as frequently happened, I chanced to be brought before him for judgment, charged with some boyish escapade or youthful folly. "I don't think I should ever be good enough to be a clergyman like you, father, however hard I might try; while, though I know I am a bad boy very often, and do lots of things that I'm sorry for afterwards, I don't believe I could ever be bad enough to make a good lawyer, if all the stories are true that they tell in the village about Mr Sharpe, the attorney at Westham."

The corners of father's mouth twitched as if he wanted to smile, but did not think it right to do so.

"You are shrewd in your opinions, Allan," he said; "but dogmatic and paradoxical in one breath, besides being too censorious in your sweeping analysis of character. I should like you to show more charity in your estimate of others. Your diffidence in respect of entering the church I can fully sympathise with, having felt the same scruples myself, and being conscious even now, after many years, of falling short of the high ideal I had originally, and have still, of one who would follow the Master; but, in your wholesale condemnation of the law and lawyers, judging on the *ex uno disce omnes* principle and hastily, you should remember that all solicitors need not necessarily be rogues because one of their number has a somewhat evil reputation. Sharpe is rather a black sheep according to all report; still, my son, in connection with such rumours we ought to bear in mind the comforting fact that there is a stratum of good even in the worst dispositions, which can be found by those who seek diligently for it, and do not merely try to pick out the bad. Who knows but that Sharpe may have his good points like others? But, to return to our theme—the vexed question as to which should be your occupation in life. As you have decided against the church and the law, giving me your reasons for coming to an adverse conclusion in each instance, pray, young gentleman, tell me what are your objections to the medical profession?"

"Oh, father!" I replied laughing, he spoke in so comical a way and with such a queer twinkle in his eye, "I shouldn't care at all to be only a poor country surgeon like Doctor Jollop, tramping about day and night through dirty lanes and sawing off people's sore legs, or else feeling their pulses and giving them physic; although, I think it would be good fun, father, wouldn't it, just when some of those stupid folk, who are always imagining themselves ill wanted to speak about their fancied ailments, to shut them up by saying, 'Show me your tongue,' as Doctor Jollop bawls out to deaf old Molly the moment she begins to tell him of her aches and pains? I think he does it on purpose."

Father chuckled.

"Not a bad idea that," said he; "and our friend the doctor must have the credit of being the first man who ever succeeded in making a woman hold her tongue, a consummation most devoutly to be wished-for sometimes—though I don't know what your dear mother would say if she heard me give utterance to so heretical and ungallant a

John Conroy Hutcheson

doctrine in reference to the sex."

"Why, here is mother now!" I exclaimed, interrupting him in my surprise at seeing her; it being most unusual for her to leave the house at that hour in the afternoon, which was generally devoted to Nellie's music lesson, a task she always superintended. "She's coming up the garden with a letter in her hand."

"I think I know what that letter contains," said father, not a bit excited like me; "for, unless I'm much mistaken, it refers to the very subject about which we've been talking, Allan,— your going to sea."

"Does it?" I cried, pitching my cap up in the air in my enthusiasm and catching it again dexterously, shouting out the while the refrain of the old song—"The sea, the sea, a sailor's life for me! Hurrah! Hurrah!"

Father sighed, and resumed his "quarter-deck walk," as mother termed it, backwards and forwards along the little path under the old elm-tree in front of the summer-house, with its bare branches stretched out like a giant's fingers clutching at the sky, always turning when he got up to the lilac bush and retracing his steps slowly and deliberately, as if anxious to tread in his former footprints in the very centre of the box-edged walk.

I think I can see him now: his face, which always had such a bright genial look when he smiled, and seemed to light up suddenly from within when he turned to speak to you, wearing a somewhat sad and troubled air, and a far-away thoughtful expression in his eyes that was generally there when he was having a mental wrestle with some difficulty, or trying to solve one of those intricate social problems that were being continually submitted for his consideration. And yet, at first glance, a stranger would hardly have taken him to be a clergyman; for he had on an old brown shooting-jacket very much the worse for wear, and was smoking one of those long clay pipes that are called "churchwardens," discoloured by age and the oil of tobacco, and which he had lit and let out and relit again half a dozen times at least during our talk.

"Very unorthodox," some critical people will say.

Aye, possibly so; but if these censors only knew father personally, and saw how he fulfilled his mission of visiting the fatherless and widow in their affliction, in addition to preaching the gospel and so winning souls to heaven, and how he was liked and loved by every one in the parish; perhaps they could condone his "sin of omission" in the matter of not wearing a proper clerical black coat with a stand-up collar of Oxford cut and the regulation white tie, and that of "commission" in smoking such a vulgar thing as a common clay pipe!

Presently, after his second turn as far as the lilac bush and back, father's face cleared, as if he had worked out the question that had been puzzling him; for, its anxious expression vanished and his eyes seemed to smile again.

"I suppose it's a family trait, and runs in the blood," he said. "Your grandfather,—my father, that is, Allan,—was a sailor; and I know I wanted to go to sea too, just like you, before I was sent to college. So, that accounts for your liking for it— eh?"

"I suppose so," I answered without thinking, just echoing his words like a parrot; although, now I come to consider the thing fully, I really can see no other reason than this heredi- tary instinct to account for the passionate longing that possessed me at that period to be a sailor, as, beyond reading

John Conroy Hutcheson

Robinson Crusoe like other boys, I was absolutely ignorant of the life and all concerning it. Indeed, up to then, although it may seem hardly credible, I had only once actually seen the sea, and a ship in the distance—far-away out in the offing of what appeared to me an immeasurable expanse of space. This was when father took my sister Nellie and me for a day's visit to Brighton. It was a wonderful experience to us, from the contrast the busy town on the coast offered to the quiet country village where we lived and of which my father was the pastor, buried in the bosom of the shires away from the bustling world, and out of contact with seafaring folk and those that voyage the deep.

Yes, there's no doubt of it. That love for the sea, which made me wish to be a sailor as naturally as a cat loves cream, ran in my blood, and must have been bred in my bone, as father suggested.

Before, however, we could either of us pursue the psychological investigation of this theory any further, our argument was interrupted by my mother's coming to where we were standing under the elm-tree at the top of the garden.

Father at once put away his pipe on her approach, always respecting and honouring her beyond all women even as he loved her; and he greeted her with a smile of welcome.

"Well, dear?" said he sympathetically as she held out the letter she carried and then placed her hand on his arm confidingly, turning her anxious face up to his in the certainty of finding him ready to share her trouble whatever it might be. "Now tell me all about it."

"It has come, Robert!" she exclaimed, nestling nearer to him.

"Yes, I see, dear," he replied, glancing at the open sheet; for they had no secrets from each other, and she had opened the letter already, although it had been addressed to him. Then, looking at me, father added: "This is from Messrs. Splice and Mainbrace, the great ship-brokers of Leadenhall Street, to whom I wrote some time since, about taking you in one of their vessels, Allan, on your expressing such a desire to go to sea."

"Oh, father!" was all I could say.

"They inform me now," continued he, reading from the broker's communication, "that all the arrangements have been completed for your sailing in the Silver Queen on Saturday next, which will be to-morrow week, your premium as a first-class apprentice having been paid by my London agents, by whom also your outfit has been ordered; and your uniform, or 'sea toggery' as sailors call it, will be down here next Monday or Tuesday for you to try on."

"Oh, father!" I cried again, in wondering delight at his having settled everything so promptly without my knowing even that he had acceded to my wishes. "Why, you seem to have decided the question long ago, while you were asking me only just now if I would not prefer any other profession to the sea!"

"Because, my son," he replied affectionately, "I know that boys, like girls, frequently change their minds, and I was anxious that you should make no mistake in such a vital matter as that of your life's calling; for, even at the last hour, if you had told me you preferred being a clergyman or a doctor or a lawyer to going to sea, I would cheerfully have sacrificed the money I have paid to the brokers and for your outfit. Aye, and I would willingly do it now, for your mother and I would be only too glad of your remaining with our other chicks at home."

"And why won't you, Allan?" pleaded mother, throwing her arms round me and hugging me to her convulsively. "It is such a fearful life that of a sailor, amid all the storms and perils of the deep."

"Don't press the boy," interposed father before I could answer mother, whose fond embrace and tearful face almost made me feel inclined to reconsider my decision. "It is best for him to make a free choice, and that his heart should be in his future profession."

"But, Robert—" rejoined mother, but half convinced of this truth when the fact of her boy going to be a sailor was concerned.

"My dear," said father gently, interrupting her in his quiet way and drawing her arm within his again, "remember, that God is the God of the sea as well as of the land, and will watch over our boy, our youngest, our Benjamin, there, as he has done here!"

Father's voice trembled and almost broke as he said this; and it seemed to me at the moment that I was an awful brute to cause such pain to those whom I loved, and who loved me so well.

But, ere I could tell them this, father was himself again, and busy comforting mother in his cheery way.

"Now, don't fret, dear, any more," he said; "the thing is settled now. Besides, you know, you agreed with me in the matter at Christmas-tide, when, seeing how Allan's fancy was set, I told you I thought of writing to London to get a ship for him, so that no time might be wasted when he finally made up his mind."

"I know, Robert, I know," she answered, trying to control her sobs, while I, glad in the new prospect, was as dry-eyed as you please; "but it is so hard to part with him, dear."

"Yes, yes, I know," said he soothingly; "I shall miss the young scaramouch, too, as well as you. But, be assured, my dear, the parting will not be for long; and we'll soon have our gallant young sailor boy back at home again, with lots of—oh! such wonderful yarns, and oh! such presents of foreign curios from the lands beyond sea for mother, when the Silver Queen returns from China."

"Aye, you will, mother dear, you will!" cried I exultingly.

"And though our boy will not wear the Queen's uniform like his grandfather, and fight the foe," continued father, "he will turn out, I hope, as good an officer of the mercantile marine, which is an equally honourable calling; and, possibly, crown his career by being the captain of some magnificent clipper of the seas, instead of ending his days like my poor old dad, a disappointed lieutenant on half-pay, left to rust out the best years of his life ashore when the war was over."

"I hope Allan will be good," said mother simply.

"I know he will be, with God's help," rejoined father confidently, his words making me resolve inwardly that I would try so that my life should not disgrace his assuring premise.

"I must go in now and tell Nellie," observed mother after a pause, in which we were all silent, and I could see father's lips move as if in silent prayer; "there'll be all Allan's shirts and socks to get ready. To-morrow week, you said, the ship was to sail—eh, dear?"

"Yes, to-morrow week," answered father bracing himself up;

"and while your mother and Nellie are looking after the more delicate portions of your wardrobe, Allan, you and I had better walk over to Westham, and see about buying some new boots and other things which the outfitters haven't got down on their list."

As he was going into such a fashionable place as Westham, the nearest county town to our parish, at mother's especial request father consented to hide the beauties of his favourite old shooting-jacket under a more clerical-looking overcoat of a greyish drab colour, or "Oxford mixture." He was induced to don, too, a black felt hat, more in keeping with the coat than the straw one he had worn in the garden; and thus "grandly costumed," as he laughingly said to mother and Nell, who watched our departure from the porch of the rectory, he and I set out to make our purchases.

Dear me! the bustle and hurry and worry that went on in the house and out of the house in getting my things ready was such that, as father said more than once in his joking way, one would have thought the whole family were emigrating to the antipodes, instead of only a mere boy like me going to sea!

And then, when everything else had been packed and repacked a dozen times or so by mother's loving hands in the big, white-painted sea-chest that had come down from London—which had my name printed on the outside in big capital letters that almost made me blush, and with such a jolly little washhand-basin and things for dressing on the top of it just inside the lid—the stupid outfitters delayed sending my blue uniform to try on in time; and it was only on the very day before I had to start that it was finished and sent home, for mother and Nellie to see how I looked in it, as I wished them to do, feeling no small pride when I put it on.

Tom, too, got away from Oxford to spend this last day with me at home; and, though he could hardly spare the time, mother believed, from his studies, I think he was more interested in some forthcoming race in which his college boat was engaged.

My last morning came round at length, and with it the final parting with mother and all at the rectory, which I left by myself. Father decided this to be the wisest course; for, as I was, as he said, making my first start in life, it was better to do so in a perfectly independent way, bidding the dear home-folks good-bye at home.

My last recollection was of father's eyes fixed on mine with a loving smile in them, and an expression of trust and hope which I determined to deserve.

The long railway journey to town, which at any other time would have been a rattle and whirr of delight and interest, seemed endlessly monotonous to me, full of sad thoughts at parting with all I loved; and I was glad enough when the train at length puffed and panted its way into the terminus at London Bridge.

Thence, I took a cab, according to father's directions, to the offices of the brokers in Leadenhall Street, handing them a letter which he had given me to establish my identity.

In return, Messrs. Splice and Mainbrace, as represented by the junior partner of the firm, similarly handed me over to the tender mercies of one of the younger clerks of the establishment, by whom I was escorted through a lot of narrow lanes and dirty streets, down Wapping way to the docks; the young clerk ultimately, anxious not to miss his dinner, stopping in front of a large ship.

"There you are, walk up that gangway," he said; and thereupon instantly bolted off!

So, seeing nothing better to be done, I marched up the broad plank he pointed out, somewhat nervously as there was nothing to hold on to, and I should have fallen into the deep water of the dock had my foot slipped, the vessel being a little way out from the wall of the wharf; and, the next instant, jumping down on the deck, I found myself on board a ship for the first time in my life.

CHAPTER TWO

MY FRIEND THE BOATSWAIN

I soon made the discovery on getting there, however, that I was neither alone nor unobserved; for a man called out to me almost the same instant that my feet touched the deck.

"Hullo, youngster!" he shouted.

"Do you mean me?" I asked him politely, as father had trained me always to address every one, no matter what their social condition might be.

"An' is it manin' yez, I am?" retorted my interlocutor sharply. "Tare an' 'ouns, av coorse it is! Who ilse should I mane?"

The speaker was a stout, broad-shouldered, middle-aged man, clad in a rough blue jersey as to the upper portion of his body, and wearing below a rather dirty pair of canvas overalls drawn over his trousers, which, being longer, projected at the bottom and overlapped his boots, giving him an untidy look.

He was busy superintending a gang of dock labourers in their task of hoisting up in the air a number of large crates and heavy deal packing-cases from the jetty alongside, where

John Conroy Hutcheson

they were piled up promiscuously in a big heap of a thousand or so and more, and then, when the crane on which these items of cargo were thus elevated had been swung round until right over the open hatchway, giving entrance to the main-hold of the ship, they were lowered down below as quickly as the tackle could be eased off and the suspending chain rattle through the wheel-block above. The clip-hooks were then unhitched and the chain run up and the crane swung back again over the pile of goods on the jetty for another load to be fastened on; and, so on, continually.

The man directing these operations, in turning to speak to me, did not pause for an instant either in giving his orders to "hoist!" and "lower away!" or in keeping a keen weather-eye open, as he afterwards explained to me, on the gang, so as to see that none of the hands shirked their work; and, as I stared helplessly at him, quite unable as yet to apprehend his meaning, or know what he wished me to do, he gave a quick side-glance over his shoulder to where I stood and renewed his questioning.

"Sure an' ye can answer me if you loike, for ye ar'n't dumb, me bhoy, an' ye can spake English fast enough. Now. I'll ax ye for the last toime—whare d'ye spring from?"

"Spring from?" I repeated after him, more puzzled than ever and awed by his manner, he spoke so sharply, in spite of his jovial face and twinkling eyes. "I jumped from that plank," pointing to the gangway by which I came on board as I said this.

This response of mine seemed, somehow, to put him into all the greater rage—I'm sure I can't tell why.

"Bad cess t'ye for an omahdawn! Sure, an' it isn't springin'—joompin' I mane," he thundered in a voice that made me spring and jump both. "Where d'ye hail from, me joker? That's what I want to know. An' ye'd bether look sharp an' till me!"

"Hail from?" I echoed, completely bewildered by this time; for, being unused to sailor's talk, as I've previously mentioned, I could not make head or tail of his language, which his strong Irish brogue, equally strange to me then, made all the more difficult to be understood. I could see, of course, that he wanted to learn something of me; but what that something was I was unable to guess, although all the time anxious to oblige him to the best of my ability. He was so impatient, however, that he would hardly give me time to speak or inquire what he wanted, besides which, he frightened me by the way in which he roared out his unintelligible questions. So, unable to comprehend his meaning, I remained silent, staring at him helplessly as before.

Strange to say, though, my answer, or rather failure to answer this last interrogatory of his—for I had only repeated his own words—instead of further exasperating him as I feared, trembling the while down to my very boots, appeared to have the unexpected effect of appeasing his sudden outburst of passion, which now disappeared as quickly as it had broken out over my unoffending head.

"Be jabers, the gossoon's a born nat'ral!" he said sympathetically in a sort of stage whisper to the stevedores, although in loud enough tones for me to hear; and then, looking at me more kindly, and speaking in a gentler key than he had yet adopted, he added, accentuating every word separately and distinctly, with a racier Milesian accent than ever: "Arrah, sure, an' I didn't mane to be rough on ye, laddie; but, till me now, whar' d'ye come from, what's y'r name, an' what for are ye doin' here?"

John Conroy Hutcheson

This was plain language, such as I could understand; and, seeing that he must be some one in authority, despite his tarred clothes and somewhat unpolished exterior, I hastened to answer his string of questions, doffing my cap respectfully as I did so.

"My name is Allan Graham," I said on his motioning to those working the crane to stop a bit while I spoke, "and I came up early this morning from the country to sail in the Silver Queen. The brokers in Leadenhall Street, Messrs. Splice and Mainbrace, to whom I went first, told me to go on down to the docks and join the ship at once, sending a clerk to show me the way, which he did, pointing out this vessel to me and leaving me after saying that I was to go on board by the 'gangway,' as he called the plank I walked up by—that is why I am here!"

I uttered these last words somewhat sturdily and in a dignified tone, plucking up courage as I proceeded; for, I began to get rather nettled at the man's suspicions about me, his questions apparently having that look and bearing.

"Och, by the powers!" he ejaculated, taking no notice of my dignified demeanour; "yis, an' that's it, is it? Sure, an' will ye till me now, are ye goin' as a cabin passinger or what, avic?"

"I'm going in the Silver Queen as a first-class apprentice," I answered with greater dignity than ever, glancing down proudly at the smart blue suit I wore, with its shining gilt buttons ornamented with an anchor in relief, which mother and sister Nellie had so much admired the day before, when I had donned it for the first time, besides inspecting me critically that very morning previous to my leaving home, to see that I looked all right—poor mother! dear Nell!

"Whe-e-e-up!" whistled my questioner between his teeth, a

broad grin overspreading his yet broader face. "Alannah macree, me poor gossoon! it's pitying ye I am, by me sowl, from the bottom av me heart. Ye're loike a young bear wid all y'r throubles an' thrials forenenst ye. Aye, yez have, as sure's me name's Tim Rooney, me darlint!"

"Why do you say so, sir?" I asked—more, however, out of curiosity than alarm, for I thought he was only trying to "take a rise out of me," as the saying goes. "Why should you pity me?"

"An' is it axin' why, yez are?" said he, his broad smile expanding into a chuckle and the chuckle growing to a laugh. "Sure, an' ye'll larn afore ye're much ouldher, that the joker who goes to say for fun moight jist as well go to the ould jintleman's place down below in the thropical raygions for divarshun, plaize the pigs!"

His genial manner, and the merry twinkle in his eyes, which reminded me of father's when he made some comical remark, utterly contradicted his disparaging comments on a sailor's life, and I joined in the hearty "ho, ho, ho!" with which he concluded his statement.

"Why, then, did you go to sea, Mr Rooney," I asked, putting him into a quandary with this home-thrust; "that is, if it is such a bad place as you make out?"

"Bedad, sorry o' me knows!" he replied, shoving his battered cheese-cutter cap further off his brows and scratching his head reflectively. "Sure, an' it's bin a poozzle to me, sorr, iver since I furst wint afore the mast."

"But—" I went on, wishing to pursue my inquiries, when he interrupted me before I was able to proceed any further.

"Whisht! Be aisy now, me darlint," he whispered, with an expressive wink; and, turning round sharply on the stevedores, who, taking advantage of his talking to me, had struck work and were indulging in a similar friendly chat, he began briskly to call them to task for their idleness, raising his voice to the same stentorian pitch that had startled me just now on our first introduction.

"What the mischief are ye standin' star-gazin' there for, ye lazy swabs, chatterin' an' grinnin' away loike a parcel av monkeys?" he cried, waving his arms about as if he were going to knock some of them down. "If I had my way wid ye, an' had got ye aboord a man-o'-war along o' me, it's 'four bag' I'd give ivery man Jack o' ye. Hoist away an' be blowed to ye, or I'll stop y'r pay, by the howly pokher I will!"

At this, the men, who seemed to understand very well that my friend of the woollen jersey and canvas overalls's hard voice and words did not really mean the terrible threats they conveyed, although the speaker intended to be obeyed, started again briskly shipping the cargo and lowering it down into the hold, grinning the while one to another as if expressing the opinion that their taskmaster's bark was worse than his bite.

"I must kape 'em stirrin' their stoomps, or ilse, sure, the spalpeens 'ud strike worrk the minnit me back's toorned," said he on resuming his talk with me, as if in explanation of this little interlude. "Yez aid y'r name's Grame, didn't ye? I once knew a Grame belongin' to Cork, an' he wor a pig jobber. S'pose now, he warn't y'r ould father, loike?"

"Certainly not!" cried I, indignantly. "My father is a clergyman and a gentleman and an Englishman, and lives down in the country. Our name, too, is Graham and not Grame, as you pronounce it."

"'Pon me conshinsh, I axes y'r pardin, sorr. Sure, an' I didn't mane no harrm," said my friend, apologising in the most handsome way for the unintentional insult; and, putting out a brawny hairy paw like that of Esau's, he gave a grip to my poor little mite of a hand that made each knuckle crack, as he introduced himself in rough and hearty sailor fashion. "Me name's Tim Rooney, as I tould you afore, Misther Gray-ham—sure, an' it's fond I am ov bacon, avic, an' ham, too, by the same token! I'd have ye to know, as ye're a foorst-class apprentice—which kills me enthirely wid the laffin' sure!— that I'm the bosun av the Silver Quane; an' as we're agoin' to be shipmets togither, I hopes things'll be moighty plisint atwane us, sure."

"I'm sure I hope so, too," I replied eagerly, thinking him an awfully jolly fellow, and very unlike the man I imagined him to be at first; and we then shook hands again to cement the compact of eternal friendship, although I took care this time that my demonstrative boatswain should not give me so forcible a squeeze with his huge fist as before, observing as I looked round the vessel and up at her towering masts overhead: "What a splendid ship!"

"Aye, she's all that, ivery inch of her from truck to kelson," he answered equally enthusiastically; "an' so's our foorst mate, a sailor all over from the sole av his fut to the crown av his hid."

"And the captain," I inquired, "what sort of a man is he?"

"Arrah, now you're axin' questions," he rejoined with a sly look from his roguish eyes. "D'ye happen to know what's inside av an egg, now, whither it's a chicken, sure, or ownly the yoke an' white, till ye bhrake the shill?"

"No," said I laughing. "But, we don't find chickens generally

John Conroy Hutcheson

in our eggs at home."

"Wait till ye thry one on shipboord," he retorted. "Still, ye can't deny now that ye don't know for sure what's insoide the shill till ye bhrake it, an' say for yoursilf—eh?"

"No," I assented to this reasoning; "but, I don't see what that's got to do with the captain."

"Don't ye, honey?" replied he with another expressive wink. "Wait till ye can say for yourself, that's all."

"Oh!" I exclaimed, understanding now that he was shrewd enough not to commit himself to any opinion on the point; so, I did not pursue the inquiry any further.

"Sure, ye'll excuse me, Misther Gray-ham," he said presently, after another word or two on irrelevant matters; "but I must stop yarnin' now, as I expexes the foorst mate aboord ivery minnit, an' he'll be groomblin' like a badger wid a sore tail if those lazy lubbers ain't hove all the cargy in. We've got to warp out o' dock this arternoon, an' the tide'll make about 'six bells'!"

"When is that?" I asked, to know the meaning of this nautical term, which I guessed referred to the time of day, as my friend the boatswain turned round again towards the stevedores, hurrying them on and making them work with a will.

"Thray o'clock. Sure, I forgot ye didn't savvy our sailor's lingo at all, at all," he explained to me between the interval of his orders to the men, shouted out in the same high key as at first. "An', be the same token, as it's now jist toorned two bells, or one o'clock, savin' your prisince, I've got no toime to lose, me bhoy. Jist d'ye go oop that ladder there, an' wait out av harum's way till I've done me job an' can come for ye."

He pointed as he spoke to the steps or stairway leading from the main-deck, where I had been standing alongside of him, to the poop.

I at once obeyed him; and, ascending with alacrity the poop ladder, was able to see from that elevated position the capital way in which he urged on and encouraged the men, until, as if by magic, the heavy boxes and lumbering crates that had but a short time before almost covered the jetty beside the ship, were all hoisted inboard and lowered down into her hold.

Here, below, another gang of stevedores, not less busy than those above, took charge of the stowage of the cargo, slamming the chests and crates about, and so ramming and jamming them between the decks by the aid of jack-screws, that they were soon packed together in one homogeneous mass—so tightly squeezed that not even a cockroach could have crawled in between them, not a single crack or cranny being left vacant.

"Thare now! Sure, an' that job's done wid anyhow for this v'yge, plaize the pigs, ma bouchal!" exclaimed the boatswain with a jolly laugh, after seeing the main-hatchway covered and battened down, and a tarpaulin spread over it to make all snug, gazing round with an air of proud satisfaction, as he slowly made his way up the poop ladder again and came up to where I was standing by the rail looking over. "Don't ye think we've made pretty sharp work of it at the last, sorr, eh?"

"I'm sure you have, Mr Rooney," I replied enthusiastically. For, I could not help admiring the way in which he had got the stevedores to work so steadily and speedily in getting in

John Conroy Hutcheson

the cargo and clearing the ship's deck, so that it was now trim and orderly in place of being littered over with lumber as previously—the active boatswain helping one here, encouraging another there, and making all laugh occasionally with some racy joke, that seemed to lighten their labour greatly and cause them to set to their task with redoubled vigour.— "It's wonderful how you managed them."

"Arrah, sure it's a way I've got wid me, honey," said he with a wink. Still, I could see he was pleased with my remark all the same, from the smile of contentment that overspread his face as he added: "Bless ye though, me darlint, sure an' it's ownly blarney arter all!"

"And what is that?" I asked.

"Faix, ya moost go owver to old Oireland to larn, me bhoy," he answered with a laugh. "Wait till ye kiss the blarney stone, an' thin ye'll know!"

"I suppose it's what father calls the *suaviter in modo*," said I, laughing also, he put on such a droll look. "And I think, Mr Rooney, you possess the *fortiter in re*, too, from the way you can speak sometimes."

"Bedad, I don't ondercumstubble," he replied, taking off his cap and scratching his head reflectively, rather taken aback by my Latin quotation; "though if that haythen lingo manes soft sawder, by the powers I've got lashins av it! Howsomedevers, youngster, we maydn't argify the p'int; but if the foorst mate were ownly aboord, d'ye know what I'd loike to do?"

"What?" I inquired.

"Why, trate them dock loompers to grog all round. They've

worruked loike blue nayghurs; specially that l'adin' man av theirs, that chap there, see him, wid the big nose on his face? I'd loike to pipe all hands down in the cabin to splice the main-brace, if ownly the foorst mate were aboord," he repeated in a regretful tone. Adding, however, the next moment more briskly: "An', by the blissid piper that played before Moses, there he is!"

CHAPTER THREE

WARPING OUT OF DOCK

While the boatswain was still speaking, and expressing his regret at not being able to show the stevedores that he properly appreciated the mode in which they had done their work, I noticed a boy come out from somewhere on the deck below, just underneath where we were standing, and make his way towards the forepart of the ship, apparently in a great hurry about something or other.

I wondered what he was going to do, and was puzzling my head about the matter, not liking to interrupt Tim Rooney, when the boy himself the next instant satisfied my curiosity by going up to the ship's bell, which was suspended in its usual place, under the break of the forecastle, just above and in front of the windlass bits away forward; when, catching hold of a lanyard hanging from the end of the clapper, he struck four sharp raps against the side of the bell, the sound ringing through the air and coming back distinctly to us aft on the poop. I should, however, explain that I, of course, was not familiar with all these nautical details then, only learning them later on, mainly through Tim Rooney's help, when my knowledge of ships and of sea terms became more extended.

Just as the last stroke of the bell rang out above the babble of the men's voices and the shuffling noise of their feet moving about, the four strokes being sounded in pairs, "cling-clang, cling-clang!" like a double postman's knock, a slim gentlemanly young man, with brown hair and beard and moustache, who was dressed in a natty blue uniform like mine, save that he wore a longer jacket and had a band of gold lace round his cap in addition to the solitary crown and anchor badge which my head-gear rejoiced in, appeared on top of the gangway leading from the wharf alongside. The next instant, jumping down from the top of the bulwarks on to the main-deck, a couple of strides took him to the foot of the poop ladder, quickly mounting which, he stood beside us.

"Sure, an' it's proud I am to say yez, sorr," exclaimed the boatswain, touching the peak of his dilapidated cheese-cutter in salute, and with a smile of welcome on his genial face; "though it's lucky, bedad, ye didn't come afore, Misther Mackay, or faix ye'd have bin in toime to be too soon."

"How's that, Rooney?" inquired the other with a pleasant laugh, showing his nice white teeth. "Instead of being too early, I'm afraid I am a little late."

"The divil a bit, sorr," replied Rooney. "We've only jist this viry minnit struck down the last av the cargo; an' if ye'd come afore, why, it's ruckshions there'd a bin about our skulkin', I know."

"No, no," laughingly said the young officer; who, I suppose, was older than he looked, for Tim Rooney told me in a loud whisper while he was speaking that he was the "foorst mate" of the ship. "I'm not half such a growler as you are, bosun; but, all the same, I'm glad you've got the job done. Who's been looking after the dock mateys below, seeing to the stowage?"

John Conroy Hutcheson

"Misther Saunders, sorr," promptly answered Rooney. Adding aside for my enlightenment as to who this worthy might be: "The 'sicond mate,' sure, mavourneen."

"Ah, then we need have no fears about its being well done," rejoined Mr Mackay, or the first mate, as I'd better call him. "Who is our friend here alongside of you, bosun? I don't recollect having the pleasure of seeing him before. Another youngster from Leadenhall Street—eh?"

He looked at me inquiringly as he asked the question.

"Yes, sorr. He's Misther Gray-ham, sorr; jist come down to jine the Silver Quane, sorr, as foorst-class apprentice," replied the boatswain with a sly wink to the other, which I was quick enough to catch. Adding in a stage whisper, which I also could not help overhearing: "An' it's foorst-class he is entoirely—a raal broth av a bhoy, sure."

"Indeed," said Mr Mackay, smiling at the Irishman's irony at my expense, in return no doubt for my whimsical assumption of dignity when telling him who I was. "I suppose he's come to fill the place of young Rawlings, who, you may remember, cut and run from us at Singapore on our last voyage out?"

"I s'pose so, sorr," rejoined Tim laconically.

"I'm very happy, I am sure, to see you on board and make your acquaintance," said the pleasant-faced young officer, turning to me in a nice cordial way that increased the liking I had already taken to him at first sight. "Have you got your traps with you all right, Mr Graham?"

"My father sent on my sea-chest containing all my clothes and things last night by the goods train from our place, addressed to the brokers in Leadenhall Street, as they directed, sir; so I hope it will arrive in time," I replied, quite proud of a grown-up fellow like Mr Mackay addressing me as "Mister."

"You needn't be alarmed about its safety, then, I suppose," observed he jokingly. But, of course, although he might have thought so from my manner, I had really no fears respecting the fate of my chest, and of its being forthcoming when I wanted it. Indeed, until that moment, I had not thought about it at all; for I knew father had despatched it all right from Westham; and when he attended to anything no mishap ever occurred—at least that was our opinion at home!

Fancying, from the expression of my face as these thoughts and the recollection of those I had left behind at the rectory flashed through my mind, that I was perhaps worrying myself about the chest, which of course I wasn't, Mr Mackay hastened, as he imagined, to allay my fears.

"There, there! don't bother yourself about your belongings, my boy," said he kindly; "your chest and other dunnage came down to the ship early this morning from the brokers along with that of the other youngsters, and you'll find it stowed in that after-deckhouse below there, where you midshipmen or apprentices will all live together in a happy family sort of way throughout the voyage."

"Thank you, sir," I answered, much obliged for his courtesy and information; although, I confess, I wondered where the "house" was of which he spoke, there being nothing like even a cottage on the deck, which with everything connected with it was utterly strange to me.

My face must again have reflected my thoughts; for even Tim Rooney noticed the puzzled expression it bore, as I

John Conroy Hutcheson

looked over the poop rail in the direction Mr Mackay pointed.

"I don't think, sorr, the young gintleman altogether onder-constubbles your manin'," he remarked to the mate in that loud whisper of his which the poor man really did not intend me to hear, as I'm sure he wouldn't have intentionally hurt my feelings. "Sure an' it s a reg'ler green hand the bhoy is entoirely."

"Never mind that now; he'll soon learn his way to the weather earring, if I don't mistake the cut of his jib," retorted Mackay in a lower tone of voice than the other, although I caught the sense of what he said equally well, as he turned to me again with the evident desire of putting me at my ease. "Have you seen any of your mess-mates yet, my boy—eh?"

"No, sir," I answered, smiling in response to his kindly look. "I have seen no one since I came on board but you and Mr Rooney, who spoke to me first; and, of course, those men working over there."

"Sure, sorr, all av 'em are down below a-grubbin' in the cuddy since dinner-toime," interposed my friend the boats-wain by way of explanation, on seeing the mate looked surprised at hearing that none of the other officers were about when all should have been so busy. "Ivery man Jack av 'em, sorr, barrin' Misther Saunders; who, in coorse, as I tould you, sorr, has bin down in the hould a-sayin' to the stowage of the cargy, more power to his elbow! An', be the same token, I thinks I sayed him jist now coom up the main-hatchway an' goin' to the cuddy too, to join the others at grub."

"Oh!" ejaculated Mr Mackay with deep meaning, swinging round on his heel, all alert in an instant; and taking hold of a short bar of iron pointed at the end, lying near, which Tim Rooney told me afterwards was what is called a "marling-spike," he proceeded to rap with it vigorously against the side of the companion hatchway, shouting out at the same time so that he could be heard all over the ship: "Tumble up, all you idlers and stowaways and everybody! Below there—all hands on deck to warp out of dock!"

"Be jabers, that'll fetch 'em, sorr," cried Tim with a huge grin, much relishing this summoning of the laggards to work. "Sure, yer honour, ye're the bhoy to make 'em show a leg when ye wants to, an' no misthake at all, at all!"

"Aye, and I want them now," rejoined the other with emphasis. "We have got no time to lose; for, the tide is making fast, and the tug has been outside the lock-gates waiting for the last half-hour or more to take us in tow as soon as we get out in the stream. Below there—look alive and tumble up before I come down after you!"

In obedience to this last hail of Mr Mackay, which had a sharp authoritative ring about it, a short, podgy little man with a fat neck and red whiskers, who, as I presently learned, was Mr Saunders, the second mate, came up the companion way; and as I perceived him to be wiping his mouth as he stepped over the coaming of the hatchway, this showed that the boatswain's surmise of his being engaged "grubbing" with the others was not far wrong.

Mr Saunders was followed up from below by a couple of sturdy youths, who appeared to be between eighteen and nineteen or thereabout; and, behind them again, the last of the file, slowly stepped out on to the deck a lanky boy of about the same age as myself—which I forgot to mention before was just fifteen, although I looked older from my build and height.

John Conroy Hutcheson

"You're a nice lot of lazy fellows to leave in charge of the work of the ship!" cried Mr Mackay on the three presenting themselves before him, slowly mounting the companion stairs, one after the other, as if the exertion was almost too great for them, poor fellows, after their dinner! "Here, you Matthews, look sharp and stir your stumps a bit—one would think you were walking in your sleep. I want you to see to that spring forwards as we unmoor!"

The boatswain had already descended from the poop and gone to his station in the fore part of the ship; and now, with the first mate's words, all was stir and action on board.

The tallest of the two youths immediately dashed off towards the bows of the ship with an alacrity that proved his slow movements previously had been merely put on for effect, and were not due to any constitutional weakness; for, he seemed to reach the forecastle in two bounds, and I could see him, from a coign of vantage to which he nimbly mounted on top of the knightheads, giving orders to a number of men on the wharf, who had gathered about the ship in the meantime, and directing them to pass along the end of the fore hawser round a bollard on the jetty, near the end of the lock-gates by which entrance was gained from the adjacent river to the basin in which the vessel was lying.

Tom Jerrold, the second youth—I heard him called by that name—was sent to look after another hawser passed over the bows of the ship on the starboard side, the end of the rope being bent round a capstan in the centre of the wharf.

Then, on Mr Mackay's word of command, the great wire cables mooring the ship to the jetty were cast off; and, a gang of the dock labourers manning the capstan, with their broad chests and sinewy arms pressed against the bars, as they marched round it singing some monotonous chorus ending in a "Yo, heave, ho!" the ship began to move—at first slowly inch by inch, and then with increased way upon her as the *vis inertiae* of her hull was overcome—towards the lock at the mouth of the basin, the gates of which had been opened, or rather the caisson floated out shortly before, as the tide grew to the flood.

Dear me! What with the constant and varied orders to the gang of men working the capstan, and the others easing off the hawser that had been passed round the bollard, keeping a purchase on it and hauling in the slack as the vessel crept along out of the dock so as to prevent her "taking charge" and slewing round broadside on at the entrance where she met the full force of the stream, I was well-nigh deafened with the hoarse shouts and unintelligible cries that filled the air on all sides, everybody apparently having something to say, and all calling out at once.

"Bear a hand with that spring!" Mr Mackay would roar out one instant in a voice that quite eclipsed that of Tim Rooney, loud as I thought that on first going on board. "Easy there!" screamed Matthews from his perch forwards, not to be outdone; while the boatswain was singing out for a "fender" to guard the ship's bows from scrunching against the dock wall, and Tom Jerrold overseeing the men at the bollard on the wharf calling out to them to "belay!" as her head swung a bit. Even lanky young Sam Weeks, the other middy like myself, had something or other to say about the "warp fouling," the meaning of which I did not catch, although he seemed satisfied at adding to the general hubbub. All the time, too, there was the red-headed Mr Saunders, the second mate, who had stationed himself in the main-chains, whence he could get a good view of what was going on both forward and aft alike, continually urging on the men at the capstan to "heave with a will!"—just as if they wanted any further urging, when they had Mr Mackay at them already and their tramping chorus, "Yo, heave, ho" to fall back upon!

It was a wonder, with so many contradictory commands, as these all seemed to my ignorant ears, that some mishap did not happen. But, fortunately, nothing adverse occurred to delay the ship; and those on shore being apparently as anxious to get rid of the Silver Queen as those on board were to clear her away from the berth she had so long occupied when loading alongside the jetty, she was soon by dint of everybody's shouting and active co-operation warped out of the basin into the lock, drifting thence on the bosom of the tideway into the stream.

Here, a little sturdy tug of a paddle steamer, which had been waiting for us the last hour or more, puffing up huge volumes of dense black smoke, and occasionally sounding her shrill steam whistle to give vent to her impatience, ranged up alongside, someone on her deck heaving dexterously a line inboard, which Tim Rooney the boatswain as dexterously caught as it circled in the air like a lasso and fell athwart the boat davits amidships.

The line was then taken forwards by Tim Rooney outside the rigging, he walking along the gunwale till he gained the forecastle; there, another man then lending a hand, the line was hauled in with the end of a strong steel hawser bent on to it, that had been already passed over the stern of the tug, and the bight carried across the "towing-horse" and firmly fastened to the tug's fore-deck, while our end on reaching the forecastle of the Silver Queen was similarly secured inboard, Tim satisfying himself that it was taut by jumping on it.

"Are you ready?" now hailed the master of the tug from the paddle-box of his little vessel, calling out to Mr Mackay who was leaning over the poop of ours which seemed so big in comparison, the hull of the ship towering above the tug and quite overshadowing her. "Are you ready, sir?"

"Aye, aye!" sang out Mr Mackay in answer. "You can start as soon as you like. Fire up and heave ahead!"

Then, the steamer's paddles revolved, the steel hawser, stretched over her towing-horse astern and attached to our bows, tightened with a sort of musical twang as it became rigid like a bar of iron; and, in another minute or so, the Silver Queen was under good way, sailing down the Thames outwards bound.

"Fo'c's'le, ahoy there!" presently shouted out Mr Mackay near me all of a sudden, making me jump round from my contemplation of the river, into which I was gazing down from over the stern, looking at the broad white foaming wake we left behind us as we glided on. "Is the bosun there?"

"Aye, aye, sorr," promptly replied Tim Rooney, showing himself from behind the deck-house between the mainmast and foremast, which had previously hidden him from the view of the poop. "I'm here, sort."

"Then send a hand aft to the wheel at once," rejoined Mr Mackay. "Look sharp, we're under steerage-way."

"Aye, aye, sorr," answered the boatswain as before; and as he spoke I could see a tall seaman making his way aft in obedience to the first mate's orders; and, before Mr Mackay had time to walk across the deck, he had mounted the poop, cast off the lashings that prevented the wheel from moving, and was whirling the spokes round with both hands in thorough ship-shape style.

This man's name was Adams, as I subsequently learnt; and he was the sailmaker—one of the best sailors on board, and

John Conroy Hutcheson

one of the old hands, having sailed with Tim Rooney, as the latter told me, the two previous voyages. That sort of man, in the boatswain's words, who was always "all there" when wanted.

I am anticipating matters, however, Mr Mackay being not yet done with Tim; for, after telling Adams to go aft to take his trick at the wheel, the worthy boatswain was just about disappearing again behind the forward deck-house as before to resume some job on which he seemed very intent, when his steps were once more arrested by the mate's hail, "Bosun!"

"Aye, aye, sorr," cried Tim Rooney rather savagely as he stopped and faced round towards the break of the poops on which Mr Mackay stood by the rail; and I'm sure I heard him mutter something else below his breath even that distance off.

"Is the anchor all clear?" asked the first mate. "You know we shall want it for bringing up at Gravesend."

"Yis, sorr," said the other. "I ased off the catfalls an' shank painter iver since the mornin'; an', sure, the blissid anchor is a-cockbill, all riddy to lit go whin ye gives the worrud."

"And the cable—how many shackles have you got up?"

"Thray lingths, sorr. I thought that enough for the river, wid a fower fathom bottom; so, I've bitted it at that, an' me an' Jackson are a-sayin' about clearin' the cable range now."

"That's right," replied Mr Mackay, apparently satisfied that at last everything forward was going on as it should; for he turned away from the poop rail and entered into conversation with a stout thickset strange man, dressed in sailor's clothes, but with a long black oilskin or waterproof over his other garments reaching down to his heels, although it wasn't raining at all, being a bright, fine afternoon.

Not only had this new-comer arrived on board without my noticing him, although I had been looking out all the time, but he managed to get up on the poop in the most mysterious way. I was certain he had not been anywhere near the moment before, and yet, now, there he was.

He must be the captain at last, I thought, having been expecting to see that personage appear on the scene every moment; and my impression of his being one in authority was confirmed a moment later, when, from his giving some order or command, Mr Mackay left him hastily, and coming further aft took up a position nearer me, close to Adams, just abaft the binnacle. The oilskin man, however, remained on the weather side of the poop at the head of the ladder, whence he had a good look-out ahead, clear of all inter-vening obstacles, and from which post he proceeded to direct the steering of the ship by waving his arms this way and that as if he were an animated windmill

The first mate interpreted as quickly these signals for the benefit of Adams, passing on the words of warning they conveyed, "Hard up!" or "Down helm!" or "Steady!" as the case might be. These frequent and often contradictory orders were necessary, when, owing to some unexpected bend in the river, the Silver Queen would luff up suddenly and shoot her head athwart stream hard a-port, or else try to "take the bit between her teeth," and sheer into the shore on the starboard hand as if she wanted to run up high and dry on the mud, loth to leave her native land.

She required good steering.

Aye, and careful watching too, on the part of the helmsman; for, in addition to the natural turnings and windings of the channel-way, which were many, the Thames curving about and twisting itself into the shape of a corkscrew between London Bridge and the Nore, the tug had besides continually to alter her course, thus, naturally, making us change ours too, as the tow-rope slackening one moment would cause the ship's bows to fall off, and then tightening like a fiddle-string the next instant her head would be jerked back again viciously into its former position, right astern of the little vessel at whose mercy we were, as if she insisted on the Silver Queen following obediently in her wake.

This eccentric mode of procedure, however, must not be altogether ascribed to any contrariness of disposition on the part of the gallant tug, which, in spite of occasional stoppages and frequent alterations of course, yet towed us along steadily down the river—a pigmy pulling a giant. Such a monster we seemed, lumbering behind her as she panted and puffed huge volumes of black smoke from her tall striped funnel, with much creaking of her engines and groaning of her poor strained timbers, and the measured rhythmical beat of her paddle-floats on the surface of the water, that sounded as if she were "spanking" it out of spite.

No, it wasn't the fault of the little, dirty, toiling tug, whose daily drudgery did not give her time to look after her toilet and study her personal appearance like those bigger craft she had always tacked on to her tail. For these turnings and twistings we had to take in our downward journey to Gravesend and the open sea beyond; the innumerable backings and fillings and bendings this way and that, now going ahead full speed for a couple of minutes, now coming to a full stop with a sharp order to let her drift astern, were all due to the fact of the tug having to keep clear, and keep us clear, too, of the innumerable inward-bound steamers, passenger boats, and other vessels coming up stream. The tideway being crowded with craft of all sorts, navigation was exceedingly difficult for a heavily-laden ship in tow, especially in that awkward reach between Greenwich and Blackwall, where the river, after trending south by east, makes an abrupt turn almost due north. This place I thought the worst part of the journey then when I first saw it; and, I am of the same opinion still, although now better acquainted with the Thames and all its mysteries.

On the bustle that ensued when she began to warp out of dock, I had left the poop, along with the boatswain and the others, going down the ladder at the side on to the main-deck; but, when arrived there, I soon discovered that an idler like myself, standing by with nothing to do, was in the way alike of the ropes that were being thrown and dragged about and of the men handling them—this knowledge being brought home very practically by my getting tripped and knocked about from pillar to post by those rushing here and there to execute the various orders hoarsely bawled out to them each instant, and which would not admit of delay.

"Look out there!" would shout one, nearly strangling me with the bight of a line circling in the air round my unfor-tunate head. "By your leave!" would cry another, jamming me, most certainly without my consent, against the bulwarks, and making me feel as flat as a pancake all over. So, first pushed this way and then driven that, and mauled about generally, I got forced away by degrees from the forward part of the deck, where I had taken up a position in the thick of the fray, back again to my original starting-point, the poop; and here, now, ensconcing myself by the taffrail at the extreme end of the vessel, I thought there was no danger of anyone asking me to get out of the way or move on any further, unless they shoved me overboard altogether.

　　　　　　John Conroy Hutcheson

CHAPTER FOUR

DOWN THE RIVER

I remained for some time very quiet on the poop, for Mr Mackay was too busy giving his orders, first as we worked out of dock and, afterwards, in directing the steersman, when we were under way, to notice me; and seeing him so occupied, of course I did not like to speak to him.

I did not like to talk to Adams either for he was equally busy, besides which I did not know him then; and the same obstacle prevented my entering into conversation with the fat man in the oilskin, although I felt sure he could tell me a lot I wanted to know, I having a thousand questions simmering in my mind with reference to the ship and her belongings, and all that was going on around me on board the Silver Queen, in and on the river, and on either shore.

Still, I had plenty to interest me, even without speaking, my thoughts being almost too full, indeed, for words; for, the varied and ever-varying panorama through which we were moving was very new and strange to one like myself who had never been on board a vessel of any sort before, never sailed down the river Thames, never before seen in all its glory that marvellous waterway of all nations.

I was in ecstasies every moment at the world of wonders in which I now found myself;—the forests of masts rising over the acres of shipping in the East and West India docks away on our right, looking like the trunks of innumerable trees huddled together, and stretching for miles and miles as far as the eye could see; the deafening din of the hammermen and riveters, hammering and riveting the frames of a myriad iron hulls of vessels building in the various shipwright yards along the river bank from Blackwall to Purfleet; the shriek of steam whistles in every key from passing steamers that seemed as if they would come into collision with us each moment, they sheered by so dangerously near; the constant succession of wharfs and warehouses, and endless rows of streets and terraces on both sides of the stream; the thousands of houses joined on to other houses, and buildings piled on buildings, forming one endless mass of massive bricks and mortar, with the river stealing through it like a silver thread, that reached back, behind, up the stream to where, in the dim perspective, the dome of Saint Paul's, rising proudly above a circlet of other church spires, stood out in relief against the bright background of the crimson sky glowing with the reflection of the setting sun just sinking in the west,—all making me wonder where the people came from who lived and toiled in the vast city, whose outskirts only I saw before me, seemingly boundless though my gaze might be.

All this flashed across me; but most wonderful of all to me was the thought that my dream of months past was at length realised; and that here I was actually on board a real ship, going towards the sea as fast as the staunch little Arrow tug could tow us down the river, aided by a good tide running under us three knots the hour at least.

It was almost incredible; and, unable to contain myself any longer I felt I must speak to somebody at all hazards.

John Conroy Hutcheson

My choice of this "somebody," however, was a very limited one, for Mr Mackay and the mysterious man in the oilskin coat, and Adams, the steersman, the only persons on the poop besides myself, were all too busy to talk to me; albeit the former good-naturedly gave me an occasional kindly glance, as if he wished me to understand that his silence was not owing to any unfriendliness, or intended to make me "keep my distance," as I might otherwise have thought.

As for Mr Saunders, the second mate, he had dived down the companion way into the cuddy below as soon as we had got out into the river and were in tow of the tug; and was probably now engaged in finishing his interrupted dinner, as his services were no longer required on deck. Matthews, the biggest of the three young fellows who had come up with him to help unmoor the ship and warp out of dock, had also followed his example in the most praiseworthy fashion.

Jerrold, the other youth, in company with the lanky boy of my own size were still hovering about, though neither had spoken to me; and the two were just now having a chat together by the door of the after-deckhouse, which Mr Mackay had pointed out to me as set apart for the accommodation of us "middies," or apprentices, although I had not yet had an opportunity of inspecting its interior arrangements.

But, strange to say, the noisy gangs of men, who had been only a short time before bustling about the deck below, rushing from the forecastle aft and then back again, and pulling and hauling and shoving everywhere, so effectively as to push me to the other end of the ship and almost overboard, seemed to have disappeared in almost as unaccountable a fashion as the man in the oilskin had made his appearance.

Beyond this latter gentleman, therefore, and Mr Mackay, and

Adams the steersman—to whom I was going to speak once only Mr Mackay shook his head—and my fellow apprentices on the main-deck below, I could only see Tim Rooney forward, with a couple of sailors helping him to range the cable in long parallel rows along the deck fore and aft, the trio lifting the heavy links by the aid of chain-hooks and turning it over with a good deal of clanking, so as to disentangle the links and make it all clear for running out without fouling through the hawse-hole when the anchor was let go.

The boatswain looked quite as busy as Mr Mackay, if not more so, his work being more noisy at any rate; but he wore so good-humoured an expression on his face, and had made friends so nicely with me after our little difficulty when I first came on board, that I thought I really could do no great harm in speaking to him and asking him to solve some of the difficulties that were troubling me about everything.

So resolving, I made my way down the poop ladder for the third time, passing my fellow apprentices, who did not speak, though the lanky one, Sam Weeks, put out his tongue at me very rudely; and, at last I came to where Rooney was standing by the windlass bitts below the topgallant forecastle.

"Hullo, Misther Gray-ham!" he cried on seeing me approach, "I was jist a wondtherin' how long ye'd be acting skipper on the poop! You looked all forlorn up there, ma bouchal, loike Pat's pig whin he shaved it, thinkin' to git a crop o' wool off av its back. Aren't ye sorry now ye came to say, as I tould ye—hey?"

"Not a bit of it," said I stoutly. "I'm more glad than ever now that I came; and I wouldn't go back on shore if I could."

"Be jabers, that's more'n you'll say, me bhoy, a fortnight hince!" he retorted with a grim chuckle, while the other men grinned in appreciation of the remark. "Sure now, though, there's no good anyhow in fore-tastin' matthers, as the ould jintleman aid whin he onhitched the rope from off his nick which he was agoin' to hang himsilf wid. Is there innythin' I can do in the manetoime to oblige ye, Misther Gray-ham?"

"I wish you would tell me a lot of things," I replied eagerly.

"Be aisy, me darlint," he rejoined in his funny way; "an' if ye can't be aisy, be as aisy as ye can! Now, go on ahid wid ye'r foorst question—'one dog, one bone,' as me ould friend Dan'l sez."

"Well, what have become of all the sailors?" I asked to begin with.

"The sailors? Why, here we are, sure, all aloive an' kickin'! What do ye take me an' me lazy mates here for, ma bouchal?"

"Oh, but I mean all those men you were ordering about when I first came on board," I said.

"Bedad, my hearty, there's no doubt but ye ought for to go to say, as ye aid y'rsilf," rejoined the boatswain indignantly. "It shows how grane yez are to misthake a lot av rowdy raps-callion dock loompers for genuine Jack Tars! Them fellers were ownly the stevedores, hired at saxpence the hour to load the ship; an' they wint off in a brace av shakes, as you must have sayn for y'rsilf, whin their job was done! No, me bhoy, them weren't the proper sort av shellbacks. There's ownly fower raal sailors, as ye call's 'em, now aboard, barrin' Misther Mackay and the second mate; an' them's Adams over thar aft at the wheel, these two idle jokers here beside me, the ship's bhoy, an' thin mesilf—though, faix, me modesty forbids me say'n it, sure!"

"And are you really the only sailors on board?" I said, much surprised at this piece of information, being under the impression that the others had all gone below.

"Iv'ry ha'porth," he answered; "that is, lavin' out ye're brother middies, or 'foorst-class apprentices' loike y'rsilf, Misther Gray-ham—faix, though, they aren't sailors yit by a long shot. There's that Portygee stooard, too, that the cap'an's got sich a fancy for, I'm sure I can't till why, as he's possissed av the timper av ould Nick himsilf, an' ain't worth his salt, to me thinkin'!"

"And is that the captain up there now with Mr Mackay?" I asked.

"That the skipper? Bless ye, no, me lad—that's ownly the river pilot!"

"Where is the captain, then?" was my next query, without stopping to think.

"By the powers, ye bates Bannagher for axin' quistions, Misther Gray-ham!" cried Tim, amused at my cross-examination of him—just as if he were in a court of justice, as he afterwards said when he brought up the matter one day.—"Sure, how can I till where he or any other mother's son is that I can't say before my eyes? I can till you, though, where I belaives him to be this blissid minnit; an' that is, by the 'Crab an' Lobster' at Gravesend, lookin' out for to say if he can say the Silver Quane a-sailin' down the sthrame."

"And will he come on board there?" I asked.

John Conroy Hutcheson

"Arrah, will a dock swim?" replied the boatswain in Irish fashion. "Av coorse he will, in a brace av shakes. Ould Jock Gillespie ain't the sort av skipper to lit the grass grow under his cawbeens, whin he says his ship forninst him!"

"Oh, he'll come on board at Gravesend," I repeated after him, my mind greatly relieved; for I had been much concerned as to how and when the captain would make his appearance as well as the remainder of the crew, having read enough about ships to know that the Silver Queen could not well be navigated with such a small number of hands as were only in her then. "And will he bring any more sailors with him?"

"Aye, sonny, the howl bilin' av the crew, barrin' us chaps here alriddy. Yis, an' our say pilot will come aboord there, the river one lavin' us there."

"I'm glad of that," I said. "I thought there weren't enough on board to sail the ship, with only you four men and the boy who struck the bell!"

"Did ye? Then, sure, ye've got the makin's av a sailor in yez afther all, as Misther Mackay aid whin he foorst clapped eyes on ye. An', sure, it's now me toorn to be afther axin' quistions, me bhoy—don't ye feel peckish loike?"

"Peckish?" I echoed, unable to understand him.

"Now, don't go on loike an omadhawn, an' make me angry, as ye did at foorst," he cried. "I mane are yez houngry? For I don't belaive you've hid a bit insoide yer little carcase since ye came aboord this forenoon; an' we're now gittin' through the foorst dog-watch."

I declare I never thought of it before, but, now he mentioned it, I did feel hungry—very much so, indeed, not having tasted a morsel since the hasty meal that morning before leaving home; when, as might be supposed, I did not have over much of an appetite, with the consciousness that it might possibly be the last time I should breakfast with father and mother and sister Nell. The parting with Tom did not affect me much, as he had got priggish and rather above a boy like me since he had been to Oxford.

"By the powers!" exclaimed the kind Irishman when I confessed to feeling "peckish," as he called it, telling him I had not had anything since eight o'clock that morning, "ye must be jist famished, me poor gossoon; an' if I'd been so long without grub, why it's atin' me grandfather I'd be, or my wife's sister's first coosin, if I had one! But, now I've got this cable snug, jist you come along o' me, me bhoy, an' we'll say what that Portygee stooard hez lift in his panthry; for I've got no proper mess yit an' have to forage in the cabin."

"I thought you said, though, he was bad tempered," I observed as I followed the boatswain along the deck towards the door opening into the cuddy from the main-deck under the break of the poop, and only used generally by the steward and cook going to and from the galley forward, the other entrance by the companion way, direct down from the poop, being reserved for the captain and officers, as a rule. "Perhaps he'll say he has nothing left, now that the others have all had their dinner?"

I said this rather anxiously; for, now that I came to think of eating at all, I felt all the hungrier, although until Tim asked me the question I had not once thought about the matter, nor experienced the slightest qualm from that neglected little stomach he had pitied!

"Bedad, whatsomedever he may say, me lad, he'll have to git somethin' for us to ate, an' purty sharp too, if he's forced to fry that oogly ould mahogany face av his!"

So saying, Tim entered the door of the passage leading into
the cuddy, which seemed very dark coming in from the open
deck, and was all the darker as we proceeded, the skylight in
the poop having been covered over to protect the glass-work
while the ship was loading in the dock, and the tarpaulin not
having been yet taken off.

It was like going from the day into the night at one jump;
but, after fumbling after my leader for a step or two, almost
feeling my way and stumbling over the coaming at the
entrance, placed there to prevent the water the ship might
take in over the side when at sea from washing in from the
main-deck, I all at once found myself in a wide saloon
stretching the whole length of the after part of the ship, with
a series of small cabins on either side and two larger ones at
the end occupying the stern-sheets. The doors of the latter,
however, were closed so that no light came through the
slanting windows that opened out on either side of the
rudder-post, above which is usually fitted what is called the
stern gallery on board of an East Indiaman or man-of-war.

The skylight above being now blocked up and the ports and
side scuttles closed, the cuddy was only dimly illuminated by
a couple of glass bull's-eyes let into the deck above, and one
of the swinging lamps that were suspended at intervals over
the long table that occupied the centre of the saloon, the rest
being untrimmed and only this one lit.

The light was certainly dim, but quite enough for me to see
how finely fitted-up the saloon was, with bird's-eye maple
panelling to the cabins and gilt-mouldings; while the butt of
the mizzen-mast that ran up through the deck and divided the
table, was handsomely decorated all round its base, the
Silver Queen having been originally intended for the

passenger trade, although since turned into a cargo ship, and now going out to Shanghai with a freight of Manchester goods, and Sheffield and Birmingham hardware.

A nicely-cushioned seat with a reversible back, so that people could either face their cabins or the table as they pleased by shifting it this way and that, was fixed along either side of the table; and at the extreme aftermost end of this, behind the mizzen-mast, I saw Mr Saunders and Matthews. They were comfortably enjoying themselves over their tea, judging by the cups and saucers before them, and other accompaniments of that meal; and evidently not hurrying themselves about it, for it was more than an hour since they had left the deck.

Our appearance did not at all discompose them; both looking up at our entrance, while Mr Saunders motioned to Tim to take a seat beside him.

"Hullo, bosun! Come in to forage—eh?" he cried, with his mouth still full and his jaws wagging away, "Bring yourself to an anchor, old ship; and bear a hand."

"Thank ye kindly, Misther Saunders; I will sorr, savin' y'r prisince," said Tim Rooney, seating himself, however, on the other side of the table close to the end of the passage way by which we had entered. "I thought it toime to have a bit atwane me teeth as I haven't tasted bit nor sup since dinner, an' that war at eight bells. This youngster, too, wor famished, an' so I brought him along o' me."

"I'm sure you're welcome," answered the second mate, losing no time though at his eating, but still keeping up his knife and fork play while talking. "Ah, the new apprentice Mr Mackay was telling me about just now—eh?"

"Yes, sir," said I for he glanced over towards me as he spoke.

"Well, I hope you'll get on well with your shipmates."

He did not say any more, completing his sentence by draining his tea-cup; and my friend the boatswain, apparently taking this as a hint, shouted out in a tone that made my ears tingle: "Ahoy there, stoo-ard!"

"Yase, yase, I coom," replied someone in a queer squeaky voice, that had a strong foreign accent, from somewhere in the darkness beyond the foot of the the companion way, where the gleam of the solitary saloon lamp did not quite penetrate; "I coom, sare, queek, queek."

"Ye'd betther come sharp, sharp, or I'll know the rayson why," growled Tim Rooney, however, before he could say any more a little dark man with black crinkly hair like a negro's emerged into the light, looking by no means amiable at being disturbed by the boatswain's hail.

"What you want—hey?" he asked angrily. "I got my bizness to do in pantry, 'fore ze cap'in coom aboard."

"What do I want, me joker?" returned Tim, in no way put out by his rude address. "I want somethin' to ate for me an' this young jintleman here. D'ye hear that?"

"Zere's nuzzing left," surlily answered the man. "You should coom down in ze propare time."

"The dickens I should? Confound y'r impudence, ye mangy Porteegee swab! Allow me to till ye, Misther Paydro Carvalho—an' be the powers it's a sin ag'in the blessed Saint Pater to name such an ugly thafe as ye afther him—that I'll pipe down to grub whin I loikes widout axin y'r laive or license. Jist ye look sharp, d'ye hear, an' git us somethin' to ate at once!"

To emphasise his words, the boatswain jumped up from his seat as he spoke; and the other, thinking he was going to make an attack on him, dodged to the opposite side of the table so as to have this as a sort of bulwark in between the irate Irishman and himself, vehemently protesting all the while that there was "nuzzing" he could put on the table.

"Nonsense, steward," interposed the second mate, who with Matthews seemed highly amused at the altercation, the two grinning between their bites of bread and butter. "There's that tin of corned-beef you opened for me just now, bring that."

"An' tay," roared out Tim Rooney, resuming his seat again, which seeing, the dark little man, who had grown almost pallid with fright, swiftly retreated into the darkness of his pantry, muttering below his breath; while Tim, turning to me, asked, "Ye'd loike some tay wid y'r grub, Misther Grayham, wouldn't ye now?"

"Yes," I said.

"Tay for two, ye spalpeen!" he thereupon roared out a second time; "an' ye'd bether look sharp, too, d'ye hear?"

The answer to this was a tremendous smash from the pantry, and the sound of things clattering about and rolling on the floor, as if all the crockery in the ship was broken, whereat Tim and the second mate and Matthews burst altogether into one simultaneous shout of laughter.

"Tare an' 'ouns, he's at it ag'in!" cried the boatswain when he was able to speak; "he's at it ag'in!"

"Aye, he's at it again. A rum chap, ain't he?" said Mr Saunders.

"It's ownly his nasty timper, though; an' he vints it on them poor harmless things bekase he's too much av a coward to have it out wid them that angers him," replied Tim Rooney, adding, as another crash resounded from the distance: "Jist he'r him now. Bedad he's havin' a foine fling this toime, an' no misthake at all, at all!"

"What is he doing?" I asked, seeing that the boatswain and the other two took the uproar as a matter of course, and were in no way surprised at it. "Is he breaking things?"

"No, ma bouchal," replied Tim carelessly. "He's ownly kickin' presarved mate tins about the flure av his panthry, which he kapes especial fur such toimes as he's in a rage wid anyone as offinds him, whin, instead av standin' up loike a man an' foightin' it out wid the chap that angers him, he goes and locks himsilf in the panthry an' kicks the harmless ould tins about, an' bangs 'em ag'in the bulkhead at the side, till ye'd think he was smashin' the howl ship!"

"What a funny man!" I exclaimed.

"He's all that," said the boatswain sententiously. "An' the strangest thing av all is, that whin he's done kickin' the tins about an' has vinted his passion, he'll come out av his panthry as cool an' calm as a Christian, an' do jist what ye wants him, as swately as if he'd nivir bin in a timper at all, at all. Jist watch him now."

It was as Tim Rooney explained.

While he was yet describing the steward's peculiar temperament and strange characteristics, the clattering sounds all at once ceased in the pantry; and the Portuguese presently appeared with a tray on which were clean plates and cups and saucers, which he proceeded to lay neatly and dexterously at one end of the table, looking as calm and quiet as if "butther wouldn't milt in his mouth, sure," as Tim remarked.

Making a second journey back to the pantry, he returned with a dish of cold beef and a cheese, besides a plate piled up with slices of bread and butter, which he certainly must have been cutting all the time he was kicking the tins about. Then, taking a large bronze teapot from the top of a stove in the after part of the cabin, where it had been keeping hot all the while without my noticing it before, the steward poured out a cup of tea apiece for Tim Rooney and myself, asking politely if there was anything more he could get us.

"No, thank ye, Paydro," replied Tim rubbing his hands at sight of the eatables; "this will do foorst rate, me bhoy. Misther Gray-ham, why don't ye fire away, ma bouchal? Sure an' y'r tay's gettin' cowld."

I hardly needed any pressing, feeling by this time as hungry as a hunter; the waiting having sharpened my appetite, as well as the sight of the second mate and Matthews at work at the other end of the table, they only just finishing their meal and going up on deck again as we commenced ours.

We did not lose any time, though, for all that, when once we began, I can tell you, following to the full the second mate's praiseworthy example.

No; for, we made such good use of our opportunities that in less than a quarter of an hour we had both assuaged our hunger—Tim appearing as bad in this respect as myself—by making a general clearance of everything eatable on the

John Conroy Hutcheson

table, the corned-beef and bread and butter and piece of cheese vanishing as if by magic, washed down by sundry cups of tea, which, if not strong, made up for this deficiency by being as sweet as moist brown sugar could make it.

"Sure, an' that Paydro ain't such a bad sort av chap afther all," observed Tim Rooney complacently as he rose from his seat, feeling comfortable as to his interior economy, the same as I did, and at peace with all mankind. "Bedad, I'd forgive him ivrythin', for a choild could play wid me now!"

Any further remark on his part, however, was cut short at the moment by a hail from Mr Mackay down the companion.

"Bosun, ahoy, below there!"

"Aye, aye, sorr!" cried Tim Rooney starting up and making a rush for the doorway leading to the main-deck from the cuddy, "I'm a-coming, sorr!"

And the next moment he was out on the deck, "two bells," or five o'clock, as I knew by this time, just striking from the fore part of the ship as we both emerged from below the break of the poop in view of those standing above—I having followed close on Tim Rooney's heels like his very shadow.

"Oh, you're there, bosun!" exclaimed Mr Mackay as soon as he caught sight of Tim out on the deck below him. "We're just abreast of Tilbury, and the pilot thinks we had better bring up in accordance with Captain Gillespie's orders. Are you ready for anchoring?"

"Quite riddy, sorr," replied Tim, looking up at the first mate and the man in the oilskin, whom I now knew to be the Thames pilot, as they leaned over the poop rail. "Lasteways, as soon as iver I can rache the fo'c's'le."

"Carry-on then. You'll find Mr Saunders already in the bows to help you," said Mr Mackay, hailing at the same time the master of the tug that had brought us so far down the river, and who was at his post on the paddle-box waiting for the pilot's orders to "stand by," the little steamer, having already stopped her engines and now busy blowing off her waste steam, waiting for us to cast off her towing-hawser from our bollard, where it was belayed on the forecastle.

While I was noticing these details, Tim was scrambling forwards towards the windlass bitts, mounting thence on to the forecastle, where Mr Saunders and Matthews, with the other middies, were assembled.

Adams, who had been relieved from the wheel, and the other two sailors, as well as the boy who remained with the rest after coming out to strike the bell, was attending to the compressor and watching the cable on the main-deck, just below the group above, which I now joined, racing after my friend Tim.

Looking back astern as soon as I attained this elevated position in the bows of the ship, I noticed the pilot on the poop bring his arm down, whereupon Mr Mackay by his side, putting both his hands to his mouth for a speaking trumpet, shouted out towards us on the forecastle:

"Are you all ready for'ard?"

"All ready!" yelled back Mr Saunders in reply.

"Let go!" then called out Mr Mackay, the second mate supplementing his cry with a second shout—

"Stand clear of the cable!"

At the same moment, Tim Rooney giving the tumbler a smart stroke with a hammer which he had picked up from off the windlass, the cathead stopper was at once released and the anchor fell from the bows into the water with a great heavy splash, the chain cable jiggle-joggling along the deck after it, and rushing madly through the hawse-hole with a roaring, rattling noise like that of thunder!

CHAPTER FIVE

CAPTAIN GILLESPIE COMES ABOARD

"Oh!" I exclaimed at the same moment, drawing back hastily and tumbling over the boatswain, who with Adams was now busy hauling inboard the tackle of the disengaged cathead stopper. "I'm blinded!"

You see, I had been leaning over the bows, watching the operation of letting go the anchor; and, as the ponderous mass of metal plunged into the river, it sent up a column of spray on to the forecastle that came slap into my face, drenching my clothes and wetting me almost to the skin at the same time.

"Whisht, ma bouchal!" cried Tim Rooney, laughing at my sorry plight as I picked myself up. "One'd think ye're kilt entoirely, wid all that row ye'r makin'! Ye'll niver be a sailor, Misther Gray-ham, if ye can't stand a bit av fun!"

"Fun, you call it?" I rejoined, rather angrily, I must confess, looking down ruefully at my soaking suit. "Why, I'm wet through!"

"Niver moind that," replied he, still grinning, as was also Adams. "Sure, it's ownly y'r say chris'nin', though it's

John Conroy Hutcheson

pricious little av the say there is, be the same token, in this dirthy shoal wather alongside av us now."

"But, it is salt for all that," said I, having had an opportunity of tasting it's flavour, my mouth being wide open when I got the ducking. "It is just like brine and even more nasty!"

Tim laughed all the more at the faces I made, as I spluttered and fumed, trying vainly to get rid of the taste; for, I had swallowed about half a pint at least of the stuff.

"It ain't as good as Paydro's tay that we had jist now, is it?" he observed consolingly. "Thare's too many did dogs an' cats an' other poor bastesesses in it for that, me bhoy; but, faix, ye jist wait till we gits into blue wather an' out av soundin's, it'll be a real trayte for ye to taste it thin."

"I don't know about that," I answered, getting over my little bit of temper and laughing too, he gave such a knowing wink and looked so comical—as I daresay I did, with all the shine taken out of my new uniform—"I think I've had quite enough of it already."

I do not believe I could forget anything, however trivial, that occurred that day, every incident connected with the ship and its surroundings being stamped indelibly on my mind.

The bright February afternoon was already drawing to a close, the sun having set, as usual at that time of year, about half-past five o'clock, going down just as we were in all the bustle of "bringing up;" and, as the Silver Queen had swung with the tide after anchoring, her head now pointing up stream, looking back as it were on the course she had gone over, I had an uninterrupted view from where I stood on the forecastle of the western horizon, with the hazy city still apparent between. I noticed how the warm crimson and orange tints of the after-glow changed gradually to the more sober tones of purple and madder and pale sea-green, marking the approach of evening, a soft semi-transparent mist the while rising from the surface of the water and blotting out one by one the distant objects. It was still light enough, however, to see everything all round near where we were lying, we being then just off the Lobster, midway in the stream, which at that point is about a mile wide, with Gravesend on our left or "port" hand, and the frowning fort of Tilbury guarding the entrance to the river on our right.

All seemed very quiet, as if old Father Thames and those who went to and fro on his broad bosom were thinking of going to sleep; and thus, the shades of night slowly descended on the scene, hushing the spirit of the waters to rest, the ebbing tide lapping its lullaby.

Two other vessels, large merchantmen both, were moored close to ours, and a tug far-away down the stream astern was toiling up wearily against the current with a long string of heavily-laden coal barges in tow, and making but poor headway judging from the long time she took to get abreast of us; while our own gallant little Arrow, which had pulled us along so merrily to our anchorage, was lying-to, about a cable's length off, waiting to see whether we would require her services any further, blowing off her superfluous steam in the meantime, with a turn of her paddles every now and then to show that she was quite ready for more work.

These were all the signs of life afloat in our immediate vicinity on the whilom teeming, busy tideway; and the shore on either side was equally still, only an occasional light, twinkling here and there like a Will o' the Wisp, bearing evidence that some people were stirring, or beginning to wake up as the darkness grew, with that topsy-turvy habit which those who live on land have sometimes of turning day

John Conroy Hutcheson

into night!

We aboard ship, though, preserved the regular ways of sea-folk; and beyond myself and Tim Rooney, who remained behind on the forecastle, to keep me company more than to act as look-out, I believe, not a soul was to be seen on the upper deck of the Silver Queen during this last half-hour of the first dog-watch, now just expiring.

No, not a soul. For Mr Saunders, the second mate, with Matthews and the other apprentices had started aft to their quarters the moment the anchor had been dropped and all things made snug forwards; Mr Mackay had disappeared from the poop, having taken our river pilot down into the cuddy for a glass of grog prior to his departure for the shore to make his way back by land to the docks he had started from, unless he could pick up a job of another vessel going up, and so "combine business with pleasure," as Sam Weeks remarked to Matthews with a snigger, as if he had said something extremely funny; while Adams and the other two sailors, the remaining hands we had aboard, had likewise proceeded towards the cuddy by the boatswain's advice to try and wheedle the steward Pedro into giving them some tea, there not being as yet any cook in the ship to look after the messing arrangements of the crew, so that they were all adrift in this respect, having no proper provision made for them.

Then, all was still inboard and out; nothing occurring, until, presently, the same boy I had noticed before, and who I found was helping the steward stowing provisions in the after-hold beneath the saloon, came out from under the break of the poop at six o'clock to strike the ship's bell, or "make it four bells," nautically speaking, in the same way as he had done previously.

I think I can hear the sound now as I heard it that calm evening when we were anchored off Gravesend. The "cling-clang, cling-clang!" of our tocsin, tolling and telling the hour, being echoed by the "pong-pang, pong-pang!" of the merchantman lying near us, and that again answered a second or so later by the "ting-ting, ting-ting!" of the other vessel further away, the different tones lingering on the air and seeming to me like the old church bells of Westham summoning the laggards of the congregation to prayers. Father wasn't an extreme high churchman, or otherwise I would have said vespers!

After sunset, it grew colder, the wind coming from the east-wards up the open reach of the river; and so, what with my wet things and standing so long on the forecastle I began to shiver. The boatswain noticed this on the sound of the ship's bell waking him up from a little nap into which he had nearly fallen when things became quiet and I ceased to talk.

"Bedad ye're tremblin' all over, loike a shaved monkey wid the ag'ey, sure," he said as he yawned and stretched himself, rising from his seat on the knightheads, where he was supposed to be keeping a strict look-out in the absence of the other men from forward. "Why the dickens don't ye go into the cuddy aft an' warrum y'rsilf, an' dhry y'r wit clothes be the stowve there, youngster?"

"I was just thinking of it," I replied.

"Ye'd betther do it, that's betther nor thinkin'," he retorted; "or ilse ye'll be catching a cowld an' gittin' them nasty screwmatics as makes me howl av a winther sometimes."

As Tim spoke, I heard a splashing noise in the distance, with the rattling sound of oars moving in the rowlocks; and, looking over the bows to the left, I noticed a large boat rowing rapidly up to us from the direction of Gravesend.

This boat, as it got nearer, seemed to be crammed full of men, its gunwale being quite down to the water's edge with the weight of its human cargo.

In an instant, the thought flashed through my mind, ridiculous though it was, that the ship was about to be boarded by pirates, my reading for some time past, and especially during the last week or so when I was assured of going to sea, having been mainly confined to stories of nautical adventure, in which such gentry generally played a prominent part.

"Look, look, Mr Rooney!" I cried stopping my shivering and feeling all aglow with excitement. "Don't you see that boat there coming towards us to capture the ship?"

"Arrah, don't make a fool av y'rsilf, Misther Gray-ham," he answered, laughing and taking the matter quite coolly. "It's ownly goin' to that Yankee astern av us; but the tide bein' on the ebb, in course, they've got to make foorther up the strame towards this vessel, so as to fetch their own craft handsomely—d'ye see?"

He was mistaken, however, for the boat approached closer and closer to us, so that the occupants could be clearly distinguished; and, just as it came alongside, a man in the stern-sheets, who had been steering, stood up, still holding the yokelines, and hailed the ship.

"Silver Queen, ahoy!"

"Begorra, it's the skipper!" ejaculated Tim, recognising the voice at once; and he then shouted out in a louder tone: "Aye, aye, Cap'en Gillespie, it's the owld barquy, sure enough. Stand by, an' I'll haive ye a rhope in a brace av shakes!"

The quiet that had reigned on board now vanished; and all was bustle and activity, the captain's loud hail having been heard by others besides the boatswain.

Almost before he had time to pitch the promised rope to the bowman of the boat so that it could drop down with the stream under the ship's counter, Mr Mackay and the pilot appeared again on the poop; while the others came out on to the main-deck, ready to receive the new-comers in seaman-like fashion, the second mate and Matthews taking up a position just amidships, abaft of the main-chains, where the side-ladder was fixed, acting as a sort of guard of honour as it were.

First to appear on board, holding on to the side lines which the second mate had thrown over within his reach, and stepping up the narrow and slippery ladder cleats as if he were ascending a comfortable staircase, only pausing an instant on the edge of the gunwale of the bulwarks before jumping down on the deck, was a tall spare man with a thin face and high cheekbones, a long pointed nose being also a most prominent feature. He had very scanty whiskers, too, and this seemed to make his face look thinner and his nose longer, so that the latter resembled a bird's beak.

This was Captain Gillespie, as I quickly learnt from the way Mr Saunders and Matthews addressed him; Mr Mackay, meanwhile, giving him a cordial salutation from the head of the poop, his proper place as the officer in command, until his superior took the reins in his own hand, which as yet the captain did not offer to do.

"I hardly expected you so soon, sir," said Mr Mackay,

John Conroy Hutcheson

leaning over the rail. "We brought up earlier than I thought we should, the tide fetching us down in capital time."

"Aye, but I was on the look-out for ye, Mackay, for I told you I'd be aboard almost as you anchored; and, you know, when I say a thing I mean a thing."

"Hear that now?" said Tim the boatswain to me in a loud whisper, he having come down from the forecastle after heaving a rope over to those in the boat, and I following him to where the others were standing on the deck. "Ye'll soon know owld Jock's ways. We allers calls him 'Sayin's an' Maynins'; for that's what he's allars a-sayin'!"

While the captain was exchanging greetings with the mates and Matthews, my other two fellow apprentices being nowhere to be seen, another thin man followed him up the side-ladder from the boat, who, wearing a thick monkey-jacket, looked a trifle less lean than Captain Gillespie; and to him succeeded a shoal of sailors, nineteen clambering in on board after him.

Tim Rooney did not notice these much, only telling me that the one who came immediately in the captain's wake was the "say," or channel pilot, who would con the ship for the remainder of her course down the river and to the Downs beyond; and I may add that this individual was the only thin pilot I have ever seen!

Rooney also said that the batch of men brought to complete our crew seemed "a tidy lot;" but when the last man stepped down from the bulwarks, he seemed a little more impressed, not to say excited.

"Bedad," he exclaimed sotto voce to me, "I'm blissid if the skipper ar'n't picked up that Chinee cook we'd aboard two v'y'ges agone, owld Ching Wang! There's his ugly yalle'r face now toorned this way foreninst you, Misther Gray-ham. Begorra hee don't look a day oulder, if a troifle uglier since I sayed him last!"

"And is he a Chinaman?" I asked, full of curiosity; "a real, live Chinaman from the East?"

"Be jabers he is, ivery inch av him from his blissid ould pigtail, tied up with a siezin' of ropeyarn, down to his rum wooden brogues an' all, the craythur!" replied Tim, stretching out his big hairy fist to the other, who had advanced on seeing him and stopped just abreast, his saffron-coloured face puckered up into a sort of wrinkled smile of pleasure at meeting an old shipmate like the boatswain, who said in his hearty way: "Hallo, ye ould son av a gun! Who'd a-thought av sayin' ye ag'in in the ould barquey, Ching Wang? Glad ye're a-comin' with us, an' hopes ye're all roight!"

"Chin-chin, Mass' Looney," answered the Chinee, putting his monkey-like paw into Tim's broad palm and shaking hands cordially in English fashion. "Me belly well, muchee sank you. Me fetchee chow-chow number one chop when you wauchee."

"Aye, that's roight, me joker; if ye say that I gits me groob whin I wants it, we'll be A1 friends an' have no squalls atwane us," said my friend the boatswain as the Chinaman passed along the deck to the forward deck-house, entering the galley as if he knew the way well, Tim adding as he got out of hearing: "The ig'rant haythin, he nivir can spake me name roight; allers callin' me 'looney,' jist as if I wor a blissid omahdawn loike himsilf!"

Meanwhile, the other men who had come on board, most of whom were fine strapping fellows, as if Captain Gillespie had selected them carefully, scrambled past us to their quarters in the forecastle, the boatswain scanning them keenly with his sharp seaman's eye as they went by, and commenting on their appearance; some being sturdy and having decent chests of clothes, which they lugged after them, while others looked lean and half starved, carrying their few belongings in bags, which showed that they had little or nothing beyond what they stood up in, and were but ill provided for the long voyage we were about to take.

Tim shook his head at these latter.

"Begorra, thay're as lane as Job's toorkey, an' that wor all skin an' faythers,' he muttered. "Thay'll pick up, though, whin they gits out to say an' has a good bit av salt joonk insoide av 'em, instid av the poor livin' thay've hid av late."

As soon as the men had all disappeared under the forecastle, leaving room for us to pass along the deck, the boatswain stepped up to the captain to present himself; and I followed his example.

"Hi, Rooney, man," said Captain Gillespie accosting Tim, "I'm glad you haven't deserted us; though I knew it before, for I heard your voice answering my hail."

"No, cap'en, I'll niver desart the ould ship so long's ye're the skipper," replied Tim. "It's goin' on foive years now since we've sailed togither."

"Aye, close on that; and I hope we'll sail together for five years more, man, for I don't wish a better bosun," responded the other pleasantly. "But, who's that you've got in tow?"

"Misther Gray-ham, sorr," said Tim, shoving me more in front as I took off my cap and bowed.

"Our new apprentice," explained Mr Mackay from the top of the poop ladder as he caught sight of me. "He came aboard just before we left the docks."

"Ah, I thought I didn't see him this morning," observed the captain. And turning to me he said: "I've read a very good letter the owners got about you, youngster, and if you only do your duty and obey orders I'll try to make a sailor out of you, and we'll get on very well together; but, mind you, if you try any tricks with me, you'll find me a scorcher."

"Oh, I think he'll turn out all right," put in Mr Mackay as I blushed and stood before the old fellow not knowing what to say, he looked so stern at me when he spoke. "I've had a chat with him already, and I think he's got the right stuff in him."

"Has he?" returned the captain. "That's got to be proved by and by. All boys promise well at first, but generally end badly! However, I only want him to understand me at the start, and know that when I say a thing I mean a thing, and stick to it, too. Where are the other 'prentices?"

"I told them they might turn in, as there was nothing else for them to do," replied the first mate, excusing them; "they were hard at it all day getting the cargo in, and helping to warp out of dock."

"H'm," muttered the captain, as if he did not like the idea of anyone having a rest off while he was about; and he compressed his lips while his long nose seemed to grow longer. "H'm!"

"What do you think of doing sir?" inquired Mr Mackay in the middle of this awkward pause, by way of changing the conversation. "The wind looks as if it was going to hold from the east'ard."

"Aye, so I think, too," assented Captain Gillespie, looking more amiable as his mind was recalled to action. "It's just the wind we want for going down Channel; and the sooner we take advantage of it, the better. What say you pilot?"

"I'm agreeable," replied the thin man alongside him in the monkey-jacket, who was giving some parting message to the one in the oilskin as he went down the side-ladder to take a passage back to Gravesend in the shoreboat that had brought his comrade off. "I think we'd better lose no time but tow on at once to the Downs."

"Just what I wish," said Captain Gillespie springing up the poop ladder and taking his place by the side of Mr Mackay; and, as the shoreboat pushed off with its now solitary passenger and only one waterman to pull, he shouted out, "Hands, up anchor!"

"Aye, aye, sorr," responded the boatswain, who, expecting the order, had already gone forwards to rouse out the men before they had stowed themselves into their bunks, quickly followed by Mr Saunders the second mate, who also anticipated what was coming; and the next moment I could hear Tim's shrill whistle and his hoarse call, which seemed an echo of the captain's, albeit in even a louder key, "A-all hands up anchor!"

Mr Mackay now hailed the tug, which had been standing by still with her steam up, awaiting our summons, and she steered up alongside shortly; so, while our portion of the crew manned the windlass, hauling in the cable with a chorus and the clink-clanking noise of the chain as the pauls gripped, another set of hands busied themselves in getting in the towing-hawser from the Arrow, and fastening it a second time around our bollards forward.

"Hove short, sir!" soon sang out the second mate from his station on the knightheads, when the anchor was up and down under our forefoot. "It'll show in a minute!"

"All right," answered Captain Gillespie from aft, "bring it home!"

More clink-clanking ensued from the windlass; and, then, as the vessel's head slewed round with the tide, showing that she was released from the ground, Mr Saunders shouted, "Anchor's now in sight, sir!"

"Heave ahead!" the captain roared in answer to the master of the tug; and, a second or two later, we were under weigh and proceeding once more down the river, Captain Gillespie calling to the second mate that he might "cat and fish" the anchor if he liked, as he did not intend to bring up again, but to make sail as soon as the tug cast off in the morning. Adding, as Mr Saunders turned away to give the order for manning the catfalls: "And you'd better see to your side-lights at once, for fear of accidents."

Mindful of my previous experiences on the forecastle, I now kept away from this part of the vessel, especially now that it was crowded with the additional hands that had come on board; and after remaining for some little time near the deck-house, I went up on the poop after the new pilot, who as soon as we were moving took up a similar position on the weather side as his predecessor had done, proceeding likewise to con the ship in the same manner.

The evening was rapidly drawing in; and the big red and green lanterns, which I noticed were placed presently in the fore-chains on the port and starboard sides respectively, began to shoot out their party-coloured gleams across the surface of the water, stretching out to meet the bright

John Conroy Hutcheson

twinkling lights ashore on either hand, which multiplied fourfold as the darkness grew.

Adams was not at the wheel now, one of the fresh hands having taken his place. But I did not mind this man being a stranger, nor did I feel so lonesome and anxious for someone to speak to as was the case earlier in the day; for Captain Gillespie having taken command of the ship, Mr Mackay the first mate was a free man, and he came and talked to me, explaining things very kindly as we pursued our way onward, the tide still with us and adding considerably to the rate we were being towed by the little Arrow, which had red and green side-lights like ours and a bright clear white one at the masthead as well, to show to other craft that she was a steamer under weigh, so that they might avoid fouling in the fairway.

An hour or so after starting from Gravesend, we passed a bright red beacon, which Mr Mackay told me was the light marking the Mucking Flat; and, later on yet, glided by the one on Chapman Head, getting abreast of the light at the head of Southend Pier on our left at ten o'clock, or "four bells" in the first watch—soon after which, the revolving light of the Nore lightship was sighted, like a single-eyed Cyclops, staring at us in the distance one moment and eclipsed the next.

The moon now rose, putting all these artificial lights to shame as it flooded the stream with its silver sheen; but I got so sleepy with the night air after all my excitement through the day, besides being thoroughly exhausted from standing so long on my legs, that, as Mr Mackay was pointing out something in connection with Sheerness and the Isle of Sheppey, and a light house on top of a church—I'm sure I can't recollect what it was all about—I made a stumble forward and nearly fell on my face on the deck, dead beat.

"Poor little chap, you're tired out," said the first mate sympathisingly, putting his arm round me and holding me up; "and when a fellow's tired out, the best thing he can do is to turn in!"

"Eh, sir," said I sleepily. "Turn where?"

"Turn in, my boy," he replied laughing. "Go to roost, I mean. To bed—if you understand that better."

"But where shall I go, sir?" I asked, catching his meaning at last.

"Come along and I'll soon show you," he answered, taking me down the poop ladder to the after-deckhouse, and hailing the steward to show a light: "There!"

It was a little narrow box of a cabin with four bunks in it, two on one side running athwart the deck and two fore and aft. The ends of these crossed each other, and they looked exactly like shelves in a cupboard; while, to add to the effect and trench on the already limited space of this apartment, the floor was blocked up by two other sea-chests besides my own, and a lot of loose clothes and other things strewn about.

The two bottom bunks were already occupied, Jerrold and Sam Weeks snoring away respectively in them; and one of the two upper ones was filled with what looked like a collection of odds and ends and crockery ware.—This was the situation.

What was I to do?

I looked at Mr Mackay appealingly.

"Well, Graham," he said in answer to my look, "you must

make the best of a bad job. These two fellows have turned in first, so, as you're the last comer you've only got Dobson's choice in the matter of bunks—that top one there, which seems a little less crowded than the other, or nothing."

"I'm so weary," I replied, "I can sleep anywhere. I don't mind."

"Then, in you go," cried he, giving me a hoist up, while he covered me over with a blanket which he pulled off young Weeks, that worthy having with his customary smartness appropriated mine as well as his own. "Are you all right now?"

"Yes—th-ank you," I answered, closing my eyes; "g-ood night, sir."

"Good night, my boy."

"Goo-goo-oo-ah!" I murmured drowsily, falling asleep in the middle both of a yawn and of my sentence, only to wake again the next moment—it seemed to me—from a horrible dream, in which I was assailed by a crowd of savages, who were dancing round me with terrible cries and just going to make an end of me, for they were pulling and hauling away at me and shaking me to pieces!

And, strange to say, my first waking impression appeared to confirm the story of my dream; for there really was an awful noise going on all round and a yellow tawny face was bending over me looking into mine, all the yellower from the bright sunlight that streamed through the open door of the cabin fall upon it, while the owner of the face was shaking me and calling out close to my ear in a strange dialect, "Hi, lilly pijjin, rousee and bittee!"

CHAPTER SIX

THE STARLING

Rubbing my eyes and then opening them to the full, wide awake at last, I at once recollected where I was, and who was speaking to me as he shook me.

It was Ching Wang, the Chinese cook, smiling all over his round yellow face, and holding out a tin pannikin with something steaming in it, that sent forth a fragrant smell which made my mouth water.

"Hi me wakee can do," he said in his broken pigeon English, although from having been several voyages he spoke more intelligibly than the majority of his countrymen, "Mass' Looney me axee lookee after lilly pijjin, and so me fetchee piecee coffee number one chop. You wanchee—hey?"

"Thank you," I cried gratefully, drinking the nice hot coffee, which seemed delicious though there was no milk in it. Then, forgetting I was in the top bunk, I sprang off the mattress on which I had been lying, falling further than I thought, it being quite six feet to the deck below; and, knocking down the good-natured Chinaman, with whom I tumbled over amongst the things scattered about the floor and landed finally outside the door of the deck-house in a

John Conroy Hutcheson

heap, rolled up with him in the blanket I had clutched as I fell!

Fortunately, however, neither of us was injured by this little scrimmage, which somehow or other seemed to smooth over the awkwardness of our making acquaintance, both of us grinning over the affair as a piece of good fun.

"Chin-chin, lilly pijjin," said my new friend, as he picked himself up from the deck and made his way back to his galley with the empty pannikin, whose contents I was glad to have swallowed before jumping out of the bunk, or else it would have been spilt in another fashion. "When you wanchee chow-chow you comee Ching Wang and he givee you first chop."

"Thank you," I replied again, not knowing then what he meant by his term "chow-chow," although I fancied he intended something kind, and probably of an edible nature, as he was the cook. But all thoughts of him and his intentions were quickly banished from my mind the moment I looked around me, and saw and heard all the bustle going on in the ship; for, men were racing here and there, and ropes were being thrown down with heavy bangs, the captain and Mr Mackay both on the poop were yelling out queer orders that I couldn't understand, and Mr Saunders and the boatswain on the forecastle were also shouting back equally strange answers, while, to add to the effect, blocks were creaking and canvas flapping aloft, and groups of sailors everywhere were hauling and pulling as if their lives depended on every tug they gave.

It was broad daylight and more; the sun having, unlike me, been up long since, it being after eight o'clock and a bright beautiful morning, with every prospect of fine weather before us for the run down the Channel.

We had come through the Bullock Channel, emerging from the estuary of the Thames ahead of the North Foreland, which proudly raised its head away on our starboard bow, the sun shining on its bare scarp and picking out every detail with photographic distinctness. Further off in the distance, on our port quarter, lay the French coast hazily outlined against the clear blue sky, from which the early mists of dawn that had at first hung over the water had withdrawn their veil, the fresh nor'-easterly breeze sweeping them away seaward with the last of the ebb. The tide was just on the turn, and the dead low water showed up the sandbanks at the river's mouth.

The little tug Arrow was right ahead; but she had eased her paddles and stopped towing us, preparatory to casting off her hawser and leaving the Silver Queen to her own devices. The good ship on her part seemed nothing loth to this; for, those on board were bustling about as fast as they could to make sail, so that they might actually start on their voyage—all the preliminary work of towing down the river by the aid of the tug being only so much child's play, so to speak, having nothing to do with the proper business of the gallant vessel.

And here I suddenly became confronted with one of the discomforts of board-ship life, which contrasted vividly with the conveniences to which I had been accustomed at home ever since childhood.

Before presenting myself amongst the others I naturally thought of dressing, or rather, as I had gone to sleep in my clothes, of performing some sort of toilet and making myself as tidy as I could; but, lo and behold, when I looked round the cabin of the deck-house, nothing in the shape of a washhand-stand was to be seen, while my sea-chest being underneath a lot of traps, I was unable to open the lid of it and make use of the little basin within, as I wished to do if

John Conroy Hutcheson

only to "christen it."

I was completely nonplussed at first; but, a second glance showing me Tom Jerrold, one of my berthmates who had turned out before me, washing his face and hands in a bucket of sea-water in the scuppers, I followed suit, drying myself with a very dirty and ragged towel which he lent me in a friendly way, albeit I felt inclined to turn up my nose at it.

"You thought, I suppose," observed Jerrold with a grin, "that you'd have a nice bath-room and a shampooing establishment for your accommodation—eh?"

"No, I didn't," said I, smiling too, and quite cheerful under the circumstances, having determined to act on my father's advice, which Tim Rooney had subsequently confirmed, of never taking umbrage at any joke or chaff from my shipmates, but to face all my disagreeables like a man; "I think, though, we might make some better arrangement than this. I've got a little washhand-basin fixed up inside my chest under there, only I can't get at it."

"So have I in mine, old fellow," he rejoined familiarly; "and it was only sheer laziness that prevented me rigging it up. The fact is, as you'll soon find out, being at sea gets one into terribly slovenly habits, sailors generally making a shift of the first thing that comes to hand."

"I see," said I meditatively; looking no doubt awfully wise and solemn, for he laughed in a jolly sort of way.

"I tell you what, Graham," he remarked affably as he proceeded to plaster his hair down on either side with the moistened palm of his hand in lieu of a brush. "You're not half a bad sort of chap, though Weeks thought you too much of a stuck-up fine gentleman for us; and, d'you know, I'll back you up if you like to keep our quarters in the deck-house here tidy, and set a better example for imitation than Master Weeks, or Matthews—though the latter has left us now, by the way, for a cabin in the saloon, the skipper having promoted him to third mate, as I heard him say just now. Do you agree, eh, to our making order out of chaos?"

"All right! I'll try if you'll help me," I answered, reciprocating his friendly advances, as he seemed a nice fellow—much nicer, I thought, than that little snob Sam Weeks, with his vegetable-marrow sort of face, my original dislike to the latter being far from lessened by the observation Jerrold told me he had made about me! "I like things to be neat and tidy; and as my father used to say, 'cleanliness is next to godliness.'"

"I'm afraid, then," chuckled Tom Jerrold, "we poor sailors are in a bad way; for, although we live on the water and have the ocean at command, I don't believe there's a single foremast hand that washes himself oftener than once a week, at least while he's at sea, from year's end to year's end."

"Oh!" I exclaimed, making him laugh again at my expression of horror.

"Aye, it is so; I'm telling the truth, as you'll find if you ask the boatswain, whom I see you've got chummy with already. But, by Jove, they're just going to set the tops'les; and we'll have the skipper or old Sandy Saunders after us with a rope's-end if we stop jawing here any longer."

From the way he spoke you would think we had been talking for a very long time; but, really, our conversation had only lasted a couple of minutes or so at the outside, while I was making myself tidy, using a little pocket-comb my mother had given me just before I left home, to arrange my hair, instead of imitating Jerrold with his palm brush. I also utilised the bucket of sea-water as an improvised looking-glass so as to get the parting of my hair straight and fix my collar.

The ropes I had heard thrown about the decks were the halliards and clewlines, buntlines, and other gear belonging to the topsails being let go, the gaskets having been thrown off before I was awake; and now at a quick word of command from Mr Mackay—"Sheet home!"—the sails on the fore and main-topsail yards were hauled out to the ends of the clews and set, the canvas being thus extended to its full stretch.

Then followed the next order.

"Man the topsail halliards!"

Thereupon the yards were swung up and the sails expanded to the breeze; and then, the outer jib being hoisted at the same time and the lee-braces hauled in, the man at the wheel putting the helm up the while, the ship payed off on the port tack, making over towards the French coast so as to take advantage of the tide running down Channel on that side. At the same time, the towing-hawser which had up to now still attached us to the tug, was dropped over the bows as we got under weigh.

The Silver Queen seemed to rejoice in her freedom, tossing her bowsprit in the air as she cast off from the tug; and then, heeling over to leeward as she felt the full force of the breeze on her quarter, she gave a plunge downwards, ploughing up the water, now beginning to be crested with little choppy waves as the wind met the current, and sending it sparkling and foaming past her bulwarks, and away behind her in a long creamy wake, that stretched out like a fan astern till it touched Margate sands in the distance.

I now went up on the poop, avoiding the weather side, which Tim Rooney had told me the previous evening was always sacred to the captain or commanding officer on duty; for I noticed that the thin pilot in the monkey-jacket, who had just mounted the companion stairs from the cuddy after having his late breakfast, was walking up and down there with Captain Gillespie, the latter smiling and rubbing his hands together, evidently in good humour at our making such a fine start.

"Good morning!" said Mr Mackay, who was standing at the head of the lee poop ladder, accosting me as I reached the top. "I hope you had a sound, healthy sleep, my boy?"

"Oh yes, thank you, sir," I replied. "I'm ashamed of being so late when everybody else has been so long astir. Isn't there something I can do, sir?"

"No, my boy, not at present," cried he, laughing at my eagerness to be useful, which arose from my seeing Jerrold nimbly mounting up the after-shrouds with Matthews and a couple of other hands to loosen the mizzen-topsail. "You haven't got your sea-legs yet, nor learnt your way about the ship; and so you would be more a hindrance than a help on a yard up aloft."

"But I may go up by and by?" I asked, a little disappointed at not being allowed to climb with the others, they looked so jolly swinging about as if they enjoyed it; with Tom Jerrold nodding and grinning at me over the yard. "Sha'n't I, sir?"

"Aye, by and by, when there's no fear of your tumbling overboard, youngster," he answered good-naturedly. "You must be content with looking on for a while and picking up

John Conroy Hutcheson

information. Use your eyes and ears, my lad; and then we'll see you shortly reefing a royal in a gale! You needn't be afraid of our not making you work when the time comes."

"I'll be very glad, sir," I said. "I do not like being idle when others are busy."

"A very good sentiment that, my boy; and I only hope you'll stick to it," he replied earnestly. "That desire to be doing something shows that you're no skulker, but have the makings of a sailor in you, as I told the captain last night; so, you see, you mustn't go back on the character I've given you."

"I won't, sir, if I can help it," said I, with my heart in my words; and, from Mr Mackay's look I'm sure he believed me, but just at that moment he crossed over to the other side of the poop, Captain Gillespie calling him and telling him what he wanted before he could take a step to reach him.

"We'd better get some more sail on her," said the captain, still rubbing his hand as if rolling pills between them; "the pilot thinks so, and so do I."

"All right, sir!" replied Mr Mackay; and going to the front by the rail, he shouted out forwards:

"Hands make sail!"

"Aye, aye, sorr,' I heard the boatswain answer in his rich Irish brogue, supplemented by his hail to the crew of: "Tumble up there, ye spalpeens! Show a leg now, smart!"

"Lay out aloft there and loose the fore and main topgallants, my men!" cried Mr Mackay, as soon as he saw the sailors out on the deck. "And, some of you, come aft here to set the spanker!"

Up the ratlines of the rigging clambered the men, racing against each other to see who would be up first, while others below cast off the ropes holding up the bunt and leech of the sail, as soon as the smart fellows had unloosed the gaskets; and then, the folds of the sails being dropped, were sheeted home with a "one, two, three, and a yo heave ho!" by those on deck, before the top men were half-way down the shrouds.

Matthews and Jerrold alone managed the mizzen topgallant-sail, after which the spanker was set, making the ship drive on all the faster through the water; though, even then, Captain Gillespie was not content yet.

"We must have the main-sail and forecourse on her," he said a few minutes later to Mr Mackay. "It would be a sin to lose this wind."

"All right, sir!" replied the other; and the order being at once given, these lower sails were soon set, adding considerably to our average of canvas, the vessel now forging ahead at a good eight knots or more; and we passed Deal, on our starboard hand, some couple of hours or so from the time of our leaving the river.

"I call this going—eh?" cried Captain Gillespie to the pilot, while he cocked his eye up aloft as if he seriously thought of setting the royals. "I said I'd get out of the Straits before the afternoon; and, you know, when I say a thing I always mean a thing!"

"Aye, aye," returned the other, motioning to the helmsman to keep her off a bit as the ship luffed up; "but we'll soon have to come about, for we'll be getting a little too near that shoal to the eastwards on this tack."

"Very good," said the captain; "whenever you please."

"I think we'll wait till we pass the South Sands light," replied the pilot. "Then we can round the Foreland handsomely on the starboard tack with the wind well abaft our beam."

"All right!" was Captain Gillespie's laconic response, rubbing his hands gleefully together again. "Carry-on."

Noticing Tom Jerrold just then on the main-deck, I went down from off the poop and joined him.

"Have you had any breakfast?" he asked when I got up to him, patting his stomach significantly. "I was just thinking of getting mine as I feel very empty here, for all the rest have had theirs."

"No, I haven't had anything but some coffee the cook brought me a long while ago, and I feel hungry too," I replied. "Where do we get our meals?"

"In the cuddy, after the captain and mates have done grubbing," he said. "Come along with me and we'll rouse up that Portugee steward."

"What! Pedro?"

"Yes; you've made his acquaintance already, I see. Did you notice anything particular about him?"

"Only his temper," I said. "Dear me, hasn't he got an awful one!"

"Bless you he only puts half of it on to try and frighten you if you're a new hand," replied Jerrold as he jauntily walked into the cuddy with the air of a commodore. "Only give him a little backsheesh and he'll do anything for you."

"Backsheesh! What is that?"

"Palm oil—tip him. Do you twig?" whispered Tom; "but, mum's the word, here we are in the lion's den!"

To my surprise, however, the whilom cranky steward made no difficulty about supplying our wants; and I strongly suspect that my fellow apprentice must have carried out his advice anent tipping Pedro that very morning, he was so extremely civil. He gave us some cold fried ham and eggs, the remains no doubt of Captain Gillespie's breakfast, with the addition of some coffee which he heated up for us especially, and which I enjoyed all the more from its having some milk in it—it was the very last milk that I tasted until I landed in England again, alas!

After making a hearty meal, I suggested to Tom that if he'd nothing to do we'd better go to work and make our cabin in the deck-house more cosy and habitable; and, on his agreeing, we left the cuddy, I taking care before going out to slip five shillings into the steward's ready palm as an earnest of my future intentions towards him should he treat me well.

"Well, you're in luck's way now, old fellow," said Jerrold when I told him of this outside the passage, Pedro retiring to his pantry to secrete my tip along with others he had probably already received. "Only a day on board, and friends with the first mate, boatswain, cook, and steward; and, last, though by no means least, your humble servant myself, I being the most important personage of all."

"Are you really such a very important personage?" I

John Conroy Hutcheson

rejoined, laughing at his affected air—"as big a man as the captain?"

"Aye, for after another voyage I'll be made third mate too, like Matthews, and then second, and then first; and after that a captain like our old friend 'sayings and meanings' here, only a regular tip-topper, unlike him."

"Aren't you anticipating matters a bit, like the Barber's Fifth Brother in the Arabian Nights," said I—"counting your chickens before they're hatched, as my father says?"

"Your father must be a wonderful man," he retorted; but he grinned so funnily that I really couldn't be angry, though I coloured up at his remark; seeing which, to change the subject, he added, "Come and let us rouse out the deck-house and make things comfortable there for ourselves."

This was easier said than done; for in the first place Weeks, who only seemed to think of eating and sleeping and nothing else, was having a quiet "caulk," as sailors call it, cuddled up in the bunk appropriated by Jerrold as being the roomiest, with all our blankets wrapped round him, although the day was quite warm and spring-like for February.

"Hullo!" cried Jerrold at the sight of the slumbering lamb, seizing hold of the blankets. "Out you go, my hearty; and confound your cheek for taking possession of my crib!"

With these words, giving a good tug, Weeks was rolled out on the deck, tumbling on his head. This angered him greatly, and he got up as red as a turkey cock, with the freckles on his face coming out in strong relief.

Seeing that Tom Jerrold was the culprit, however, he soon quieted down, being an arrant sneak and afraid of him.

"What did you do that for?" he whined. "I was only having a nap."

"You're always napping," retorted Tom; "and I should like to know what the dickens you mean by going snoozing in my bunk? I've half a mind to punch your head. The next time I catch you at it I'll keelhaul you, Master Sammy, by Jupiter!"

Jerrold kept on grumbling away, pretending to be very angry; and he frightened Weeks so that he forgot the ugly knock he had received on his own head, and apologised abjectly for the offence he had committed. Tom then allowed his assumed indignation to pass away, and forgave him on the condition that he took away all the spare crockery ware, which the steward had stowed in the top bunk of the deck-house, into the cuddy, giving it to the Portuguese with his, Tom's, compliments.

Weeks thereupon proceeded to execute this mission, Jerrold and I awaiting the result with much anticipated enjoyment, Tom saying to me confidentially as he started for the cuddy, "Won't Pedro carry-on at him! I wouldn't be in the young fool's shoes for something."

The denouement justified our expectations; for, no sooner had Weeks entered the passage way than he came flying out again looking awfully scared, a tremendous crash following as if all the crockery ware was pitched after him, bang! Next, we heard Pedro swearing away in his native tongue, and kicking his preserved meat tins about his pantry at such a rate that Captain Gillespie sang out on the poop above, and sent Matthews down the companion to find out what he was making all the row about. This finally quieted the steward down, but subdued mutterings came to our ears from the cuddy for long afterwards, Pedro never having been so roused up before, not even when Tim Rooney tackled him on the previous day.

Weeks got very angry on our laughing at him when he returned crestfallen to the deck-house, and he went off forwards in high dudgeon; but this did not make any difference to us, we being rather pleased at getting rid of his company—at least I was, for one. So we went on arranging the chests and things in the little cabin until we ultimately made it quite ship-shape and comfortable. As Jerrold had proposed, he had his chest on one side of the doorway and mine and Weeks's were now stowed alongside our bunks, just sufficient space and no more being left for us to open them without having to shift them, and also to get in and out of the cabin.

"Be jabers ye've made a tidy job av it, lads," said the boatswain, coming up as we finished, and surveying approvingly our arrangements. "I couldn't have done it no betther mesilf! Ye can well-nigh swing a cat round, which it would a poozled ye to a-done afore, faix. An' sure, Misther Grayham, does ye loike bayin' at say yit?"

"Of course I do," I answered. "Why shouldn't I?"

"Begorra, ye're a caution!" he ejaculated. "An', did that haythin, Ching Wang, wake ye up this mornin' wid some coffee, as he promised me. I wor too busy to say you or ax you afore?"

"Yes," I replied; "and many thanks for your kind thoughtfulness."

"Stow that flummery," he cried; and to prevent my thanking him he began to tell Jerrold and me one of his funny yarns about a pig which his grandmother had, but unfortunately the story was nipped in the bud by a roar from the captain on the poop.

"Hands 'bout ship!"

In a second the boatswain was away piping on the forecastle, and ropes cast off and sails flapping again.

"Helms a-lee!" was the next order from the captain, followed by a second which grew familiar enough to me in time. "Raise tacks and sheets!" and the foretack and main-sheet were cast off with the weather main-brace hauled taut.

Then came the final command, "Main-sail haul!" and the Silver Queen came up to the wind slowly. The foretack being then boarded and the main-sheet hauled aft, she heeled over on the starboard tack with the wind well on her starboard beam, heading towards the South Foreland, which she rounded soon after.

Off Dungeness, which we reached about three in the afternoon, or "six bells," exactly twenty-four hours from the time of our leaving the docks, we hove-to, backing our main-topsail and hoisting a whiff at the peak as a signal that we wanted a boat from the shore to disembark our pilot.

A dandy-rigged little cutter soon came dancing out to us; when the thin man in the monkey-jacket took his farewell of Captain Gillespie and went on board to be landed, the Silver Queen filling again and shaping a course west by south for Beachy Head, and so on down channel, free now of the last link that bound her to old England.

The afternoon, however, was not destined to pass without another incident.

It was getting on for sunset; and, steering more to the west

John Conroy Hutcheson

well out from the land so as to avoid the Royal Sovereign shoal, we must have been just abreast of Hastings, although we could not see it, the weather thickening at the time, when suddenly a strange bird settled on the rigging utterly exhausted. It had evidently been blown out to sea and lost its reckoning.

"Here's a Mother Carey's chicken come aboard!" cried Sam Weeks, making for the poor tired thing to catch it. "I'll have it."

"Don't hurt it, it's a starling," I said. "Can't you see its nice shiny black-and-green plumage, and its yellow bill like a blackbird? Leave the poor little thing alone, it's tired to death."

"A starling! your grandmother!" he retorted, nettled at my speaking, and bearing me a grudge still for what had recently occurred in the deck-house. "A fine lot you know about birds, no doubt! I tell you I'll catch it, and kill it too, if I like."

So saying, he made another grab at the little creature, which, just fluttering off the rigging in time, managed for the moment to escape him and perched on the backstay, when the cruel lad hove a marlin-spike at it. He again missed the bird, however, and it then flew straight into the bosom of my jacket as I stood in front of it, whistling to entice it in that chirpy kissing way in which you hear starlings call to each other, having learnt the way to do so from a boy at Westham.

Weeks was furious at my succeeding in the capture of the poor bird when he had failed; although he would not understand that I had only coaxed it to protect it from his violence. Poor little thing. I could feel its little heart palpitating against mine as it rested safe within the breast of my jacket, nestling close to my flannel shirt!

"Why, you've caught it yourself after all, you mean sneak!" he cried; and thinking he was more of a match for me than he was for Tom Jerrold, and could bully me easily, he made a dash at my jacket collar to tear it open, exclaiming at the same time, "I will have it, I tell you. There!"

He made a wrong calculation, however, for, holding my right arm across my chest so as to keep my jacket closed and protect the poor bird that had sought my succour, I threw out my left hand; and so, as he rushed towards me, my outstretched fist caught him clean between the eyes, tumbling him backwards, as if he had been shot, on to the deck, where he rolled over into a lot of water that had accumulated in the scuppers to leeward—the pool in the scuppers washing forwards and then aft as the ship rose and fell and heeled over to port on the wind freshening with the approach of night.

CHAPTER SEVEN

AT SEA

"Hullo, Weeks!" cried Tom Jerrold, coming up at the moment and grinning at him rolling in the scuppers. "What's the matter, old fellow? You seem rather down."

"Begorra, he's ownly havin' a cooler to aise that nashty timper av his own," said the boatswain from the door of his cabin, which was just next ours in the deck-house, only more forward. And then, turning to me, he added, "Sure an' that wor a purty droive, Misther Gray-ham; ye lit him have it straight from the shouldher."

"I'm sure I didn't mean to hurt him," I answered, sorry now for my opponent as he scrambled at last up on his feet, looking very bedraggled and showing on his face the signs of the fray. "I only held out my hand to save the poor bird, and he ran against my fist."

"Oh, did you?" slobbered Weeks, half crying, in a savage, vindictive voice, and rushing at me as soon as he rose up. "You spiteful beggar! Well, two can play at that game, and I'll pay you out for it if you've got pluck enough to fight!"

"Be aisy now," interposed Tim Rooney, stepping between us

and holding him back. "Sure an' if y're spilin' for a batin' I'm not the chap to privint you; but, if you must foight, why ye'll have to do it fair an' square. Misther Gray-ham, sorr, jist give me the burrd as made the rumpus, I've a little cage in me bunk that'll sarve the poor baste for shilter till ye can get a betther one. It belonged to me ould canary as toorned up its toes last v'y'ge av a fit av the maysles."

"The measles?" exclaimed Tom Jerrold, bursting into a laugh. "I never heard of a bird dying of that complaint before."

"Faix, thin, ye can hear it now," said the boatswain with some heat. "An', sure, I don't say whare the laugh comes in, me joker! Didn't its faythers dhrop off av the poor craythur, an' its skin toorn all spotty, jist loike our friend Misther Wake's phiz here; an' what could that be, sure, but the maysles, I'd loike to know?"

"All right, bosun; I daresay you're right," hastily rejoined Jerrold to appease him; but he made me smile, however, by his efforts to look grave, although my own affairs were just then in such a critical position, with the prospect of a battle before me. "I was only laughing at the idea of a canary with the measles; but I've no doubt they have them the same as we do, and other things like us, too."

"In coorse they does, an' plinty of tongue, too, loike some chaps I've come across on shipboard!" replied Tim, all himself again in all good humour; and then, popping into his cabin, he reappeared quickly with the cage he had mentioned, saying to me, "Sorr, give me the burrd."

I had a little difficulty in extricating the starling from its safe retreat, for it had crept within my flannel shirt inside my jacket, tickling me as it moved; but, going carefully to work,

I finally succeeded in taking it out without hurting it. Then, placing the little fluttering thing in the cage, the boatswain bore it off to his bunk, giving me an expressive wink as he took it away, as if to say that it would be safer and more out of harm's way in his keeping, albeit I was quite at liberty to reclaim the bird when I pleased.

"Now, jintlemin," said Tim, addressing Weeks and myself after putting the innocent cause of our quarrel inside his cabin and locking the door to prevent accidents, as he shrewdly observed, "if ye're both av ye riddy an' willin', as it's goin' on for the sicond dog-watch, whin all hands are allers allowed at say to skoilark an' devart theirsilves, ye can follow me out on the fo'c's'le, me jokers, an' have y'r shindy out fairly in a friendly way."

I didn't want to fight Weeks, I'm sure; for I was not of a quarrelsome disposition, besides which my father had cautioned me against ever having any disputes with my comrades, if I could avoid such; although he told me also at the same time always to act courageously in the defence of my principles and of my rights, or when I took the part of another unable to defend himself. Here, therefore, was a quarrel forced upon me, almost against my will, to save the poor starling's life; and, beyond that, the aggravating way in which Weeks looked at me and shook his fist in my face would have provoked even a better-tempered boy than I. Tom Jerrold said afterwards that I turned quite white, as I always did when excited; while Weeks, on the contrary, was naming with fury and as red as a lobster.

"Come on, you coward!" he blustered, thinking I was afraid of him. "I'll soon let you know what it is to have a good hiding, my fine gentleman of a parson's son. You only floored me just now because you caught me unawares."

"I'm quite ready, Mr Rooney," said I to the boatswain, paying no attention to the cur's snobbish bravado; but I felt his sneer against my father's profession keenly, and had to bite my lip to prevent myself from replying to it. I added, however, for his personal benefit as I turned my back on him in contempt, "Those who crow the loudest, I've heard, generally do the least when the time for real action comes!"

"Thrue for ye, Mister Gray-ham," cried Tim Rooney. "Brag's a good dog, but Howldfast's the bist for my money. Come on wid ye, though, to the fo'c's'le if ye manes foightin'; for we've had palaverin' enough now in all conshinsh!"

So saying, the boatswain led the way forward, Tom Jerrold, who dearly loved anything in the way of a spree, and was overjoyed at the prospect of what he called "a jolly row," following with Weeks, to make sure that he did not back out of the contest at the last moment, which, knowing his cowardly character very well, as Tom told me afterwards, he anticipated his doing. I brought up the rear—and so we proceeded towards the bows of the ship along the lee-side of the deck, so as to escape the observation of Captain Gillespie and Mr Mackay. These were standing together, I noticed when the starling flew on board, by the rail on the weather side of the poop, where they were having a good look-out to windward, and watching some clouds that were piling themselves in black masses along the eastern sky—shutting out the last vestiges of land in the distance, already now become hazy from the mist rising from the sea after sunset.

Passing under the bellying main-sail, whose clew-garnet blocks rattled as it expanded to the breeze, which was now blowing pretty stiff, with every indication of veering more round to the north, causing the yards to have a pull taken at the braces every now and then, our little procession soon got clear of the deck-house that occupied the centre of the main-deck, finally gaining the more open space between the cook's galley at the end and the topgallant forecastle.

Here, the folds of the foresail, swelled out like a balloon, interposed like a curtain betwixt the after-glow of the setting sun and ourselves, the shadows of the upper sails, too, making it darker than on the after part of the deck whence we had started; but it was still quite light enough for me to see the expression on Weeks' mottled face as he stood opposite me.

Not much time was wasted in preliminaries, the boatswain, who acted as master of the ceremonies, placing me against the windlass bitts while my opponent had his back to the galley, what light there was remaining shining full upon him.

I had been present at one or two fights before, at the school I used to attend at Westham, where the boys used to settle their differences generally at the bottom of the playground under a little clump of shady trees that were grouped there, which shut off the view of the house and the headmaster's eye; but never previously had the surroundings of any similar pugilistic encounter seemed so strange as now!

As usual in such cases, the news had circulated through the ship with astonishing rapidity, considering that only a couple of minutes or so at most had elapsed since I had saved the starling and knocked down Weeks; for the whole crew, with the exception of two or three hands standing by the braces and the man at the wheel, appeared to scent the battle from afar, and were now gathered near the scene of action—some on the forecastle with their legs dangling over, others in the lower rigging, whence they could command the issues of the fray.

It was a pitiful contrast!

Here was the noble vessel surging through the gradually rising sea, with her towering masts and spreading canvas, and the wind whistling through the cordage, and the water coming every now and then over her bows in a cascade of iridescent spray, as the fast-fading gleams of the sunset lit it up, or else rushing by the side of the ship like a mill-race as we plunged through it, welling in at the scuppers as it washed inboard. All illustrated the grandeur of nature, the perfection of art; while there, on the deck, under the evening sky and amid all the glories of the waning glow in the western horizon and the grandeur of the sea in its might and the ship in its beauty and power over the winds and waves alike, were we two boys standing up to fight each other, with a parcel of bearded men who ought to have known better grouped round eagerly awaiting the beginning of the combat.

A contrast, but yet only an illustration of one of the ordinary phases of human nature after all, as father would have said, I thought, this reflection passing through my mind with that instantaneous spontaneity with which such fancies do occur to one, as Rooney placed me in my assigned position. Then, recalling my mind to the present, I noticed that Matthews, my whilom fellow apprentice and lately promoted third mate, sinking the dignity of his new rank, had come forward to act as the second, or backer, of my opponent, who must have sent some message aft to summon him.

"Now, me bhoys, are ye riddy?" sang out the boatswain, who stood on the weather side of the deck, glancing first at me and then at Weeks. "One, two, thray—foire away!"

I was not quite a novice in the use of my fists, my brother Tom, who, before he went to Oxford and got priggish, had bought a set of boxing-gloves, having made me put them on with him, sometimes, and showed me how to keep a firm guard and when to hit. My experience was invariably to get

John Conroy Hutcheson

the worst of these amicable encounters, for I used to be knocked off my pins, besides feeling my forehead soft and pulpy; for, no matter how well padded gloves may be, a fellow can give a sturdy punch with them, or appreciate one, all the same. Still, the practice stood me in good stead on this eventful occasion, especially as my brother had well drilled me into being light on my feet and dexterous in the art of stepping forward to deliver a blow and backward to avoid one—no small advantage, and the resource of science over brute force.

So, holding my right arm well across my chest and just about level with it, so that I could raise it either up or down as quick as lightning, to protect my face or body, I advanced my left fist, and waited for Sam Weeks to come on with a rush, as I was certain he would do, bracing myself well on my legs to receive the shock, although the pitching of the ship made me somewhat more uncertain of my equilibrium than if the combat had taken place ashore.

My antagonist acted exactly as I had expected.

Whirling his arms round like those of a windmill, he beat down my guard and gave me a nasty thump with one of them on the side of the head, for being lanky, as I said, he had a longer reach than I; however, as he got in close enough, my left fist caught him clean between the eyes again, landing on the identically same spot where I had hit him before, the place being already swollen, and whereas I only staggered against the windlass from his blow, mine sent him tumbling backwards, and he would have fallen on the deck if Matthews had not held him up just in time.

"Bray-vo, dark 'un!" shouted one of the men standing around, complimenting me on having the best of this first exchange, and alluding no doubt to the colour of my hair, which was dark brown while that of Weeks was quite sandy, like light Muscovado sugar. "Give him a one-two next time; there's nothing like the double!"

"I'll back freckles," cried another; "he's got more go in him!"

"Arrah, laive 'em alone, can't ye?" said the boatswain, as we faced each other again. "Don't waste y'r toime, sure. Go it, ye chripples; an' may the bist av ye win, sez I!"

The next two rounds had somewhat similar results to the first, I keeping up a steady defence and hitting my antagonist pretty nearly in the same place each time, while he gave me a couple of swinging blows, one of which made my mouth bleed, whereat his admirers were in high glee, especially Matthews, his second, for I heard the latter say to him, "Only go on and you'll soon settle him now, Sam!"

My friend the boatswain, however, was equally sanguine as to the result, as his encouraging advice to me showed.

"Kape y'r pecker up, Misther Gray-ham. Sure, he's gittin' winded, as all av thim lane an' lanky chaps allers does arter a bit," said Tim, wiping the blood away that was trickling from my lip with his soft silk handkerchief, which he took off from his own neck for the purpose. "Begorra, ye've ownly to hammer at his chist an' body, me lad; an' ye'll finish him afore ye can say 'Jack Robinson,' an' it's no lie I'm tellin'!"

Hitherto I had been merely acting on the defensive, and parrying the blows rained on me by Weeks in his impetuous rushes, more than hitting in return; for only keeping my left fist well out and allowing him to meet it as he so pleased, and which, strange to say, whether he wished it or not, he did so meet.

But now, thinking it time to end matters, the sight of the blood the boatswain had wiped from my face somehow or other bringing out what I suppose was the innate savagery of my nature, I determined to carry the war into the enemy's camp; or, in other words, instead of standing to be struck at, to lead the attack myself.

As Weeks, therefore, advanced with a grin, confidently as before, thinking that I should merely remain on guard, I threw my left straight out, swinging all the weight of my body in the blow; and then, stepping forwards, I gave him the benefit of my right fist, the one following up the other in quick succession, although I acted on Tim's advice, and directed my aim towards his body.

The result of these new tactics of mine altered alike the complexion not only of the fight but that of my antagonist as well; for he went down on the deck with a heavy dull thud, almost all his remaining breath knocked out of him.

"Hurrah, the little un wins!" cheered some of the hands; while others rejoined in opposition, "The lanky one ain't licked yet!"

But, to my especial friend the boatswain the end of the contest was now a foregone conclusion and victory assured to me.

"Bedad, me bhoy," he whispered in my ear as he prepared me for what turned out to be the final round of the battle, "that last dhroive av yourn wor loike the kick av a horse, or a pony anyhow! One more brace av them one-twos, Misther Gray-ham, an' he'll be kilt an' done wid!"

It was as Rooney said.

Matthews forced Weeks well-nigh against his will to face me once more, when my double hit again floored him incontinently, when the ship, giving a lurch to leeward at the same time, rolled him into the scuppers, as before at our first encounter.

This settled the matter, for, with all the pluck taken out of him and completely cowed, Master Sammy did not offer to rise until Matthews, catching hold of his collar, forcibly dragged him to his feet.

"Three cheers for the little un!" shouted one of the hands, as I stood triumphant on the deck in their midst, the hero of the moment, sailors following the common creed of their fellow men in worshipping success. "Hooray!"

A change came over the scene, however, the next instant.

For, ere the last note of the cheer had ceased ringing out from their lusty throats, Captain Gillespie's long nose came round the corner of the cook's caboose, followed shortly afterwards by the owner of the article—causing Ching Wang, who had been surveying the progress of the fight with much enjoyment, to retreat instantly within his galley, the smile of satisfaction on his yellow oval face and twinkle of his little pig-like eyes being replaced by that innocent look of one conscious of rectitude and in whom there is no guile, affected by most of his celestial countrymen.

"Hullo, bosun!" cried the captain, addressing Tim Rooney, who was helping me to put on my jacket again, and endeavouring, rather unsuccessfully, to conceal all traces of the fray on my person. "What the dickens does all this mean?"

"Sorry o' me knows, sorr, why them omahdawns is makin' all av that row a-hollerin'," said Tim, scratching his head as he always did when puzzled for the moment for an answer. "It's ownly Misther Gray-ham, sorr, an' Misther Wakes havin' a little bit of foon togither, an' settlin' their differses in a frindly way, loike, sorr."

"Fighting, I suppose,—eh?'

An ominous stillness succeeded this question, the men around following Ching Whang's example and sneaking inside the forecastle and otherwise slily disappearing from view. Presently, only Tim Rooney and Matthews remained before the captain besides us two, the principals of the fight, and Tom Jerrold, who, blocked between Captain Gillespie and the caboose, could not possibly manage to get away unperceived.

"Yes, there's no doubt you've been fighting," continued the captain, looking from Weeks to me and from me to Weeks, and seeming to take considerably more interest than either of us cared for in our bruised knuckles and battered faces and generally dilapidated appearance; for his long nose turned up scornfully as he sniffed and expanded his nostrils, comp-ressing his thin lips at the end of his inspection with an air of decision. "Well, youngsters, I'd have you to know that I don't allow fighting aboard my ship, and when I say a thing I mean a thing. There!"

"But, sir," snivelled Weeks, beginning some explanation, intended no doubt to throw all the blame on me. "Graham—"

Captain Gillespie, however, interrupted him before he could proceed any further.

"You'd better not say anything, Weeks," said the captain. "Graham's a new hand and you're an old one; at least, you've already been one voyage, whilst this is his first. I see you've had a lickin' and I'm glad of it, as I daresay it's been brought about by your own bullying; for I know you, Master Samuel Weeks, by this time, and you can't take me in as you used to do with your whining ways! If I didn't believe you were pretty well starched already, I'd give you another hiding now, my lad. Please, my good young gentleman, just to oblige me, go up in the mizzen-top so that I can see you're there, and stop till I call you down! As for you, Matthews, whom I have just promoted I'm surprised at your forgetting yourself as an officer, and coming here forrud, to take part with the crew in a disgraceful exhibition like this. I—"

"Please, sir—" expostulated the culprit. But the captain was firm on the matter of discipline, as I came to know in time.

"You'll go aft at once, Mr Matthews," he said, waving him away with his outstretched arm. "Another such dereliction from duty and you shall come forrud altogether, as you appear to like the fo'c's'le so well. I have made you third officer; but bear in mind that if I possess the power to make, I can break too!"

It was now Tim Rooney's turn, the captain wheeling round on him as soon as he'd done with Matthews.

"Really, bosun," he said, "I didn't think a respectable man like you would encourage two boys to fight like that!"

"Bedad it wor ownly to privint their bein' onfrindly, sorr," pleaded Tim, looking as much ashamed as his comical twinkling left eye would permit. "I thought it'd save a lot av throuble arterwards, spakin' as regards mesilf, sorr; fur I'm niver at paice onless I'm in a row, sure!"

"Ha, a nice way of making friends—pummelling each other to pieces and upsetting my ship," retorted Captain Gillespie.

John Conroy Hutcheson

But, as Tim Rooney made no answer, thinking discretion the better part of valour in this instance, and going up into the bows as if to look out forward, the captain then addressed me: "Graham!"

"Yes, sir," said I, awaiting my sentence with some trepidation. "I'm very sorry, sir, for what has happened, I—"

"There, I want no more jaw," he replied, hastily snapping me up before I could say another word. "I saw all that occurred, though neither of you thought I was looking. Weeks rushed at you, and you hit him; and then this precious hot-headed bosun of mine made you 'have it out,' as he calls it, in 'a friendly way,' the idiot, in his Irish bull fashion! But, as I told you, I won't have any fighting here, either between boys or men, and when I say a thing I mean a thing; so, to show I allow no relaxation of discipline on board so long as I'm captain, Master Graham, you'll be good enough to remain on deck to-night instead of going to bed, and will keep the middle watch from 'eight bells' to morning."

"Very good, sir," I replied, bowing politely, having already taken off my cap on his speaking to me; and I then went back to our deck-house cabin and had a lie down, as I felt pretty tired. Ching Wang, however, came to rouse me up soon afterwards with a pannikin of hot coffee, his way of showing his appreciation of my conduct in the fray, and I subsequently went with Tim Rooney to see the starling—which made me quite forget all about being tired and having to stop up all night, and that Tom Jerrold had escaped any punishment for his presence at the fight!

At eight o'clock, when it was quite dark, we passed Beachy Head, seeing the light in the distance; and then, feeling hungry again, I went to the steward in the cuddy and got something to eat, meeting there poor Weeks, whom the captain had only just called down from his perch in the mizzen-top, very cold and shivery from being so long up there in his wet clothes in the night air.

He looked rather grimly at me, and from the light in the saloon I noticed that he had a lovely pair of black eyes; but, on my stretching out my hand to him, we made friends, and agreed to bury all the disagreeable occurrences of the day in oblivion.

We had a lot of yarning together until midnight inside the deck-house, where Tom Jerrold lay an his bunk snoring away, utterly regardless of our presence; and then, on Mr Mackay's summoning me, by the captain's order as he told me, to keep watch with him on the poop, I went up the ladder and remained with him astern, watching the ship bowling along under all plain sail, with the same buoyant breeze behind her with which we had started.

"Now, Graham," said Mr Mackay at daybreak, when we were just off Saint Catharine's Point in the Isle of Wight, as he informed me, "you can go and turn in. Bosun, call the starboard watch!"

"Aye, aye, sorr," answered Tim Rooney from the bows, where he had been keeping his vigils, too, like us aft. "Starbowlines, ahoy—!"

I only remained on the poop while the man at the wheel was being relieved, and Mr Saunders, the second mate, came on deck to take Mr Mackay's place; when, going below to the deck-house cabin, I was soon in my little shelf of a bed, falling asleep more quickly, I think, than I had ever done before; doing so, indeed, almost the instant I got within the blankets.

John Conroy Hutcheson

The next day, at noon, we tore by the Start, and, later on, that noblest monument a man could have, the Eddystone, Smeaton's glory; the ship racing down Channel as if all the sea-nymphs were chasing us, and old Neptune, too, at their heels to hurry them on, with his tritons after him.

Our average speed all that day was a good ten knots, the wind never shifting and every sail drawing fore and aft. Sometimes it was even more, according to Tom Jerrold's calculations, he having to heave the log at intervals and turn the fourteen-second glass, his especial duty, in order to determine our rate of progress through the water; but I don't think it was ever less from the time the sun rose in the morning.

At all events, the Silver Queen made such good use of her time that, at six o'clock on this evening of our second day under sail, we were up to the Lizard, the last bit of English shore we should see in a hurry; and at "six bells" in the first watch, were speeding along some ten miles south of the Bishop's Rock lightship in the Scilly Isles, really, at last, at sea!

CHAPTER EIGHT

A SUDDEN INTERRUPTION

"Now, my boy," said Mr Mackay, who had the "first watch," from eight o'clock till midnight that is, I sharing it with him, speaking as we were just abreast of the light I've mentioned, although so far to the southward that it could only be seen very faintly glimmering on the horizon like a star, a trifle bigger than those which twinkled above it and on either side in the clear northern sky—"we've run exactly forty-six miles from our departure point."

"Departure point, sir!" I repeated after him, my curiosity aroused by the use of such a term. "What is that?"

"The last land sighted before a ship gains the open sea," replied he kindly, always willing to give me any information, although I'm afraid I caused him a good deal of trouble with my innumerable questions, in my zeal to get acquainted with everything connected with the ship and my profession as an embryo sailor. "Ours was the Lizard; didn't you notice Cap'en Gillespie taking the bearings of it as we passed this afternoon?"

"Yes, sir. I saw him with his sextant, as you told me that queer triangular thing was," said I; "but I didn't know what he was doing. I thought our starting-place was the Thames? We must have gone miles and miles since we left the Downs."

"So we have, my boy; still, that was only the threshold of our long journey, and sailors do not begin to count their run until fairly out at sea as we are now. When you came up to town the other day from that place in the country—West something or other?"

"Westham, sir," I suggested; "that's where we live."

"Well, then," he went on, accepting my correction with a smile, "when you were telling your adventures and stated that you came from Westham to London in three hours, say, you would not include the time you had taken in going from the door of your house to the garden gate and from thence to the little town or village whence you started by the railway—eh?"

"No, sir," said I, laughing at his way of putting the matter. "I would mean from the station at Westham to the railway terminus in London."

"Just so," he answered; "and, similarly, we sailors in estimating the length of a voyage, do not take into consideration our passage along the river and down channel, only counting our distance from the last point of land we see of the country we are leaving and the first we sight of that we're bound to. Our first day's run, therefore, will be what we get over from the Lizard up to the time the cap'en takes the sun at noon to-morrow, which will tell us our latitude and longitude then, when, by the aid of this fixed starting-point or 'point of departure,' and calculating our dead reckoning and courses steered, we will be enabled to know our precise position on the chart."

"I see, sir," said I. "I won't forget what you've told me another time, and shall know in future what the term means, sir, thank you."

"You're quite welcome, Graham," he replied pleasantly as he resumed his walk up and down the deck, with an occasional glance to windward and a look at the compass in the binnacle to see that the helmsman was keeping the ship on the course the captain had directed before going below a short time before—west-sou'-west, and as close up to the wind as we could sail, so as to avoid the French coast and get well across the mouth of the Bay of Biscay into the open Atlantic. "I hope to make a good navigator of you in time, my boy."

"I hope so, too, sir," said I, trying to keep pace with his measured tread, although I always got out of step as he turned regularly at the end of his walk, which was backwards and forwards between the cabin skylight and the binnacle. "I will try my best, sir."

While bearing in mind the "departure point," however, I must not forget to mention, too, that immediately after Captain Gillespie had taken our bearings off the Lizard, he sang out to Tim Rooney the boatswain to send the hands aft.

"Aye, aye, sorr," responded Tim, at once sounding his shrill whistle and hoarse shout. "A-all ha-ands aft!"

"Now for a bit of speechifying," said Tom Jerrold, who was along with me on the lee-side of the poop, watching the crew as they mustered together on the main-deck underneath. "The 'old man' loves a jaw."

But Tom was mistaken; for the captain's speech was laconic in the extreme, being "much shorter, indeed, than his nose," as my fellow mid was forced to acknowledge in a whisper to me!

"My men," said he, leaning over the brass rail at the head of the poop, and gazing down into the faces of the rough-and-ready fellows looking up at him expectantly, with all sorts of funny expressions on their countenances, as they wondered what was to come—"we're now at sea and entering on a long voyage together. I only wish you to do your duty and I will do mine. If you have anything to complain of at any time, come to me singly and I will right it; but if you come in a body, I'll take no notice of ye. Ye know when I say a thing I mean a thing."

"Aye, aye sir!" shouted the hands, on his pausing here as if waiting for their answer. "Aye, aye, sir!"

"All right then; ye understand me, I see. That will do the watch."

Whereupon, half of them went back into the forecastle to finish their tea, while the remainder took their stations about the ship, remaining on deck until their span of duty was out, the whole lot having been divided into two groups, styled respectively the port and starboard watches, under charge of Mr Mackay and the second mate, Mr Saunders—Tom Jerrold and I being in the port watch with the first mate; while Sam Weeks and Matthews, who was like the fifth wheel of a coach as "third mate," a very anomalous position on board-ship, mustered with the starbowlines under Mr Saunders.

Counting in Captain Gillespie, with the three mates, us apprentices, the boatswain, sailmaker Adams and carpenter Gregory—the three latter all "old hands," having sailed several voyages previously together in the ship—the steward Pedro Carvalho, Ching Wang our cook, Billy the boy, our "second-class apprentice," and the eighteen fresh men who had come aboard with the Chinaman at Gravesend, our crew mustered all told some thirty-one hands; and, to complete the description of the vessel and her belongings, the Silver Queen was a sharp-bowed, full-rigged ship, with a tremendous bilge, built for carrying a goodish cargo, which consisted, as I believe I mentioned before, mainly of Manchester goods and Birmingham hardware, besides a private speculation of our captain consisting of a peculiarly novel consignment of Dundee marmalade, packed up in tins like those used for preserved meats and such like dainties.

About this marmalade I shall have something to say by and by; but I think I had better go on with my yarn in proper ship-shape fashion, narrating events in the order in which they occurred—merely stating, in order to give a full account of all concerning us, that, in addition to the particulars of our cargo as already detailed, we had sundry items of live freight in the shape of some pigs, which were stowed in the long-boat on top of the deck-house; three cats, two belonging to the Portuguese steward and messing in the cuddy, while the third was a vagrant Tom that had strayed on board in the docks, and making friends with the carpenter Gregory, or "old chips" as he was generally called, was allowed to take up his quarters in the forepeak, migrating to the cook's cabin at meal-times with unwavering sagacity; a lot of fowls, accommodated aristocratically in coops on the poop; and, lastly, though by no means least, the starling which I'd caught coming down Channel, and which now seemed very comfortable in the boatswain's old canary cage, hung up to a ringbolt in his cabin next to mine, and regarded as a sort of joint property between us two.

There, you have our list of passengers; and, now, to continue my story.

John Conroy Hutcheson

Shortly after passing the Bishop's Rock lighthouse, which we did some few minutes before "Billy," the ship's boy, came out of the forecastle and struck "six bells," eleven o'clock, near the end of the port watch's spell on deck, the wind, which had freshened considerably since sunset, began to blow with greater force, veering, or "backing" as sailors say, more and more round to the north; so that, although our yards were braced up to the full and the vessel was sailing almost close-hauled, we had to drop off a point or two within the next half-hour from our true western course.

Within the next half-hour, south-west by west was as close as we could now keep her head outward across "The Bay," the wind even then continuing to show a tendency to shift further round still to the northwards and westwards, and naturally forcing us yet more in a southerly direction before gaining the offing Captain Gillespie wished.

The sea, too, had got up wonderfully during the short period that had elapsed from our leaving the Chops of the Channel—I suppose from its having a wider space to frolic in, without being controlled by the narrow limits of land under its lea; for, the scintillating light of the twinkling stars and pale sickly moon, whose face was ever and anon obscured by light fleecy clouds floating across it in the east, showed the tumid waste of waters heaving and surging tempestuously as far as the eye could reach. The waves were tumbling over each other and racing past the ship in sport, sending their flying scud high over the foreyard, or else trying vainly to poop her; and, when foiled in this, they would dash against her bows with the blow of a battering-ram, or fling themselves bodily on board in an angry cataract that poured down from the forecastle on to the main-deck, flooding the waist up to the height of the bulwarks to leeward, for we heeled over too much to allow of the sea running off through the scuppers, these and our port gunwale as well being well-nigh under water.

Presently, we had to reduce sail, brailing up the spanker and taking a single reef in the topsails; but still keeping the topgallant-sails set above them, a thing frequently done by a skipper who knows how to "carry-on."

Then, as the wind still rose and as with less canvas the ship would go all the better and not bend over or bury herself so much, the topgallants were taken in. At length, when Mr Mackay and I quitted the deck at midnight, the men were just beginning to clew up the main-sail, the captain, who had come up from below with Mr Saunders when the starboard watch relieved us, having ordered it to be furled and another reef to be taken in the topsails, as it was then blowing great guns and the ship staggering along through a storm-tossed sea, with the sky overcast all round—a sign that we had not seen the worst of it yet!

The Silver Queen pitched so much—giving an occasional heavy roll to starboard as her bows fell off from the battering of the waves, with her stern lifting up out of the water, and rolling back quickly to port again on her taking the helm as the men jammed it hard down—that I found it all I could do to descend the poop ladder safely. I climbed down gingerly, however, holding on to anything I could clutch until I reached the deck-house, which was now nearly knee-deep in the water that was sluicing fore and aft the ship with every pitch and dive she gave, or washing in a body athwart the deck as she rolled, and dashing like a wave against the bulwarks within.

I went to turn in to my bunk, which was on top of that occupied by Sam Weeks, who, very luckily for him, had to turn out, going aft on duty with the rest of the starboard watch; for, in my struggles to ascend to the little narrow

　　　　John Conroy Hutcheson

shelf that served me for a bed, and which from the motion of the ship was almost perpendicular one moment and the next horizontal, I would have pretty well trampled him to jelly, having to stand on the lower bunk to reach the upper one assigned to me.

Ultimately, however, I managed to climb up to my perch and pulled my blankets about me; and then I tried to sleep as well as the roaring of the wind and rushing wash of the sea, in concert with the creaking of the chain-plates and groaning of the ship's timbers and myriad voices of the deep, would let me.

But, it was all in vain!

Hitherto, although I had been more than two days and two nights on board and had sailed all the way from the docks along the river and down the Channel, I had never yet been sea-sick, smiling at Tim Rooney's stereotyped inquiry each day of me, "An' sure, Misther Gray-ham, aren't ye sorry yit ye came to say?"

Since the afternoon, however, when the water had become rougher and the ship more lively, I had begun to experience a queer sensation such as I recollect once having at home at Christmas-time—on which occasion Dr Jollop, who was called in to attend me, declared I had eaten too much plum-pudding, just in order to give me some of his nasty pills, of course!

I hadn't had the chance of having anything so good as that now; but, at tea-time Tom Jerrold, who, like myself, had made friends with Ching Wang, had induced him to compound a savoury mess entitled, "dandy funk," composed of pounded biscuits, molasses, and grease. Of this mess, I am sorry to say, I had partaken; and the probable source of my present ailment was, no doubt, the insidious dandy funk wherewith Jerrold had beguiled me.

Oh, that night!

Dandy funk or no, I could not soon forget it, for I never was so sick in my life; and what is more, every roll of the ship made me worse, so that I thought I should die—Tom Jerrold, the heartless wretch, who was snoring away as usual in the next bunk to Weeks' below, not paying the slightest attention to my feeble calls to him for help and assistance between the paroxysms of my agonising qualms.

Somehow or other a sympathetic affinity seemed to be established between the vessel and myself, I rolling as she rolled and heaving when she heaved; while my heart seemed to reach from the Atlantic back to the Channel, and I felt as if I had swallowed the ocean and was trying to get rid of it and couldn't!

Ille robur et aes triplex, as Horace sang on again getting safely ashore—for he must have been far too ill when afloat in his trireme—and as father used to quote against me should I praise the charms of a sailor's life, "framed of oak and fortified with triple brass" must have been he who first braved the perils of the sea and made acquaintance with that fell demon whom our French neighbours style more elegantly than ourselves *le mal de mer*!

Weeks had his revenge upon me now with a vengeance indeed for all he might have suffered from my pummelling of the previous day; yes, and for the reproach of the two black eyes I had given him, which had since altered their colouring to the tints of the sea and sky, they being now of a bluish-purple hue shaded off into green and yellow, so that the general effect harmonised, as Tom Jerrold unkindly remarked, with his sandy hair and mottled complexion.

But, my whilom enemy and now friend Sammy must have been amply indemnified for all this when, at the end of the middle watch, he came in due course to rouse me out again for another turn of duty, not knowing that Mr Mackay, as if anticipating what would happen after the shaking up I had had, had given me leave to lie-in if I liked and "keep my watch below;" for, when Weeks succeeded in opening the door of the deck-house, which he did with much difficulty against the opposing forces of the wind and the water that united to resist his efforts, he found me completely prostrate and in the very apogee of my misery.

"Hullo, Graham!" he called out, clutching hold of the corner of the blanket that enveloped one of my limp legs, which was hanging down almost as inanimate over the side of the bunk, and shaking this latter, too, as vigorously as he did the blanket. "Rouse out, it's gone eight bells and the port watch are already on deck, with Mr Mackay swearing away at a fine rate because you're not there—rouse out with you, sharp!"

There was no rousing me, however, pull and tug and shake away as much as he pleased both at my leg and the blanket.

"Leave me alone," I at last managed to say loud enough for him to hear me. "Mr Mackay told me I needn't turn out unless I felt well enough; and, oh, Weeks, I do feel so awfully ill!"

"Ill! what's the row with you?"

"I don't know," I feebly murmured. "I think I'm going to die; and I'm so sorry I hurt your eyes yesterday, they do look so bad."

"Oh, hang my eyes!" replied he hastily, as if he did not like the subject mentioned; and I don't wonder at this now, when I recollect how very funny they looked, all green and yellow as if he had a pair of goggle-eyed spectacles on. "Why can't you turn out? You were well enough when you called me four hours ago—shamming Abraham, I suppose,—eh?"

I was too weak, though, to be indignant.

"Indeed I'm not shamming anything," I protested as earnestly as I could, not quite knowing what his slang phrase meant, but believing it to imply that I was pretending to be ill to shirk duty when I was all right. "Weeks, I'm terribly ill, I tell you!"

He scrutinised me as well as he could by the early light of morning, now coming in through the open cabin door, which he had not been able to close again, the wind holding it back and resisting all his strength.

Tom Jerrold, too, aroused by Weeks' voice and the cold current of air that was blowing in upon him, rubbed his eyes, and standing up in his bunk while holding on to the top rail of mine, had also a good look at me.

"Bah!" cried he at length. "You're only sea-sick."

That was all the consolation he gave me as he shoved himself into his clothes; and then, hastily lugging on a thick monkey-jacket hurried out on deck.

"A nice mess you've made, too, of the cabin."

This was Master Weeks' sympathy as he took possession of Jerrold's vacated bunk and quietly composed himself to sleep, regardless of my groans and deaf to all further appeals for aid.

Tim Rooney, however, was the most unkind of all.

Later on in the morning he popped in his head at the cabin door.

"Arrah, sure now, Misther Gray-ham, arn't ye sorry ye iver came to say, at all at all?"

I should like to have pitched something at him, although I knew what he would say the moment he opened his mouth, with that comical grin of his and the cunning wink of his left eye.

"No," I cried as courageously as I was able under the circumstances, "I'm not sorry, I tell you, in spite of all that has happened, and when I get better I'll pay you out for making fun of me when I'm ill!"

"Begorra don't say that now, me darlint," said he, grinning more than ever. "Arrah, though, me bhoy, ye look as if ye'd been toorned insoide out, loike them injy-rubber divils childer has to play wid. 'Dade an' I'd loike to say ye sprooce an' hearty ag'in; but ownly kape aisy an' ye'll be all roight in toime. D'ye fale hoongry yit?"

"Hungry!" I screamed, ill again at the very thought of eating. "Go away, do, and leave me alone—o-oh!"

And then I was worse than ever, and seemed afterwards to have no heart, or head, or stomach left, or legs, or arms, or anything.

The boatswain did not forget me though, in spite of his fun at my expense; and he must have spoken to Ching Wang again about me, for the Chinaman came to the cabin after giving the men their breakfast at eight bells, bringing me a pannikin of hot coffee, his panacea for every woe.

"Hi, lilly pijjin, drinkee dis chop chop," said he, holding the pannikin to my mouth. "Makee tummy tummy number one piecee!"

I could not swallow much of the liquid; but the drop or two that I took did me good; for, after Ching Wang had gone away I fell asleep, not waking till the afternoon, when, the ship being steadier, I managed to scramble out of my bunk and made a late appearance on deck, feeling decidedly weak but considerably better than in the morning.

"Hullo, found your sea-legs already?" cried Mr Mackay on my crawling up the poop ladder. "I didn't expect to see you out for another day at least."

"I don't feel all right yet, sir," said I, and I'm sure my pale face must have shown this without any explanation; "but, I didn't like to give way to being ill, thinking it best to fight against it."

"Quite right, my boy," he replied. "I've never been sea-sick myself, not even the first time I went afloat; but, I've seen a good many suffering from the complaint, and I have noticed that the more they humoured it, the worse they became. You're getting used to the motion of the ship by this time—eh?"

"Yes, sir," said I, holding on tightly, however, to the bulwarks as I spoke, the Silver Queen just then giving a lurch to starboard that nearly pitched me overboard. "I'll soon be able to stand up like you, sir."

John Conroy Hutcheson

"Well, at all events, you've got plenty of pluck, Graham; and that's the sort of material for making a good sailor. You were asking me last night about the course of the ship, if your sickness hasn't put our talk out of your head. How far do you think we've run?"

"A good way, I suppose, sir," I answered, "with that gale of wind."

"Yes, pretty so so," he said. "When the cap'en took the sun at noon to-day we were in latitude 48 degrees 17 minutes north and longitude just 8 degrees 20 west, or about two hundred miles off Ushant, which we're to the southward of; so, we've run a goodish bit from our point of departure."

"Oh, I remember all about that, sir," I cried, getting interested, as he unfolded the chart which was lying on top of the cabin skylight and showed me the vessel's position. "And we've come so far already?"

"Yes, all that," replied he laughing as he moved his finger on the chart, pointing to another spot at least a couple of inches away from the first pencil-mark; "and we ought to fetch about here, my boy, at noon to-morrow—that is, if this wind holds good and no accident happens to us, please God."

The ship at this time was going a good ten knots, he further told me, carrying her topgallants and courses again; for, although the sea was rough and covered with long rolling waves, that curled over their ridges into valleys of foam like half-melted snow, and it was blowing pretty well half a gale now from the north-west, to which point the wind had hauled round, it was keeping steady in that quarter, for the barometer remained high, and the Silver Queen, heading south-west by south, was bending well over so that her lee-side was flush almost with the swelling water. She was racing along easily, and presented a perfect picture, with the sun bringing out her white clouds of canvas in stronger contrast against the clear blue sky overhead and tumbling ocean around, and making the glass of the skylight and bits of brass-work about on the deck gleam with a golden radiance as it slowly sank below the horizon, a great globe of fire like a molten mass of metal on our weather bow, the vessel keeping always on the same starboard tack, for she wore round as the wind shifted.

Oh, yes, we were going; and so, evidently, Captain Gillespie thought when he came up the companion presently and took his place alongside Mr Mackay on the poop.

"This is splendid!" said he, rubbing his hands as usual and addressing the first mate, while I crept away further aft, holding on to the bulwarks to preserve my footing, the deck being inclined at such a sharp angle from the ship heeling over with the wind. "I don't know when the old barquey ever went so free."

"Nor I, sir," replied the other with equal enthusiasm; "she's fairly outdoing herself. We never had such a voyage before, I think, sir."

"No," said the captain. "A good start, a fairish wind and plenty of it, a decent crew as far as I can judge as yet, and every prospect of a good voyage. What more can a man wish for?"

"Nothing, sir."

"And I forgot, Mackay, while speaking of our luck, for you know I like to be particular, and when I say a thing I mean a thing—no stowaways on board!"

John Conroy Hutcheson

"True, sir," responded the first mate with a laugh, knowing the captain's great abhorrence of these uninvited and unwelcome passengers. "I think it's the first voyage we've never been troubled with one."

"Aye, aye, they're getting afraid of me, Mackay, that's the reason," said Captain Gillespie chuckling at this. "They've heard tell of the way I treat all such swindling rascals, and know that when I say a thing I mean a thing!"

His satisfaction, however, was short-lived; for, just then, several confused cries and a general commotion was heard forward.

"Hullo!" cried the captain, staggering up to the poop rail and looking towards the bows, "what's the row there?"

"Bedad, sorr," shouted back the boatswain, yelling out the words as loudly as he could, like Captain Gillespie, and putting his hands to his mouth to prevent the wind carrying them away seaward, "there's a did man in the forepake!"

CHAPTER NINE

OUR STOWAWAY TUMBLES INTO LUCK

"A man in the forepeak—eh?" yelled out Captain Gillespie, all his complacency gone in a moment, his voice sounding so loudly that it deadened the moaning of the wind through the shrouds and the creaking of the ship's timbers, whose groans mingled with the heavy thud of the waves against her bows as she breasted them, and the angry splash of the baffled billows as they fell back into the bubbling, hissing cauldron of broken water through which the noble vessel plunged and rolled, spurning it beneath her keel in her majesty and might. "A man in the forepeak, and dead, is he, bosun? I'll bet I'll soon quicken him into life again with a rope's-end!"

He muttered these last words as he hastily scrambled down the poop ladder and along the weather side of the main-deck towards the forecastle, making his way forward with an activity which might have shamed a younger man.

Mr Mackay at once tumbled after him, and I followed too, as quickly as I could get along and the motion of the ship would allow me, being buffeted backwards and forwards like a shuttlecock between the bulwarks and deck-house in my progress onwards, as well as drenched by the spray, which came hurtling inboards over the main-chains from windward

John Conroy Hutcheson

as it was borne along by the breeze, wetting everything amidships and soaking the main-sail as if buckets of water were continually poured over it, although the air was quite dry and the sun still shining full upon its swelling surface.

"Begorra, he's as did as a door-nail, sorr," I heard Tim Rooney saying on my getting up at last to the others, who were grouped with a number of the crew round the small hatchway under the forecastle leading down to the forehold below, the cover of which had been slipped off leaving the dark cavity open. "I ownly filt him jist move once, whin I kicked him wid me fut unknowns to me, as I wor sayin' about stowin' the cable."

"Dead men don't move," replied the captain sharply, the hands round grinning at the boatswain's Irish bull. "Some of you idlers there, go down and fetch this stowaway up and let us see what he's made of."

The boatswain, spurred by Captain Gillespie's rejoinder, was the first to dive down again into the dark receptacle, where he had previously been searching to find room for stowing the cable, the anchor having been hoisted inboard and the chain unshackled on the ship now getting to sea; and, Tim was quickly followed below by a couple of the other hands, as many as could comfortably squeeze into the narrow space at their command.

"On deck, there!" presently called out Tim Rooney from beneath, his voice sounding hollow and far off.

"Some av ye bind owver the coamin' av the hatch an' hilp us to raise the poor divil!"

A dozen eager hands were immediately stretched down-wards; and, the next instant, between them all they lifted out of the forepeak the limp body of a ragged youth, who seemed to be either already dead or dying, not a movement being discernible in the inert, motionless figure as it was laid down carefully by the men on the deck, looking like a corpse.

Captain Gillespie, however, was not deceived by these appearances.

"Sluice some water over his face," cried he, after leaning down and putting his hand on his chest; "he's only swooned away or shamming, for he's breathing all right. Look, his shirt is moving up and down now."

"I think he must be pretty far gone with starvation," observed Mr Mackay, bending over the unconscious lad, too, and scrutinising his pinched features and bony frame. "He could only have stowed himself down there when we were loading in the docks, and it is now over three days since we cleared out and started down the river."

"Humph!" growled Captain Gillespie, "the confounded skulker has only brought it on himself, and serve him right, too."

"Shame!" groaned one of the men, a murmur of reproach running round amongst the rest, in sympathy with this expression of opinion against such an inhuman speech, making the captain look up and cock his ears and sniff with his long nose, trying to find out who had dared to call him to account. But, of course, he was unable to do so; and, after glaring at those near as if he could have "eaten them without salt," as the saying goes, he bent his eyes down again on Mr Mackay and the boatswain. These were trying to resuscitate the unfortunate stowaway in a somewhat more humane way than the captain had suggested; for, while the mate opened

John Conroy Hutcheson

his collar and shirt and lifted his head on his knee, Tim Rooney sprinkled his face smartly with water from the bucket that had been dipped over the side and filled.

At first, Tim's efforts were unsuccessful, causing Captain Gillespie to snort with impatience at his delicate mode of treatment; but, the third or fourth dash of the cold water at last restored the poor fellow to consciousness, his eyelids quivering and then opening, while he drew a deep long breath like a sigh.

He didn't know a bit, though, where he was, his eyes staring out from their sockets, which had sunk deep into his head, as if he were looking through us and beyond us to something else—instead of at us close beside him.

In a moment, however, recollection came back to him and he tried to raise himself up, only to fall back on Mr Mackay's supporting knee; and, then, he called out piteously what had probably been his cry for hours previously as he lay cramped up in the darkness of the forepeak:

"Hey, let Oi out, measter, and Oi'll never do it no more! Oi be clemmed to da-eth, measter, and th' rats and varmint be a-gnawing on me cruel! Let Oi out, measter, Oi be dying here in the dark—let Oi out, for Gawd's sake!"

"It is as I told you," said Mr Mackay looking up at the captain; "he is starving. See, one of you, if the cook's got anything ready in his galley."

"Begorra, it wor pay-soup day to-day," cried Tim Rooney getting up to obey the order; "an' Ching Wang bulled it so plentiful wid wather that the men toorned oop their noses at it, an' most of it wor lift in the coppers."

"The very thing for one in this poor chap's condition," replied Mr Mackay eagerly. "Go and bring a pannikin of it at once."

Captain Gillespie sniffed and snorted more than ever of being baulked for the present in his amiable intention of giving the stowaway a bit of his mind, and, possibly, something else in addition.

He saw, though, that his unwelcome passenger was too far gone to be spoken to as yet; and so, perforce, he had to delay calling him to account for his intrusion, putting the reckoning off until a more convenient season.

"Ah, well, Mackay," said he, on Tim Rooney's return presently with a pannikin of pea-soup and a large iron spoon, with which he proceeded to ladle some into the starving creature's mouth, which was ravenously opened, as were his eyes, too, distended with eager famine craving as he smelt the food—"you see to bringing the beggar round as well as you can, and I'll talk to him bye and bye."

So saying, Captain Gillespie returned to his former place on the poop, and contented himself for the moment with rating the helmsman for letting the ship yaw on a big wave catching her athwart the bows and making her fall off; while the first mate and Tim Rooney continued their good Samaritan work in gently plying the poor creature, who had just been rescued from death's door, with spoonful after spoonful of the tepid soup. Presently a little colour came into his face and he was able to speak, recovering his consciousness completely as soon as the nourishment affected his system and gave him strength.

In a little time, he also was able to raise himself up and stand without assistance; and, then, Mr Mackay asked him who he was and why he came on board our ship without leave or license.

He said that he was a country bricklayer, Joe Fergusson by name; and that, not being able to get work in London, whither he had tramped all the way from Lancashire, he had determined to go to Australia, hearing there was a great demand for labour out there. By dint of inquiries he had at length managed to reach the docks, hiding himself away in the forepeak of the Silver Queen, she being the first ship he was able to get on board unperceived, and the hatchway being conveniently open as if on purpose for his accommodation.

"But, we're not going to Australia," observed Mr Mackay, who had only contrived to get all this from the enterprising bricklayer by the aid of a series of questions and a severe cross-examination. "This ship is bound for China."

"It don't matter, measter," replied Mr Joe Fergusson with the most charming nonchalance. "Australy or Chiney's all the same to Oi, so long as un can git wa-ark to dew. Aught's better nor clemming in Lonnon!"

"You've got no right aboard here, though," said Mr Mackay, who could not help smiling at the easy way in which the whilom dying man now took things. "Who's going to pay your passage-money? The captain's in a fine state, I can tell you, about it, and I don't know what he won't do to you. He might order you to be pitched overboard into the sea, perhaps."

The other scratched his head reflectively, just as Tim Rooney did when in a quandary, looking round at the men behind Mr Mackay, who were grinning at his blank dismay and the perturbed and puzzled expression on his raw yokel face.

"Oi be willin' to wa-ark, measter," he answered at length, thinking that if they were all grinning, they were not likely to do him much harm. "Oi'll wa-ark, measter, loike a good un, so long as you gie Oi grub and let Oi be."

"Work! What can you, a bricklayer according to your own statement, do aboard ship? We've got no bricks to lay here."

"Mab'be, measter, you moight try un, though," pleaded the poor fellow, scratching his head again; and then adding, as if a brilliant thought all at once occurred to him from the operation, "Oi be used to scaffoldin' and can cloimb loike sailor cheaps."

"Ah, you must speak to the captain about that," replied Mr Mackay drily, turning aft and giving some whispered instructions to Tim Rooney to let the stowaway have some more food later on and give him a shake-down in the forecastle for the night, so that he might be in better fettle for his audience with Captain Gillespie on the morrow. "You can stop here with the men till the morning, and then you will know what will be done in the matter."

"Well," cried Captain Gillespie as soon as Mr Mackay stepped up the poop ladder, "how's that rascal getting on?"

"I think he'll come round now, sir," said the first mate, thinking it best not to mention how quickly his patient had recovered, so that he might have a few hours' reprieve before encountering the captain's wrath. "I've told the boatswain to give him a bunk in the fo'c's'le for the night, and that you'll talk to him in the morning."

"Oh, aye, I'll talk to him like a Dutch uncle," retorted the captain, sniffing away at a fine rate, as if Mr Mackay was as much in fault as the unfortunate cause of his ire. "You know

John Conroy Hutcheson

I never encourage stowaways on board my ship, sir; and when I say a thing I mean a thing."

"Yes, sir; certainly, sir," said Mr Mackay soothingly, taking no notice of his manner to him and judiciously turning the conversation. "Do you think, though, sir, we can carry those topgallants much longer? The wind seems to have freshened again after sunset, the same as it did last night."

"Carry-on? Aye, of course we can. The old barquey could almost stand the royals as well, with this breeze well abeam," replied "Old Jock," who never agreed with anyone right out if he could possibly help, especially now when he was in a bit of temper about the stowaway; but, the next instant, like the thorough seaman he was, seeing the wisdom of the first mate's advice, he qualified what he had previously said. "If it freshens more, though, between this and eight bells, you can take in the topgallants if you like, and a reef in the topsails as well. It will save bother, perhaps, bye and bye, as the night will be a darkish one and the weather is not too trustworthy."

Captain Gillespie then went down the companion into the cuddy to have his tea; and Mr Mackay, thinking I ought to be hungry after all my sacrifices to Neptune, advised me to go down below and get some too.

I was hungry, but I did not care about tea, the flavour of the pea-soup the stowaway had been plied with having roused my appetite; so, receiving Mr Mackay's permission, instead of seeking out the steward Pedro, I paid a visit to Ching Wang in his galley forward.

"Hi, lilly pijjin," cried this worthy, receiving me far more pleasantly than I'm sure the Portuguese would have done, for as I passed under the break of the poop I heard the latter clattering his tins about in the pantry, as if he were in a rage at something. "What you wanchee—hey?"

I soon explained my wants; and, without the slightest demur, he ladled out a basinful of soup for me out of one of the coppers gently stewing over the galley fire, which looked quite bright and nice as the evening was chilly. The good-natured Chinaman also gave me a couple of hard ship's biscuits which he took out of a drawer in the locker above the fireplace, where they were kept dry.

"Hi, you eatee um chop chop," said he, as he handed me the basin and the biscuits and made me sit down on a sort of settle in the galley opposite the warm fire—"makee tummee tummee all right."

The effects of this food were as wonderful in my instance as in that of the poor starved bricklayer shortly before; for, when I had eaten the last biscuit crumb and drained the final drop of pea-soup from the basin, I felt a new man, or rather boy—Allan Graham himself, and not the wretched feeble nonentity I had been previously.

Of course, I thanked Ching Wang for his kindness as I rose up from the settle to go away, on the starboard watch, who were just relieved from their duty on deck, coming for their tea; but the Chinee only shook his head with a broad smile on his yellow face, as if deprecating any return for his kind offices.

"You goodee pijjin and chin chin when you comee," he only said, "and when you wanchee chow-chow, you comee Ching Wang and him gettee you chop chop!"

Then, I stopped in front of the forecastle, as Tim Rooney giving me a cheery hail, and saw to my wonder Joe Fergusson looking all hale and hearty and jolly amongst the men, without the least trace of having been, apparently, at his last gasp but an hour or so before.

He was half lying down, half sitting on the edge of one of the bunks, nursing the big stray tortoise-shell tom-cat which had shared his lodgings in the forepeak, and he had mistaken it for a rat as it crept up and down the chain-pipe to see what it could pick up in the cook's galley at meal-times, which it seemed to know by some peculiar instinct of its own; and although thus partially partial to Ching Wang's society, the cat now appeared to have taken even a greater fancy to his bed-fellow in his hiding-place below than it had done to the cook, looking upon the stowaway evidently as a fellow-comrade, who was unfortunately in similar circumstances to himself.

Joe Fergusson not only looked all right, but he likewise was in the best of spirits, possibly from the tot of rum Tim Rooney had given him after his soup, to "pull him together," as the boatswain said; for, ere I left the precincts of the forecastle he volunteered to sing a song, and as I made my way aft I heard the beginning of some plaintive ditty concerning a "may-i-den of Manches-teer," followed by a rousing chorus from the crew, which had little or nothing to do with the main burden of the ballad, the men's refrain being only a "Yo, heave ho, it's time for us to go!"

A hint which I took.

The wind did not freshen quite so soon as either Mr Mackay or the captain expected; but it continued to blow pretty steadily from the north-west with considerable force, the ship bending over to it as it caught her abaft the beam, and bowling along before it over the billowy ocean like a prancing courser galloping over a race-course, tossing her bows up in the air one moment and plunging them down the next, and spinning along at a rare rate through the crested foam.

As it got later, though, the gale increased; and shortly after "two bells in the first watch," nine o'clock that is in landsman's time, Captain Gillespie, who was on deck again, gave the order to shorten sail.

"Stand by your topgallant halliards!" cried Mr Mackay, giving the necessary instructions for the captain's order to be carried into effect, following this command up immediately by a second—"Let go!"

Then, the clewlines and buntlines were manned, and in a trice the three topgallants were hanging in festooned folds from the upper yards, I doing my first bit of service at sea by laying hold of the ropes that triced up the mizzen-topgallant-sail, and hauling with the others, Mr Mackay giving me a cheery "Well done, my lad," as I did so.

Tom Jerrold, who now appeared on the poop, and whom I had fought shy of before, thinking he had behaved very unkindly to me in the morning, was one of the first to spring into the mizzen-shrouds and climb up the ratlines on the order being given to furl the sail, getting out on the manrope and to the weather earing at the end of the yard before either of the three hands who also went up.

Seeing him go up the rigging, I was on the point of following him; but Mr Mackay, whose previous encouragement, indeed, had spurred me on, stopped me.

"No, my boy," said he kindly, "you must not go aloft yet, for you might fall overboard. Besides, you would not be of the slightest use on the yard even if you didn't tumble. Wait till you've got your sea-legs and know the ropes."

John Conroy Hutcheson

I had therefore to wait and watch Tom Jerrold swinging away up there and bundling the sail together, the gaskets being presently passed round it and the mizzen-topgallant made snug. When Tom and the others came down, he grinned at me so cordially that I made friends with him again; but I was longing all the time for the blissful moment when I too could go aloft like him.

Previously to this, I had given Billy, the ship's boy, a shilling to swab out our cabin and make it all right, so that neither Tom nor Weeks could grumble at the state it was in; and Sam Weeks, at all events, seemed satisfied, for he turned into his bunk as soon as Billy had done cleaning up, having begged Tom Jerrold to take his place for once with the starboard men, who had the first watch this evening instead of the "middle watch," as on the previous night. This shifting of the watches, I may mention here, gives all hands in turn an opportunity of being on deck at every hour of the night and day, without being monotonously bound down to any fixed time to be on duty throughout the voyage, as would otherwise have been the case.

This alternation of the four hours of deck duty is effected by the dog-watches in the afternoon, which being of only two hours duration each, from four o'clock till six the first, and the second from six to eight o'clock, change the whole order of the others; as, for instance, the port watch, which has the deck for the first dog-watch to-night, say, will come on again for the first night watch from eight o'clock till twelve, and the morning watch from four o'clock until eight, the starboard watch, which goes on duty for the second dog-watch, taking the middle watch, from midnight till four o'clock, and then going below to sleep, while the port watch takes the morning one. The arrangement for the following night is exactly the reverse of this, the starbowlines starting with, the first dog-watch and taking the first and the evening watch;

while the port watch has only the second dog-watch and the middle one, from midnight till morning.

I thought I had better explain this, as it was very strange at first to me, and I could not get out of the habit of believing sometimes that I ought to be on deck when it was really my turn to have my "watch in" below.

This evening, as I felt all right and hearty after my pea-soup and had a good sleep in the afternoon, I remained on deck, although the port watch, to which I belonged, was not on duty, Mr Mackay, who had only stayed on the poop to see the topgallants taken in, having at once gone below on this operation being satisfactorily performed.

I was glad I stopped, though; for, presently, Captain Gillespie, ignoring Mr Saunders the second mate, who was now supposed to be in charge of the deck, sang out in his voice of thunder, his nose no doubt shaking terribly the while, albeit I couldn't see it, the evening being too dark and lowering for me even to distinguish plainly that long proboscis of his:

"Hands reef topsails!"

The men, naturally, were even more spry than usual from the fact of "Old Jock" having given the order; so, they were at their posts before the captain could get at his next command.

"Stand by your topsail halliards—let go!"

The yards tumbled down on the caps in an instant as the last word came roaring from Captain Gillespie's lips; and at almost the same moment parties of the men raced up the fore and main and mizzen-shrouds, each lot anxious to have their sail reefed and rehoisted the first.

The foretop men, however, this time, bore away the palm over those attending to the main-topsail; while those on the cro'jack-yard were completely out of the running with only four hands against the fourteen in the other top—although Tom Jerrold was pretty quick again, and if those helping him had been but equally sharp they might, in spite of being short-handed, have achieved the victory.

Urged on by Tim Rooney, though, the men forward were too smart for those aft, and had handed their topsail and were hoisting away at the halliards again before those reefing the main-topsail were all in from their yard. The last man, indeed, was just stepping from the yard into the rigging again, when an accident happened that nearly cost him his life, although fortunately he escaped with only a fall and a fright.

In order to render the work of reefing easier for the hands, the captain had directed the men at the wheel by a quick motion which they understood to "luff her up" a bit, so as to flatten the sails; and now, on the folds of the main-topsail ballooning out before being hoisted again as it caught the wind, the sail flapped back and jerked the unfortunate fellow off the yard, his hands clutching vainly at the empty air.

We could see it all from the poop, although the night was darkish, because the whiteness of the sails made everything stand out in relief against their snowy background; and, as he fell, with a shriek that seemed to go through my heart, I held my breath in agonised suspense, expecting the next moment to hear the dull thud of his mangled body on the deck below.

But, in place of this, a second later, a wild hurrah burst from the men at the halliards and from those coming down the rigging, who had remained spellbound, their descending footsteps arrested in the ratlines in awful expectancy and horror. It was a cheer of relief on their anxious fears being dispelled.

I never heard such a hearty shout in my life before, coming, as it did, as if all the men had but one throat!

I seem to hear it now.

"Hurrah!"

It rang through the ship; and we on the poop soon saw the reason for the triumphant cry and shared the common feeling of joy.

The main-sail had jibed and then bellied out again in the same way as the topsail above it had done; and when the man fell, a kind Providence watching over him caused it to catch him in its folds, and then gently drop him into the long-boat above the deck-house below, right in the midst of the captain's pigs there stowed—thus breaking his fall, so that he absolutely escaped unhurt, with the exception of a slight shaking and of course a biggish fright at falling.

"Who is the man?" sang out Captain Gillespie as soon as some of the hands had clambered up on top of the deck-house and released their comrade from the companionship of the pigs, who were grunting and squealing at his unexpected descent in their midst. "Who is that man?"

"Joe Fergusson," cried out one of the men. "It's Joe Fergusson, sir."

Captain Gillespie was bothered, thinking he could not hear aright.

"Joe Fergusson?" he called back. "I don't know any man of

John Conroy Hutcheson

that name, or anything like it, who signed articles with me, and is entered on the ship's books. Pass the word forrud for the bosun—where is he?"

"Here, sorr," cried out Tim Rooney, who of course was close at hand, having bounded to the scene of action the moment he heard the man's wild weird shriek as he fell, arriving just in time to see his wonderful escape. "Here I am, sorr."

"Who is the man that fell?"

"Our new hand, sorr."

"New hand?" repeated Captain Gillespie after him, as perplexed as ever. "What new hand?"

"Joe Fergusson, sorr. Himsilf and no ither, sure, sorr."

"What the dickens do ye mean, man?" said the captain, angry at the mystification. "I don't know of any Joe Fergusson or any new hands save those I brought on board myself at Gravesend; and there was no one of that name amongst 'em, I'm certain."

"Aye, aye, thrue for ye, cap'en," answered Tim, and although, of course, I couldn't see him, I'm sure he must have winked when he spoke, there was a tone of such rich jocularity in his voice; "but, sure, sor this is the chap as brought himsilf aboard. He's the stowaway, sorr; Joe Fergusson, by the same token!"

CHAPTER TEN

CROSSING THE LINE

"Humph!" grunted Captain Gillespie, astounded by this information. "That's the joker, is it?"

"Aye, aye, sorr," said Tim Rooney, thinking he was asked the question again as to the other's identity; "it's him, sure enough."

"Then I should like to know what the dickens he means by such conduct as this? The beggar first comes aboard my ship without my leave or license, and then tries to break his neck by going aloft when nobody sent him there!"

"Arrah sure, sorr, the poor chap owny did it to show his willin'ness to worruk his passige, sayin' as how Mr Mackay tould him ye'd blow him up for comin' aboard whin he came-to this arternoon, sorr," pleaded Tim, not perceiving, as I did, that all the captain's anger against the unfortunate stowaway had melted away by this time on learning that he had shown such courage. "Begorra, he would cloimb up the shrouds, sorr, whin ye tould the hands to lay aloft; an' the divil himsilf, sorr, wouldn't 'a stopped him."

"He's a plucky fellow," cried the captain in a much more

John Conroy Hutcheson

amiable tone of voice, to Tim's great surprise.

"Send him aft, bosun, and I'll talk to him now instead of to-morrow, as I said."

"Aye, aye, sorr," replied Tim; and, presently, the stowaway, who looked none the worse for his fall, came shambling sheepishly up the poop ladder, Tim following in his wake, and saying as he ushered him into the captain's presence, "Here he is, sorr."

"Well, you rascal," exclaimed Captain Gillespie, looking at him up and down with his squinting eyes and sniffing, taking as good stock of him as the faint light would permit, "what have you got to say for yourself—eh?"

"Oi dunno," answered the ragged lad, touching his forelock and making a scrape back with his foot, in deferential salute. "Of's got nowt ter say, only as Oi'll wark me pessage if you'll let me be, and dunno put me in that theer dark pit agin."

"Do you know you're liable to three months imprisonment with hard labour for stowing yourself aboard my ship?" replied Captain Gillespie, paying no attention to his words apparently, and going on as if he had not spoken. "What will you do if I let you off?"

"Oi'll wark, measter," cried the other eagerly. "Oi'll wark loike a good un, Oi will, sure, if you lets Oi be."

"Ha, humph! I'll give you a try, then," jerked out Old Jock with a snort, after another nautical inspection of the new hand; "only, mind you don't go tumbling off the yard again. I don't want any accidents on board my ship, although I expect every man to do his duty; and when I say a thing I mean a thing. What's your name—eh?"

"Oi be called Joe Fergusson, measter," replied the shock-headed fellow, moving rather uneasily about and shuffling his feet on the deck, the captain's keen quizzical glance making him feel a bit nervous. "My mates at whoam, though, names me, and the folk in Lancacheer tew, 'Joey the moucher.'"

"Oh, then, Master Joey, you'll find you can't mooch here, my lad," retorted Old Jock, glad of the opportunity of having one of his personal jokes, and sniggering and snorting over it in fine glee. "However, I'll forgive you coming aboard on the promise of your working your passage to China; but, you won't find that child's play, my joker! Fergusson, I'll enter you on the ship's books and you'll be rated as an able seaman, for you look as if you had the makings of one in you from the way you've tried already to earn your keep."

"Thank ye koindly, measter," stammered out the redoubtable Joe, seeing from the captain's manner that his peace was made, and that nothing dreadful was going to be done to him, as he had feared from all that Tim Rooney and the hands forward had told him of Old Jock's temper—although he did not understand half what the captain said—"Oi'll wark, measter."

"There, that will do," said Captain Gillespie interrupting him ere he could proceed any further with his protestations of gratitude; "the proof of the pudding lies in the eating, and I'll soon see what you're made of. Bosun, take him forrud and rig him out as well as you can. I'll send you an old shirt and trousers by the steward."

"Aye, aye, sorr," answered Tim obediently, pleased at "the ould skipper behavin' so handsomely," as he afterwards said; "an' I'll give him an ould pair av brogues av me own."

"You can do as you like about that," said Captain Gillespie, turning on his heel and calling the watch to tauten the lee-braces a bit, telling the men at the wheel at the same time to "luff" more; "but, you'd better let the chap have a good lie-in to-night and put him in the port watch to-morrow so that Mr Mackay can look after him."

"Aye, aye, sorr," replied Tim, leading his charge down the poop ladder again. "I'll say to that same, sorr."

"And, bosun—"

"Aye, aye, sorr."

"Just see if those pigs in the long-boat got damaged by that fellow tumbling on top of them. His weight ought to have been enough to have made pork of some, I should think!"

"Aye, aye, sorr," said Tim as he went off laughing; and I could hear his whispered aside to Adams, who was standing by the deck-house. "Begorra, I'd have betted the ould skipper wouldn't forgit thim blissid pigs av his. He wor thinkin' av thim all the toime that poor beggar wor fallin' from aloft, I belave!"

Much to the captain's satisfaction, though, the grunting inhabitants of the long-boat were found to be all right, escaping as harmlessly as Joe Fergusson; and so, with his mind relieved Old Jock went below soon after "six bells," or two o'clock, leaving the charge of the deck to Mr Saunders—who, grumbling at the captain's rather insidious usurpation of his authority, had betaken himself to the lee-side of the taffrail, whence he watched the ship's wake and the foaming rollers that came tumbling after her, as she drove on before the stiff nor'-wester under reefed topsails and courses, the waves trying to poop her every instant, though foiled by her speed.

So things went on till midnight, when the men at the wheel were relieved, as well as the look-out forward, and the port watch came on deck; while, the starbowlines going below, Mr Mackay took the place of the second mate as the officer on duty. Tom Jerrold, too, lugged out Sam Weeks and made him put in an appearance, much against his will; but nothing subsequently occurred to vary the monotony of the life on board or interfere with the vessel's progress, for, although it was blowing pretty nearly "half a gale," as sailors say, we "made a fair wind of it"—keeping steadily on our course, south-west by west, and getting more and more out into the Atlantic with each mile of the seething water the Silver Queen spurned with her forefoot and left eddying behind her.

The wind, somehow or other, seemed to get into my head, like a glass of champagne I had on Christmas-day when father and all of us went to Westham Hall and dined with the squire. I can't express how jolly it made me feel—the wind I mean, not the champagne; for it was as much as I could do to refrain from shouting out aloud in my exultation, as it blew in my face and tossed my hair about, pressing against my body with such force that I had to hold on by both hands to the weather bulwarks to keep my feet, as I gazed out over the side at the magnificent scene around me—the storm-tossed sea, one mass of foam; the grand blue vault of heaven above, now partially lit by the late rising moon and twinkling stars, that were occasionally obscured by scraps of drifting clouds and flying scud; and, all the while, the noble ship tearing along, a thing of beauty and of life, mastering the elements and glorying in the fight, with the hum of the gale in the sails and its shrieking whistle through the rigging, and the ever-murmuring voices of the waters, all filling the air around as they sang the dirge of the deep!

John Conroy Hutcheson

"You seem to like it, youngster," observed Mr Mackay, stopping his quarter-deck walk as he caught sight of my face in the moonlight and noticed it's joyous glow, reflecting the emotions of my mind. "You look a regular stormy petrel, and seem as if you wanted to spread your wings and fly."

"I only wish I could, sir," I cried, laughing at his likening me to a "Mother Carey's chicken," as the petrel is familiarly termed, a number of them then hovering about the ship astern. "I feel half a bird already, the wind makes me so jolly."

Mr Mackay quietly smiled and put his hand on my shoulder.

"Take care, my boy," said he good-humouredly, "you'll be jumping overboard in your enthusiasm. You seem to be a born sailor. Are you really so fond of the sea?"

"I love it! I love it!" I exclaimed enthusiastically. "Now, I can imagine, sir, the meaning of what I read in Xenophon with father, about the soldiers of Cyrus crying with joy when they once more beheld the sea after their toilsome march for months and months, wandering inland over a strange and unknown country without a sight of its familiar face to tell them of their home by the wave-girt shores of Greece!"

"You're quite a poet, Graham," observed Mr Mackay, laughing now, though not unkindly. There was, indeed, a tone of regret and of sadness, it seemed to me, in his voice. "Ah, well, you'll soon have all such romantic notions taken out of you, my boy, when you've seen some of the hardships of a sailor's life, like others who at one time were, perhaps, as full of ardour for their profession at the start as yourself."

"I hope not, sir," I replied seriously. "I should never like to believe differently of it to what I do now. I think it is really something to be proud of, being a sailor. It is glorious, it—it—it's—jolly, that's what it is, sir!"

"A jolly sight jollier being in bed on a cold night like this," muttered Weeks, who was shivering by the skylight, the tarpaulin cover of which he had dragged round his legs for warmth. "Don't you think so, sir?"

"That depends," replied Mr Mackay on Sammy putting this question to him rather impudently, as was his wont in speaking to his elders, his bump of veneration being of the most infinitesimal proportions. "I think, though, that a fellow who likes being on deck in a gale of wind will turn out a better sailor than a skulker who only cares about caulking in his bunk below; and you can put that in your pipe, Master Sam Weeks, and smoke it!"

This had the effect of stopping any further conversation on the part of my fellow apprentice, who retired to the lee-side of the deck in high dudgeon with this "flea in his ear;" and, it being just four o'clock in the morning now and the end of the middle watch, eight bells were struck and the starbowlines summoned on deck again to duty, we of the port watch getting some hot coffee all round at the galley and then turning in. For this I was not sorry, as I began now to feel sleepy.

"I'd rather be a dog with the mange than a sailor," yawned Tom Jerrold when Sam Weeks roused him out of his nice warm bunk to go on duty in the cold grey morning. "Heigh-ho, it's an awful life!"

So, it can be seen that all of us were not of one opinion in the matter.

But, in spite of sundry drawbacks and disagreeables which I

subsequently encountered, and which perhaps took off a little of the halo of romance which at first encircled everything connected with the sea in my mind, I have never lost the love and admiration for it which I experienced that night in mid Atlantic when I kept the middle watch with Mr Mackay, nor regretted my choice; neither have I ever felt inclined, I may candidly state, to give an affirmative answer to Tim Rooney's stereotyped inquiry every morning—"An' ain't ye sorry now, Misther Gray-ham, as how ye iver came to say?"

The next day, our third out from the Lizard, we spoke the barque Mary Webster from Valparaiso for London, sixty days at sea.

She signalled that she had broken her chronometer and had to trust only to her dead reckoning, so Captain Gillespie hove-to and gave them our latitude and longitude, 45 degrees 15 minutes North and 10 degrees 20 minutes West, displaying the figures chalked on a black-board over our quarter, in order that those on board the other vessel might read the inscription easily with a glass, as we bowed and dipped towards each other across the rolling waves, both with our main-topsails backed.

Before the following morning we had weathered Cape Finisterre, Mr Mackay told me, having got finally beyond the limits of the dread Bay of Biscay, with all its opposing tides and contrary influences of winds and currents which make it such a terror to navigators passing both to and from the Equator; and, in another two days, we had reached as far south as the fortieth parallel of latitude, our longitude being now 13 degrees 10 minutes west, or about some five hundred miles to the eastward of the Azores, or Western Islands.

As we worked our way further westwards I noticed a curious thing which I could not make out until Mr Mackay enlightened me on the subject.

On my last birthday father had given me a very nice little gold watch, similar to one which he had presented to my brother Tom, much to my envy at the time, on his likewise obtaining his fifteenth year.

This watch was a very good timekeeper, being by one of the best London makers; and, hitherto, had maintained an irreproachable character in this respect, the cook at home, whenever the kitchen clock went wrong, always appealing to me to know what was the correct time, with the flattering compliment that "Master Allan's watch, at all events," was "sure to be right!"

But now, strange to say, although my watch kept exactly to railway time up to the day of my arrival in London and while we were on our way down the river, I found that, as we proceeded into the Channel and out to sea it began to gain, the difference being more and more marked as we got further to the westward; until, when the captain, after taking the sun on our fifth day out, told Tom Jerrold who was on the deck beside him to "make it eight bells," or strike the ship's bell to declare it was noon, I was very nearly an hour ahead of that time—my watch, which I was always careful about winding up every evening as father enjoined me when giving it to me, pointing actually to one o'clock!

I could not understand it all.

Mr Mackay, however, made it clear to me after a little explanation, showing me, too, how simple a matter it was with a good chronometer to find a ship's position at sea.

"For every degree of longitude we go westwards from the meridian of Greenwich, which is marked with a great round

John Conroy Hutcheson

0 here, you see, my boy, we gain four minutes," said he, pointing out the lines of longitude ruled straight up and down the chart as he spoke, for my information; "and thus, the fact of the hands of your watch telling, truly enough, that it is now about eight minutes to one o'clock in London, shows that we are thirteen degrees further to the west than at the place where your time is set—for we are going with the sun, do you see?"

"Yes, I see, sir," said I; "but suppose we were going to the east instead of the west?"

"Why then, my boy," he replied, "your watch, in lieu of gaining, would appear to lose the same number of minutes each day, according to our rate of sailing. A ship, consequently, which goes round the world from the east to the west will seem to have gained a clear day on circumnavigating the globe; while one that completes the same voyage sailing from the west continually towards the east, loses one."

"How funny!" cried I. "Is it really so?"

"Yes, really," said he; "and I've seen, on board a ship I was once in, the captain skip a day in the log, to make up for the one we lost on the voyage, passing over Saturday and writing down the day which followed Friday as 'Sunday'—otherwise we would have been all out of our reckoning with the almanac."

"How funny!" I repeated. "I never heard that before."

"Probably not, nor many other things you'll learn at sea, my boy, before you're much older," answered Mr Mackay, as he turned to the log slate on which Captain Gillespie had been putting down his calculation about the ship's position after taking the sun and working out his reckoning. "Let us see, now, if your watch is a good chronometer for telling our longitude. Ha, by Jove, 13 degrees 10 minutes west, or, nearly what we made out just now. Not so bad, Graham, for a turnip!"

"Turnip, sir!" cried I indignantly. "Father told me it was one of Dent's best make, and to be careful of it."

"I'm sure I beg both your father's and Dent's pardon," said Mr Mackay, laughing at my firing up so quickly. "I was only joking; for your watch is a very good one, and nicely finished too. But I must not stop any more now. I hope you won't forget your first lesson in navigation and the know-ledge you've gained of the difference between 'mean time' and what is called 'apparent time' on board a ship, and how this will tell her correct longitude—eh?"

"Oh, no, sir," I answered as he went off down the companion way below, to wind up the chronometers in the captain's cabin, a task which he always performed every day at the same hour, having these valuable instruments under his especial charge; "I won't forget what you've told me, sir."

Nor did I.

Shortly afterwards Mr Mackay showed me how to use the sextant and take the sun's altitude, on his learning that I was acquainted with trigonometry and rather a dab at mathe-matics, the only portion indeed of my studies, I'm sorry to confess, in which I ever took any interest at school. I was thus soon able under his instruction to work out the ship's reckoning and calculate her position, just like the captain, who sniffed and snorted a bit and crinkled his nose a good deal on seeing me engaged on the task; although he gave me some friendly commendation all the same, when he found

John Conroy Hutcheson

that I had succeeded in actually arriving at a similar result to himself!

Wasn't I proud, that's all.

But, before advancing so far in my knowledge of navigation, I had to be initiated into my regular duties on board, and learn the more practical parts of seamanship; however, having willing tutors in Mr Mackay and the boatswain, and being only too anxious myself to know all they could teach me, it was not long before I was able to put it out of the power of either Tom Jerrold or Weeks to call me "Master Jimmy Green," as they at first christened me—just because they had the advantage of going to sea a voyage or two before me! I may add, too, that my progress towards proficiency in picking up the endless details of nautical lore was all the more accelerated by the desire of excelling my shipmates, so as to have the chance of turning their chaff back upon themselves.

Spurred on by this motive, I quickly learnt all the names of the ropes and their various uses from Mr Mackay; while Tim Rooney showed me how to make a "reef knot," a "clove hitch," a "running bowline," and a "sheep-shank," explaining the difference between these and their respective advantages over the common "granny's knot" of landsmen—my friend the boatswain judiciously discriminating between the typical peculiarities of the "cat's-paw" and the "sheet bend," albeit the one has nothing in connection with the feline tribe and the other no reference to one's bed-covering!

The wind moderated when we got below the Azores, while the sea also ceased its tumultuous whirl, so that we were able to make all plain sail and carry-on without rolling as before; so, now, at last, I was allowed to go aloft, my first essay being to assist Tom Jerrold in setting the mizzen-royal.

Really, I quite astonished Tom by climbing up the futtock shrouds outside the top, instead of going through "the lubber's hole," showing myself, thanks to Tim Rooney's private instructions previously, much more nimble in casting off the gaskets and loosening the bunt of the sail than my brother mid expected; indeed, I got off the yard, after the job was done, and down to the deck a good half minute in advance of him.

On our sixth day out, we reached latitude 35 degrees north and 17 degrees west, drifting past Madeira a couple of days later, the temperature of the air gradually rising and the western winds growing correspondingly slack as we made more southing; until, although it was barely a week since we had been experiencing the bitter weather of our English February, we now seemed to be suddenly transported into the balminess of June. The change, however, took place so imperceptibly during our gradual progress onward to warmer latitudes, that, in looking back all at once, it seemed almost incredible.

I found the work which we apprentices had to do was really very similar to that of the hands forward, Tom Jerrold and I in the port watch, and Weeks and Matthews—who, although styled "third mate," had still to go aloft and do the same sort of duties as all the rest of us—in the starboard watch under the second mate, having to attend to everything connected with the setting and taking in of sail on the mizzen-mast, as well as having to keep the ship's time, one of us striking the bell every half-hour throughout our spell on deck.

After the first few days at sea, too, I came to the conclusion that if our work was like that of the sailors our food was not one whit the better; albeit, one of the stipulations in the contract when my father paid the premium demanded by the owners of the ship for me as a "first-class apprentice," was that I should mess aft in the cabin.

I certainly did so, like Tom Jerrold and the two others; but all that either they or I had of cabin fare throughout the entire voyage was an occasional piece of "plum duff" and jam on Sundays—on which day, by the way, we had no work to do save attending to the sails and washing decks in the morning; while, in the afternoon, Captain Gillespie read prayers on the poop, his congregation being mainly limited to ourselves and the watch on deck, the crew spending their holiday, on this holy day, in mending their clothes in the forecastle.

Yes, our rations were the same as those of the ordinary hands; namely, salt junk and "hard tack," varied by pea-soup and sea-pie occasionally for dinner, with rice and molasses as a treat on Saturdays. Our breakfast and tea consisted of a straw-coloured decoction known on board-ship as "water bewitched," accompanied by such modicums of our dinner allowance as we were able to save conscientiously with our appetites. This amounted to very little as a rule, for, being at sea makes one fearfully hungry at all hours, and, fortunately, seems to endow one, also, with the capacity for eating anything!

Really, if it had not been by currying favour with Ching Wang and bribing the steward, Pedro Carvalho, between whom there were continual rows occurring about the provisions, which it was the duty of the Portuguese to serve out, we must have starved ere reaching the Equator; for Captain Gillespie, in order to "turn an honest penny" and make his Dundee venture prove a success, persuaded the men forward and ourselves to give up a pound and a quarter of our meat ration for a pound tin of his marmalade, which he assured us would not only be more palatable with our biscuit, being such "a splendid substitute for butter," as the advertisements on the labels say, but would also act as an antiscorbutic to prevent the spread of scurvy amongst us—it being, as he declared, better than lime-juice for this purpose!

The hands consented to this arrangement at first as a welcome change; but, when they presently found themselves mulcted of their salt junk, they grumbled much at Old Jock for holding us all to the bargain, and he and his marmalade became a by-word in the ship. I did not wonder at all, after a bit, that Pedro the steward got into the habit of venting his wrath when vexed by kicking the empty tins about!

I cannot say, however, that I disliked my new life, in spite of these drawbacks in the way of insufficiency of food and constancy of appetite, throughout which Ching Wang remained my staunch friend, bringing me many a savoury little delicacy for supper when it was my night watch on deck. These tit-bits in the "grub" line I conscientiously shared with Tom Jerrold, who received similar favours from the steward, with whom he was a firm favourite, the only one, indeed, to whom the Portuguese appeared to take kindly on board.

No, on the contrary, the charm of being a sailor grew more and more upon me each day as the marvels of the deep became unfolded to me, and the better I became acquainted with the ship and my companions.

All was endless variety—the sky, the sea, and our surroundings changing apparently every moment and ever revealing something fresh and novel.

It did not seem real but a dream.

Could that be the Madeira I had read about in the distance, and that the Bay of Funchal of which I had seen pictures in books; and that the little nautilus or "Portuguese man-of-war"

John Conroy Hutcheson

floating by the side of the vessel, now almost becalmed, with its cigar-shaped shell boat and pink membraneous sail all glowing with prismatic colouring? Was it an actuality that I saw all these things with my own eyes; or, was I dreaming? Was it really I, Allan Graham, standing there on the deck of the good ship Silver Queen, or somebody else?

An order from the captain, who came up from his cabin just then and caught me mooning, to go forward and "make it eight bells," stopped my reflections at this interesting point; and the next moment I was more interested in a most appetising odour of lobscouse emanating from Ching Wang's galley than in poetical dreams of Atlantic isles and ocean wonders!

On passing Madeira, we soon got out of the Horse Latitudes, a soft breeze springing up from the west again towards evening, which wafted us down to the Canaries within the next two days. Here we picked up the north-east trades south of Palma, just when we could barely discern the Peak of Teneriffe far-away off high up in the clouds, and then we went on grandly on our voyage once more with every sail set, logging over two hundred miles a day and going by the Cape de Verde Islands in fine style. We did not bring up again until we reached "the Doldrums," in about latitude 5 degrees north and 22 degrees west, where the fickle wind deserted us again and left us rolling and sweltering in the great region of equatorial calm. The north-east and south-east trades here fight each other for the possession of their eventful battle-ground, the Line, and old Neptune finds the contest so wearisome that he goes to sleep while it lasts, the tumid swelling of his mighty bosom only showing to all whom it may concern that he merely dozes and is not dead!

The temperature of the sea seemed to increase each day after we lost sight of the Peak of Teneriffe until it was now lukewarm, if one drew a bucket from over the side; although Captain Gillespie said it was "quite cold" for that time of year!

Talking about this, Mr Mackay told me that sea-water is composed of an awful lot of things such as I would not have supposed—oxygen and hydrogen, with muriate of soda, magnesia, iron, lime, copper, silica, potash, chlorine, iodine, bromide, ammonia and silver being amongst its ingredients, and the muriate of soda forming the largest of the solid substances detected in it. With such a mixture of things as this, it is not surprising that it should taste so nasty when swallowed—is it?

With the enforced leisure produced by the calm, I had plenty of opportunity for observing the various strange varieties of animal life which came about the ship—the flying-fish with beautiful silvery wings that sparkled in the sunlight coming inboard in shoals, pursued by their enemies the albacores, who drove them out of the sea to take refuge in the air; besides numbers of grampusses and sharks swimming round us. Adams, the sailmaker, killed one of these latter gentry with a harpoon, spearing him from the bowsprit as he came past the ship. He looked up with his evil eye, fancying perhaps that he would "catch one of us napping," but no one was unwary enough to get within reach of his voracious maw; and Mr Shark "caught a tartar" instead and got a taste of cold steel for his pains, much to our delight, though the captain was chagrined at the loss of the harpoon, the shark parting the line attached to it in his death struggles, and carrying it below with him when he sank. The brute, to end the story, was eaten up at once by his affectionate comrades, the sea being dyed red with his blood.

We had not all leisure, though, thus hanging about the Equator under the scorching sun, now at noon precisely perpendicular over our heads, the heat at night too being almost as stifling and the stars as bright as moons; for Captain Gillespie took advantage of our inaction to "set up" the rigging, which had slackened considerably since we entered the tropics, the heat making the ropes stretch so that our masts got loose and the upper spars canted.

While doing this, of course, I had another practical lesson in seamanship, learning all about "double luffs" and "toggles," "salvagee strops" and "Burton tackles," and all the rest of such gear, whose name is legion.

But I must go on now to a more important incident.

One morning, about a week after the wind left us, with the exception of an occasional cat's-paw of air which came from every point of the compass in turn, we ultimately drifted to the Line; accomplishing this by the aid of the swell ever rolling southward and the eddy of the great south equatorial current, setting between the African continent and the Caribbean Sea. This meets the Guinea current running in the opposite direction in the middle of the Doldrums, and helps to promote the pleasant stagnation, of wind and water and of air alike, of this delightful region so dear to mariners!

I recollect the morning well; for the night was unusually oppressive, the heat between the middle watch and eight bells having been more intense than at any period, I thought, during the week.

So, after tossing about my bunk, unable to get to sleep I was only too glad when the time came to turn out for duty, the task of washing decks and paddling about in the cool water—for it was cool at the earlier hours of the morning if tepid at noon—being something to look forward to.

I forgot, however, all about the terrible rites of Neptune for those crossing the Line for the first time, and neither Tom Jerrold nor Weeks, naturally, enlightened me on the subject; so that I was completely taken by surprise when a loud voice hailed us from somewhere forward, just about "four bells," as if coming from out of the sea.

"What ship is that?"

"The Silver Queen," answered Mr Saunders, who was on the poop and of course in the joke, answering the voice, which although portentously loud, had a familiar ring about it suspiciously like Tim Rooney's Irish brogue. "Bound from London to Shanghai."

"Have ye minny of me unshaved sons aboard?"

"Aye, two," shouted back Mr Saunders, "a stowaway and an apprentice."

"Ye spake true," returned the voice. "I knows 'em both, Misther Allan Gray-ham an' Joe Fergusson. I will come aboard an' shave 'em."

Then it all flashed upon me, and I tried to run below and hide; but two of Neptune's tritons seized me and pushed me forward to where the boatswain, capitally got up in an oakum wig with an enormous tow beard, was seated on the windlass, trident in hand. Joe Fergusson, who had been made prisoner before me, lay bound at his feet, close to an improvised swimming bath made out of a spare fore-topsail, rigged up across the deck on the lee-side and filled with water to the depth of four feet or more.

The ceremonies were just about to begin; and, I could readily imagine what was in store for both me and my companion in distress, the ex-bricklayer, who, like myself, having never been to sea before would have to go through the painful ordeal as well as being made fools of and laughed at by all our grinning shipmates around; so, seeing Tom Jerrold and Sam Weeks conspicuous right in front of me, and Mr Saunders looking on too with much gusto, I made another desperate attempt to free myself from those holding me, urging on Joe Fergusson to try and save himself and me too.

Our struggles were in vain; but, strange to say, help came for us from a most unexpected quarter.

As I have said before, the night had been extremely hot and the morning lowering; and now, all at once, a violent squall caught the ship in the midst of Neptune's carnival.

"Stand by your royal halliards!" roared out Captain Gillespie, who coming up quickly behind Mr Saunders on the poop made him jump round in consternation at his neglect in not keeping a look-out overhead while watching the game going on in the bows amongst the crew.

Neptune darted down from his perch instanter in the most ungodlike fashion; and, the rest of the men rushing to their stations, left Joe Fergusson and I rolling on the deck.

"Let go!" next cried the captain; adding a moment later, "Bosun, go forward and slack off the head sheets!"

And then the rain came down in a perfect deluge, as if it were being emptied out of a tub, and as it only can pour down in the tropics; and that is how we "crossed the Line!"

CHAPTER ELEVEN

"ONE PIECEE COCK-FIGHTEE"

The ship had nearly all her canvas spread, so as to take advantage of the first puff of air which came to waft us beyond the Doldrums towards the region of the south-east trades, then beginning to blow just below the calm belt; consequently, it took all hands some time to clew up and furl all the light upper sails, and squall after squall burst over us ere we could reduce the ship to her proper fighting trim of reefed topsails and courses, our outer jib getting torn to shreds before it could be handed.

"Begorra, it's a buster an' no mishtake!" exclaimed Tim Rooney coming off the forecastle as soon as he had seen the other head sails attended to, and setting me free from the lashings with which his whilom tritons had bound my hands and legs. "Sp'ilin' all av our fun, too, Misther Gray-ham, jist whin I wor goin' to shave ye!"

I did not regret this, though, I'm sure. Still, I did not stop to answer him, being in too great a hurry to join Tom Jerrold and the others aft in taking in the mizzen-royal and topgallant—my fellow apprentices having had time already to get aloft while I was rolling on the deck forward like a trussed fowl!

John Conroy Hutcheson

"Take it aisy, me darlint," shouted Tim after me as I rushed up the poop ladder and swung myself into the shrouds; but, I was half-way up the ratlines before he could get out the end of his exordium, "Aisy does it!"

I was too late to help hand the royal, my especial sail since I had got familiar with my footing aloft; but the mizzen-topgallant sheets, bowlines and halliards having been hardly a second let go, and the men on the poop having only just begun to haul on the clewlines and buntlines, I was quite in time to get out on this yard. My aid, indeed, came in usefully in assisting to stow the sail; although, in my haste not to be eclipsed by Tom Jerrold, I nearly got knocked off my perch on the foot-rope through the canvas ballooning out, in the same way as it did when Joe Fergusson so narrowly escaped death only three weeks or so before!

The fright, as I clutched hold of a rope and saved myself, made my heart come in my mouth; and what with this, and the turmoil of the elements around me as I clung to the yard, with the deck of the ship so small and far-away below, and saw the immense area of the swelling sea as far as the eye could reach—now chopped up into short rolling waves, crowned with foam, almost in an instant, and the black cloud-covered dome of the heavens that was almost as dark as at midnight—I could not help thinking of the grandeur of the works of God, and the insignificance of man and his pigmy attempts to master the elements.

For, beyond the quick sharp puffs of wind that came with the squalls of rain from almost every point of the compass in succession, the downpour which descended from the over-cast sky was accompanied with terrible ear-splitting peals of thunder. This seemed to rattle and roll almost immediately above our heads, as if the overhanging black vault was about to burst open every moment; while dazzling forked flashes of bluish lightning zigzagged across the horizon from the zenith, first blinding our eyes with its brilliancy for a second and then making the darkness all around the darker as the vivid glare vanished and the accompanying thunderbolt sank into the sea—providentially far off to leeward, where the full force of the tropical storm was spent, and not near our vessel.

The sight was an awful and magnificent one to me suspended there in mid-air, as it were; but I confess I was not sorry when, presently, the mizzen-topgallant was snugly stowed, with the gaskets put round it, and I was able to get down to the more substantial deck below, where I was not quite so close to the cloud war going on above!

When I reached the poop, as the Silver Queen was now stripped of her superfluous canvas and ready for anything that might happen should the squalls last, Mr Mackay seeing that I was wet through told me that I might go down and change my clothes. This I gratefully did, feeling all the better on getting into a dry suit, over which I took the precaution before coming out of the deck-house again of rigging my waterproof and a tarpaulin hat; for the rain was still coming down in a regular deluge, "as if the sluice-valve of the water tank above had somehow or other jammed foul, so that the water couldn't be turned off for a while"—this being Tom Jerrold's explanation of it.

Feeling chilled from the damp after the great heat of the morning, as soon as I had doffed my wet things I went round to the galley to see if I could discover a drop of hot coffee knocking about, as it was getting on for tea-time, being now late in the afternoon; but when I got there, instead of finding Ching Wang, who was always punctuality itself in the matter of meal-times, busy with the coppers, there he was flat on his stomach on the floor of his caboose, with a hideous little brass image or idol, which might have been Buddha for all that I know to the contrary, set up in the corner—the Chinese cook being so actively engaged in salaaming in front of this image, by touching the deck with his forehead and burning bits of gilt paper before it, as incense I suppose, that he did not notice me.

"Hullo, Ching Wang," I said, "what are you about?"

"Me chin chin joss, lilly pijjin," he answered, turning to me his round, unconscious, and imperturbable face as if he were engaged in some ordinary occupation of everyday life. "Me askee him me watchee if kyphong catchee ship, no sabey?"

The poor fellow evidently believed more in his god than I did in mine; for here he was in a moment of danger, as he thought, praying for help, while I, who had almost lost my life when I so nearly escaped tumbling from the topgallant yard only a moment or so since, had thoughtlessly forgotten Him who had saved me!

I think of this now, but I didn't then. Nay, I even laughed at Ching Wang's ignorance when speaking to Tim Rooney, whom I met as I retreated from the galley, telling him that I wondered how the generally astute Chinaman could really fancy he was propitiating Buddha, or whoever else he believed in as his sovereign deity, by burning a few scraps of tinsel paper to do honour to the senseless image.

"Be jabers, though," argued Tim on my giving him this opinion of mine, "I can't say, sorr, as how we Christians be any the betther."

"Why!" I exclaimed indignantly. "How can you say so?"

"Begorra, sure we all thry to have our ray-ligion as chape as we can," replied he coolly. "Don't we, Cath'lics an' Protistints aloike, for there's little to choose atwane us on the p'int, contint oursilves wid as little as we can hilp, goin' once to chapel or church, mebbe, av a Sunday an' thinkin' we've wiped out all the avil we may a-done in the wake, an' have a clane sheet for the nixt one—jist as this poor ig'rant haythin booms his goold paper afore his joss an' thinks that clears off all his ould scores. I say no differ, sure, mesilf, Misther Gray-ham, atwane us, that same, as I tould ye."

I did not answer Tim, but his words affected me more than any sermon I ever heard from the pulpit; and, as I went back to my cabin I determined to try and keep to something I had promised father before parting from him, and which I had neglected up to then—my promise being never to forget my daily prayer to "Him who rules the waves," even should I have no time to look at my Bible.

The weather cleared up before sunset, and the wind subsequently began to blow steadily from the southward and eastward, showing that we had at length got into the wished-for "trade;" so the ship soon had all plain sail set on her again, now heading, though, sou'-sou'-west on the port tack, and making a bee-line almost for the island of Trinidad off the South American coast.

Having lost our outer jib, however, from its blowing away in the first squall, a new one had to be fitted and bent on; and as we were hoisting studding sails, too, the jewel block on the main-topsail yard carried away. So, another block had to be got up and secured to the end of the yard-arm before the halliards could be rove afresh for getting up the stu'n'sail; and, I had opportunities in both instances for acquiring better knowledge of seamanship—gaining more by watching Adams the sailmaker and Tim Rooney at work on their respective jobs, than I could have obtained in a twelvemonth by the perusal of books or from oral information.

We had long lost sight of our old friend the North Star and his pointers, who guide the mariner, should he be without a compass, in northern latitudes, making acquaintance now with a new constellation, the Southern Cross, which grew more brilliant each night as we ran further and further below the Equator. Other stars, too, of surpassing brightness made the heavens all radiant as soon as the sun set each evening, there being no twilight to speak of—the night and its glories coming upon us as quickly as the last scrap of daylight fled. In the morning it was the same, the firmament being still bright with starlight when the glorious orb of day rose in all his majesty and paled into insignificance his lesser rivals, who, however, twinkled up to the very last.

This was by far the jolliest part of our voyage; for, although the weather was nice and warm, it had not that disagreeable, clammy heat we experienced at the Line, on account of the fresh south-east breeze tempering the effect of the sun, which, however, still shone down on us at noon with tropical force, its rays being as potent almost as at the Equator.

But the sea had lost all that glassy brazen look it had in the calm latitudes, now dancing with life and as blue as the heavens above it; while as our gallant ship sailed on, running pretty large on the port tack with everything set that could draw—skysails being hoisted on top of the royals and staysails, and trysails on every mast, with the foretopmast staysail, jib and flying jib forward, and upper and lower stu'n'sails spread out to windward—she looked like some beautiful bird in full flight with outstretched wings, her motion through the water being so easy and graceful, while the sparkling spray was tossed up sometimes over the sprit-sail yard as she ever and anon dipped her bows, as if curtsying to Neptune. It seemed to me the most delightful thing in the world to be there, ship and sea and air and sky being all alike in harmony, expressing the poetry of progression!

My work, too, although we had plenty to do, to "keep us out of mischief," as the captain said, was not too hard, especially at this period.

In the morning, after an early coffee, when few thought of turning in again although it might be their watch below, the weather was so enjoyable, the order was given for "brooms and buckets aft," and the first duty of the day was attended to. This was to scrub decks, just as in a well-ordered household the servant cleans the door-step before anyone is astir; the decks of a ship giving as good a notion of what her commander is like, as the door-step of a house does of its mistress!

For this job the men forward rigged the head pump and sluiced the forecastle and main-deck; while we apprentices had to wash down the poop, having a fine time over it dowsing one another with buckets of water, and chasing each other round the mizzen-mast and binnacle, or else dodging the expected deluge behind the skylight—sometimes awaking Captain Gillespie up, and making him come up the companion in a towering rage to ask "what the dickens" we were "kicking up all that row for?"

Once, as he came up in this way, Tom Jerrold caught him full in the face with a bucket of water he was pitching at me; and wasn't there a shindy over it, that's all! "Old Jock" was unable to find out who did it, for of course none of us would tell on Tom, and the water in the captain's eyes prevented him from seeing who was his assailant; but, he immediately ordered Tom, as well as Weeks and I, all up into the cross-trees, Tom at the fore, Sam at the main, and I on the mizzen-mast, to "look out for land," instead of having our breakfast.

As we were some hundreds of miles off the nearest coast, our task of looking out for land was entirely a work of supererogation; still, we did not realise this, and strained our eyes vainly until we were called down from aloft at "two bells," after the hands had all had their breakfast and there was nothing left for us. This was "Jock's" satisfaction in return for the shower bath he had been treated to so unceremoniously. Tom Jerrold afterwards said that he did not notice Jock coming up the companion way, and that of course he would never have dreamt of treating the captain so disrespectfully; but, as Master Tom invariably grinned whenever he made this declaration, Weeks and I, as well as Tim Rooney, who somehow or other got hold of the yarn, all had our suspicions on the point.

However, this is a digression from the description of our daily duties.

After scrubbing decks, each watch alternately had breakfast; and then, as now, when the wind was fair and hardly a brace or rope required to be handed from morning till night or from night till morning, we and the rest of the crew were set to work unravelling ends of junk and picking oakum, like convicts.

After being thus disintegrated, the tow was spun into sennit or fine twine and yarn which is always of use on board, quantities of it being used in "serving" and "parcelling" for chafing gear.

At noon, the crew had their dinner, watch in and watch out, but we apprentices had to wait till the captain and mates had theirs; although, as I've already mentioned, we saw little of the delicacies of the cabin table except occasionally of a Sunday, on which day, sometimes, Captain Gillespie's heart was more benevolently inclined towards us apparently. During the afternoon watch on week-days we were allowed to amuse ourselves as we liked, and I frequently took advantage of this opportunity to learn all that Tim Rooney and Adams could teach me forward—the two being great cronies, and busying themselves at this period of the day, if there were nothing to call their attention elsewhere, in doing odd jobs on the forecastle, the one in the sailmaking line and the other attending to his legitimate occupation of looking after the weak points of the rigging, all concerning which came within his special province as boatswain.

After tea, all hands were allowed to skylark about the decks below and aloft until the end of the second dog-watch at "eight bells;" when, the night being fairly on us in the southern latitudes we were traversing, those whose turn it was to go below turned in, and the others having the "first watch" took the deck until they were relieved at midnight and retired to their well earned rest. But, of course, should "all hands" be called to take in sail, on account of the wind shifting or a sudden squall breaking over the ship, which fortunately did not happen at the time of which I am speaking, those who might only have just turned in had to turn out again instanter. In the same way, I may add, had the weather been stormy and changeable all of us would have had plenty to do in taking in and setting sail, without leisure for sennit reeving and yarn spinning and playing "Tom Cox's traverse" about the decks from morning till night, as we did in those halcyon days between the tropics.

We sighted Martin Vas Rocks, to the eastward of Trinidad Islands, in latitude 20 degrees 29 minutes south and longitude 28 degrees 51 minutes west, a little over a week from our leaving the Line, having made a very good passage

John Conroy Hutcheson

so far from England, this being our thirty-sixth day out.

Soon after this, the south-east trades failing us and varying westerly breezes taking their place, we hauled our wind, altering our course to south-east by south, and making to pass the meridian on the forty-seventh parallel of latitude. This we did so as to get well to the southward of the Cape of Good Hope, between which and ourselves a long stretch of some three thousand miles of water lay; although both Captain Gillespie and Mr Mackay appeared to make nothing of this, looking upon it as the easiest part of our journey.

Indeed, the latter told me so.

"Now, it's all plain sailing, my boy, and we ought to run that distance in a fortnight or so from here, with the strong westerly and sou'-western winds we'll soon fetch into on this tack," said he; "but, wait till we come to the region of the Flying Dutchman's Cape, and then you'll make acquaintance with a sea such as you have never seen before, all that we've gone through as yet being merely child's play in comparison."

"What, worse than the Bay of Biscay?" I cried.

"Why, that was only a fleabite, youngster," he replied laughing. "I suppose you magnified it in your imagination from being sea-sick. The weather off the Cape of Storms, however; is a very different matter. It is quite in keeping with its name!"

But, still, for the next few days, at first proceeding close-hauled on the starboard tack and then, as the wind veered more round to the west, running free before it, with all our flying kites and stu'n'sails set, the time passed as pleasantly as before; and we had about just as little to do in the way of seamanship aboard, the ship almost steering herself and hardly a tack or a sheet needing to be touched. I noticed, though, Adams a little later on with a couple of men whom he requisitioned as sailmakers' mates busy cutting out queer little triangular pieces of canvas, which he told me were "storm staysails," the old ones having been blown away last voyage; while I saw that Tim Rooney, besides assuring himself of the security of the masts and setting up preventer stays for additional strength by the captain's orders, rigging up life-lines fore and aft, saying when I asked him what they were for, "To hould on wid, sure, whin we toombles into Cape weather, me darlint!"

There were no signs of any change yet, though; and the hands got so hard up for amusement with the small amount of work they had to perform, in spite of Captain Gillespie hunting up all sorts of odd jobs for them to do in the way of cleaning the brass-work of the ship and polishing the ring-bolts, that they got into that "mischief," which, the proverb tells us, Satan frequently "finds for idle hands" to do.

Tom Jerrold and I were in the boatswain's cabin one after-noon teaching the starling to speak a fresh sentence—the bird having got quite tame and learnt to talk very well already, saying "Bad cess to ye" and "Tip us yer flipper," just like Tim Rooney, with his brogue and all; when, all at once, we heard some scrambling going on in the long-boat above the deckhouse, and the sound of men's voices whispering together.

"Some of the fellows forrud are having a rig with the skipper's pigs," cried Tom. "Let us watch and see what they're up to."

"They can't be hurting the poor brutes," said I, speaking in the same subdued tone, so as not to alarm the men and make

John Conroy Hutcheson

them think anyone was listening; "I'm sure of that, or they would soon make a noise!"

"I suppose I was mistaken," observed Tom presently, when we could not hear the sailor's whispering voices any longer nor any grunting from the pigs; although we kept our ears on the alert. "I fancy, though, they were up to something, from a remark I heard just now when I passed by the fo'c's'le as the starboard watch were having their tea."

"What was that?" I asked. "Did they speak of doing anything?"

"No-o," replied Tom hesitatingly, as if he did not quite like telling me all he knew, being afraid perhaps of my informing Mr Mackay, from the latter and I being now known to be close friends albeit I was only an apprentice and he the first mate. "I only heard them joking about that beastly marmalade the skipper has palmed off on them, and us, too, worse luck, in lieu of our proper rations of salt junk; and one of them said he'd 'like to swap all his lot for the voyage for a good square meal of roast pork,' that's all."

"Why, any of us might have said that," cried I laughing, and not seeing any harm in the observation. "I'm sure I would not object to a change of diet."

Later on in the evening, though, what Tom had related was brought back to me with much point; for, a curious circumstance occurred shortly after "four bells," when it was beginning to get dark after sunset, the night closing in so rapidly.

The captain was then on the poop talking to Mr Saunders about something or other in which they both seemed deeply interested, the one sniffing and twitching his long nose about, and the other wagging his red beard as he moved his jaws in talking. I was just above their heads in the mizzen-top, my favourite retreat of an evening, whither I had taken up a book to read, although I could barely distinguish the print by this time, daylight had disappeared so quickly on the sun's sinking in the deep astern; when, all at once, a violent squealing and grunting broke out from the long-boat, sufficient for more than a herd of porkers all in their last agony, instead of its coming from one or even all three of the pigs Captain Gillespie had stowed there, fattening them up until he thought them big enough to kill for the table.

"Who the dickens is that troubling my pigs?" roared the captain, clutching hold of the brass rail of the poop in front of him, and squinting forwards as well as he could in the dim light to where the clew of the main-sail just lifting disclosed the fore part of the deck-house with the long-boat on top. "None of your sky-larking there, d'ye hear? Leave 'em alone!"

But, there was no one to be seen either on top of the deck-house or in the long-boat, although the squealing still continued.

"D'ye hear me there, forrud?" shouted Captain Gillespie again in a voice of thunder, having now worked himself up into one of his tornado-like rages. "Leave those pigs alone, I tell ye!"

"Sure, sorr, there's nobody there," said Tim Rooney, who was on the main-deck below, just under the break of the poop. "There's divil a sowl botherin' the blissid pigs, sorr, as ye can say for y'rsilf. Faix, they're ownly contrary a bit, sorr, an' p'raps onaisy in their moind!"

"Nonsense, man!" cried Captain Gillespie stamping his foot.

"It is some of those mutinous rascals carrying on their games, I—I know! Just look, will ye, bosun?"

"There ar'n't a sowl thare, I tell ye, sorr," protested Tim, rather a bit vexed at his word being doubted, as he turned to go forward where the row was still going on. "Ain't I jist come from there, sorr, an' can't I say now wid me own eyes there ain't nobody not nigh the long-boat nor the pigs neither—bad cess to 'em!"

He muttered the last words below his breath, and getting up into the main-rigging he climbed half-way up the shrouds, so as to be able to drop from thence on to the deck-house, this being his quickest mode of reaching the roof of that structure; and from thence, as he knew, he would of course be able to see right into the long-boat as well as inspect its four-footed tenants.

"There's not a sowl in the boat or near it, sorr, at all, at all, cap'en dear, barrin' the pigs sure, as I towld ye," he repeated on getting so far; and he was just proceeding to lower himself down to the top of the deck-house by a loose rope that was hanging from aloft, when he swung himself back into the rigging in alarm as a dark body jumped out of the long-boat right across his face, uttering the terrified ejaculation, "Murther in Irish! Howly Moses, what is that?"

It was one of the pigs, which, giving vent to a most diabolical yell, appeared to leap from the long-boat deliberately over the port side of the ship into the sea, sinking immediately with a stifled grunt, alongside.

Then more weird squeaking was heard, and a second pig imitated his comrade's example, jumping also from the boat overboard—just as if they were playing the game of "follow my leader" which we often indulged in when sky-larking in the second dog-watch!

This was no sky-larking, however, for the captain on the poop, as well as Mr Saunders and myself up in the mizzen-top, had witnessed the whole of the strange occurrence the same as Tim Rooney, and all of us were equally astonished.

As for Captain Gillespie, being a very superstitious man, he seemed strongly impressed by what had happened. His voice quite trembled as he called out to Tim Rooney after a moment's pause, during which he was too much startled to speak:

"Wha—what's the matter with them, bosun?"

"Sorry o' me knows," replied Tim in an equally awestruck voice, either full of real or very well assumed terror, "barrin' that the divil's got howld av 'em; an' it's raal vexed I am, sorr, av spakin' so moighty disrespectful av his honour jist now. Aye, take me worrud for it, cap'en, they're possiss'd, as sure as eggs is mate!"

"I think the same, and that the deil's got into 'em," said Captain Gillespie gravely, wrinkling up his nose so much and nodding his head, and looking so like an old owl in the bright light of the moon which had rapidly risen, and was already shining with all the fulness and brilliancy it has in these southern latitudes, that it was as much as I could do to keep from bursting out laughing and so betraying my presence in the top above his head. I was all the more amused, too, when "Old Jock" turned to the second mate and added: "I look upon this as a visitation, and am glad I never killed the animals; for I would not touch one now for anything! Have the remaining brute chucked overboard, Saunders; it would be unlucky to keep it after what has happened. I'm sure I could not bear the sight of it or to hear it

John Conroy Hutcheson

grant again!"

So saying, Captain Gillespie went below and took a stiff glass of grog to recover his nerves. He must then have got into his cot for he did not appear on deck again until the middle watch—a most unusual thing for him to do.

"It's an ill wind that blows nobody any good," however, and the aptness of the adage was well illustrated in the present instance, the men feasting on roast pork, besides putting by some tit-bits salted down for a rainy day, at the expense of "Old Jock's" superstitious fears.

It was wonderful, though, how many legs were owned by that one "last pig" which the captain had ordered to be chucked overboard, and which Mr Saunders had, instead, given over to Ching Wang's tender mercies for the benefit of himself and the crew, stipulating, however, that he was to have one of the best pieces stuffed and baked, the second mate being a great glutton always, and fond of good living. Yes, it was wonderful for one pig to have no less than twelve legs!

I will tell you how this was.

Tom Jerrold let me into the secret. It seems that the apparent suicidal tendencies of the pigs who jumped into the sea in that mysterious way was caused by the fore-topgallant stu'n'sail halliards being dexterously fastened round them by a couple of the hands previously in sling fashion; and when the poor brutes were jerked overboard by the aid of these, they were allowed to tow under the keel of the ship until their squeals were hushed for ever, and then drawn inboard again and cut up in the forecastle. When they were carved properly into pork, the men thought them none the less delicious because they had come to their death by water instead of by the ordinary butcher's knife; and, as I had the opportunity of testing this opinion in a savoury little pig's fry which Ching Wang presented me with the same evening for supper, I cannot but acknowledge that I agreed thoroughly with the judgment of the hands in the matter of "spiflicated pork," as Tom Jerrold called it.

"Dick, Dick, what do you think of it all?" said I, chirping to the starling, who was whistling wide awake when I turned out next morning at "eight bells" after dreaming of the poor murdered pigs, on my way to the galley to get some hot coffee. "What do you think of it all—eh, Dick?"

"Tip us your flipper!" hoarsely croaked the bright-eyed little bird with the voice of Tim Rooney, only seeming to be a very long way off. He also seemed to have the nose of Captain Gillespie, which we all said his long beak strongly resembled. "Tip us your flipper!"

That was all I could get out of him; but I thought that, really, a wrong had been righted, and the captain's marmalade imposition on us and on the hands forward been amply avenged.

Poor "Old Jock's" live stock of late appeared to be in a very bad way; for, not only was he deprived of his favourite pigs so unfortunately, but since we had begun to run more to southward after leaving the Line, his supply of eggs from the collection of hens he had in the coops on the poop daily dwindled down to nothing, although they had previously been good layers.

Somehow or other the fowls seemed to have the pip, while the three cocks, one a splendid silver and gold fellow, who lorded over the harem of Dorkings and Brahmas, all looked torn and bedraggled as if they had given way to dissipated

John Conroy Hutcheson

habits. Besides this, they took to crowing defiance against each other at the most unearthly hours, whereas, prior to this, their time for chanticleering had been as regular as clockwork, in the afternoon and in the "middle watch" generally.

Captain Gillespie couldn't make it out at all.

One fine morning, however, coming on the deck through the cuddy doors below the break of the poop instead of mounting up to the latter by the companion way as usual, before the time for washing down, he surprised a number of the men assembled about the cook's galley.

There was Ching Wang in the centre of the group, holding Captain Gillespie's pet gold and silver crower and urging it on to fight one of the other cocks, which the carpenter was officiating for as "bottle holder" in the most scientific way, he apparently being no novice at the cruel sport.

The captain did not see what they were about at first; but the delinquent was soon pointed out by Pedro Carvalho, between whom and the Chinaman the most deadly enmity existed, and who had indeed already informed the captain of the cook's treatment of his fowls, the Portuguese steward doing this with much alacrity, as if proud of being the informer.

"Look dere, sah!" cried Pedro. "Dere is dat Ching Wang now, sah! Oh, yase, dere he was, sah, as I say, killin' your cockles magnificent—oh!"

The captain's appearance at once broke up the ring, the carpenter dropping his bird incontinently and fleeing into the forecastle with the other men; but, the Chinaman never moved a muscle of his countenance when he turned his round innocent-looking, vacuous, Mongolian face and caught sight of "Old Jock's" infuriated look bent on him.

He did not even let go the gold and silver cock, whose plumage had been sadly tarnished by a previous tournament with the Dorking which the carpenter had squired. No, he held his ground there before the galley with a courage one could not but admire, the only sign he gave of an inward emotion being the occasional twinkling of his little beady Chinese eyes.

"Wh-wha-what the dicken's d-d-d'ye mean by this?" stuttered and stammered Captain Gillespie, his passion almost stopping his speech. "Wh-wh-what d'ye mean, I say?"

"Me only hab piecee cocky-fightee," answered Ching Wang as calmly as possible. "Me chin chin you, cap'en."

Captain Gillespie fairly boiled over with rage.

"This beats cock-fighting!" he cried, stating the case inadvertently in his exclamation. "I thought it was those confounded cats we have aboard the ship that ill-treated the poor fowls and prevented them from laying me any eggs, till Pedro here told me it was you, though I didn't believe it. I wouldn't have believed it now if I hadn't seen you at it. By jingo, it's shameful!"

Ching Wang, however, paid no attention to this violent tirade, only salaaming humbly and looking the very picture of meekness and contrition.

But his eyes, as I could see, being close by, having been attracted by the row as most of us were, had altered their expression, now flashing with a peculiar glare as the Chinaman, with a more abject bow than before to the captain, asked him deferentially:

"And dis one manee you tellee Ching Wang cocky-fightee

John Conroy Hutcheson

one piecee—hi?"

"Yes, Pedro told me," replied Captain Gillespie, sniffing and snorting out the words. "And a good job too; for, else, I wouldn't have known of your goings on!"

Ching Wang's yellow face almost turned white with anger.

"Hi, blackee-brownee manee," he yelled, springing upon Pedro like a tiger. "You takee dat number one, chop chop!"

CHAPTER TWELVE

A STRANGE SAIL

Although a coward at heart, the Portuguese steward, nerved by his intense hatred of the cook, made a bold resistance to his first onslaught, clutching at Ching Wang's pigtail with one hand and clawing at his face with the other; while the Chinaman gripped his neck with his sinewy fingers, the two rolling on the deck in a close embrace, which was the very reverse of a loving one.

"Carajo!" gurgled out Pedro, half-strangled at the outset, but having such a tight hold of Ching Wang's tail, of which he had taken a double turn round his wrist, that he was able to bend his antagonist's head back, almost dislocating his neck. "Matarei te, podenga de cozenheiro!"

"Aha cutus pijjin, me catchee you, chop chop!" grunted the other through his clenched teeth; and then, not another word escaped either of them as they both sprawled and tumbled about in front of the galley, locked together, the Chinee finally coming up on top triumphantly, with Pedro, all black in the face and with his tongue protruding, below his lithe enemy.

"Take him off the man, some of you," cried Captain

John Conroy Hutcheson

Gillespie, who had not made any effort to stop the combat until now that it bad arrived at such an unsatisfactory stage for the steward. "Don't you see that yellow devil's murdering him? He looks more than half dead already!"

Tim Rooney hereupon stepped forwards; but Ching Wang did not need any force to compel him to quit his powerless foe.

Disengaging his pigtail from Pedro's limp fingers, he arose with a sort of native dignity from his prostrate position over the Portuguese, his round face all one bland smile—although it bore sundry scratches on its otherwise smooth surface, whose oiliness had probably saved it from greater hurt.

"Him no sabbey," he exclaimed, pointing down to the still prostrate Pedro, who, now that the Chinaman's grip had been released from his throat, began to show signs of returning life, "what me can do. Him more wanchee, Ching Wang plenty givee chop chop!"

"I tell ye what, me joker," cried "Old Jock" after him as the victorious cook retired into his galley on making this short speech, with all the honours of war—the hands raising a cheer, which the presence of the captain could not drown, at the result of the encounter; for all of them looked on the steward as one opposed to their interests, and who cheated them in their provisions when serving them out, regarding the Chinaman, on the other hand, as their friend and ally, he always taking their part in this respect. "I tell ye what, me joker, I'll stop your wages and make ye pay for my fowls when we get to Shanghai! I don't mind your basting the steward, for a thrashing will do him good, as he has wanted one for some time; but I do mind your knocking those fine birds of mine about with your confounded 'one piecee cock-fightee.' Look at this one, now; he's fit for nothing but the pot, and the sooner you cook him the better."

Ching Wang only smiled more blandly than ever as the captain, who had picked up the two cocks, flung the silver and gold one into the galley, taking the other aft and restoring it to its coop; while Pedro, rising presently to his feet, amidst the grins of the men around, sneaked after "Old Jock," saying never a word but looking by no means amiable. His departure ended the incident of the morning, and we immediately finished sluicing the decks, the cook and steward fight having somewhat delayed this operation, as it was getting on for "eight bells" and nearly breakfast-time.

Towards noon, on the same day, we passed by the island of Tristan da Cunha, the land bearing on our port quarter sou'-west by south when seen; and, on the thirteenth day after turning our backs on the Martin Vas Rocks, we crossed the meridian of Greenwich in latitude 46 degrees 58 minutes south, steering almost due east so as to weather the Cape of Good Hope. The westerly wind was dead aft, which made us roll a bit; but we "carried on," with the ship covered with sail from truck to kelson and stu'n'sails all the way up both on our weather side and to leeward, as well as spinnakers and a lot of other things in the sail line whose names I can't remember.

Proceeding thus gaily along, with our yards squared and every stitch of canvas drawing fore and aft, in another couple of days or so the Cape pigeons and shearwaters began to come about the ship, showing that we were approaching the stormy region Mr Mackay had warned me of; and on the fourth night the sky ahead of us became overcast, while a lot of sheet and zig-a-zaggy "chain lightning," as sailors call it, told us to look out for squalls.

John Conroy Hutcheson

This was a true portent; for the wind freshened during the first watch, causing us to take in all of our stu'n'sails before midnight. Then followed the royals and topgallants in quick succession, the main-sail and inner and outer jibs being next furled and the foresail reefed, the vessel at "four bells" being only under topsails and fore-topgallant staysail and reefed foresail.

As I had noticed previously, when crossing the Bay of Biscay, the sea got up very quickly as the wind increased, only with much more alarming rapidity now than then; for, while at sunset the ocean was comparatively smooth, it became covered with big rolling waves by the time that we began to reduce sail, the billows swelling in size each moment, and tossing and breaking against each other as the wind shifted round dead in our teeth to the north-east, the very quarter where we had seen the lightning.

"We're going to have a dirty night of it, sir," said Mr Mackay to the captain, who after turning in for a short time when the starboard watch was relieved had come on deck again, anxious about the ship. "I thought we'd have a blow soon."

"Humph, Cape weather!" snorted out Captain Gillespie. "We're just in the proper track of it now, being nearly due south of Table Mountain, as I make it. I think you'd better get down our lighter spars, Mackay, for this is only the beginning of it—the glass was sinking just now."

"Aye, aye sir," returned the first mate, who had previously called the watch aft for this very purpose, crying out to the men standing by: "Lay aloft there, and see how soon you can send down those royal yards!"

Matthews, who was trying all he could to deserve his promotion and had remained up after the rest of his watch had gone below, helped Tom Jerrold and me in sending down ours; and, when up aloft, the most active topman I noticed was Joe Fergusson, the bricklayer. As "Old Jock" with his shrewd seaman's eyes had anticipated, he had developed into a smart sailor, considering the short time he was learning, being now quicker than some of those who had been to sea for years and were thought good hands.

On the present occasion he ran us a rare race with the main-royal yard, we getting the mizzen spar below but a second or two in advance of his party.

After this the topgallant yards were sent down likewise on deck and the masts struck, "all hands" being called to get the job done as soon as possible. Indeed this was vitally necessary, for the storm was increasing in force every moment, and our topsails had to be reefed immediately the royal yards were down and the topgallants lowered.

Getting rid of all this top hamper, however, made the ship ride all the easier over the heavy waves that met her bows full butt; and, now, she did not roll half as much as she had done while she had all those spars up, although what she lost in this respect she made up for in pitching—diving down as the big seas rolled under her keel and lifted up her stern as if she were about paying a visit to the depths below, and then raising her bowsprit the next instant so high in the air that it looked as if she were trying to poke a hole in the sky with it!

Shortly before "six bells" the gale blew so fiercely that it was as much as we could do to stand on the poop; and when, presently, Mr Mackay gave the order for us to take in the mizzen-topsail, we had to wait between the gusts to get up aloft, for the pressure of the wind flattened us against the rigging as if we had been "spread-eagled," making it impossible to move for the moment.

But sailors mustn't be daunted by anything to be "worth their salt;" so, watching an opportunity, we climbed up by degrees to the top and then on to the upper rigging until we gained the cross-trees, being all the while pretty well lashed by the gale. Our eyes were blinded, and our faces all made sore and smarting by it, I can tell you, while we were well out of breath by the time we had got so far.

The topsail sheets and halliards, of course, had been let fly before we left the deck; but in order not to expose the sail more than could be helped to the force of the storm, the clewlines and buntlines were not hauled open until we were up on the yard, so that the topsail should not remain longer bagged in folds than necessary before we could furl it out of harm's way.

Still, the precaution was of no avail; for hardly had the men on deck handed the clewlines, when the sail, bulging out under our feet like a huge bag, or rather series of bags, as the wind puckered its folds, burst away from its bolt-ropes with a noise like the report of a gun discharged close to our ears, just as if we had cut it from off the yard, thus saving us any further trouble in furling it.

Casting my eyes round ere beginning the perilous task of climbing down the shrouds again, for it was as much as one could do to hold on, the sharp gusts when they caught one's legs twirling them about like feathers in the air, the outlook was not merely grand but positively awful. The sea was now rolling, without the slightest exaggeration but literally speaking, mountains high as far as the eye could reach, and the scud flying across my face in the mizzen cross-trees; while the waves on either side of the ship, as we descended into the hollow between them every now and then, were on a level with the yard-arms below and even sometimes rose above these.

"Come, my men," I heard Mr Mackay calling out, as I at last put my foot down to feel for the nearest ratline before commencing to descend the rigging, "look sharp with that fore-tops'le or we'll have it go like the mizzen!"

His words were prophetic.

"R-r-r-r-r-ip!" sounded the renting, tearing noise of the sail, almost as soon as he spoke; and then, with a greater "bang!" than that of the mizzen-topsail, the main topsail split first from clew to earing and the next second blew away bodily to leeward, floating like a cloud as it was carried along the crests of the rollers out of our ken in a minute. The fore-topsail imitated its example the next moment, leaving the ship now with only the reefed foresail on her in the shape of canvas, a wonderful metamorphosis to the appearance she presented the previous evening at sunset!

We had been trying to beat to windward, so as not to fall off our course; but now that we had hardly a rag to stand by, the captain put up the helm and let her run for it, the foresail with the gale that was blowing sending her at such a rate through the water as to prevent any of the following seas from pooping her. The fear alone of this had prevented him doing so before, "Old Jock" being as fond of scudding as he was of carrying on when he had a fair wind.

Adams and the hands forward, though, were busy getting ready the storm staysails I had seen the former cutting out some days previously so as to be prepared to hoist them on the first available opportunity, as it would never do to run too far off our course, which many hours going at that rate before the nor'-easter would soon have effected; and so, during a slight lull that occurred about breakfast-time, a mizzen staysail and foretopmast staysail, each about the size of a respectable pocket-handkerchief, were got aloft

John Conroy Hutcheson

judiciously and the foresail as carefully handed, when the ship was brought round again head to wind and lay-to on the port tack.

A little later there was one terrific burst, the tops of the waves being cut off as with a knife and borne aboard us in sheets of water, while the Silver Queen heeled over to starboard so greatly that it seemed as if she would "turn the turtle" and go down sideways with all hands; but it was the last blast of the storm, for each succeeding hour lessened its force, although the sea continued high. After that it grew gradually calmer and calmer, until we were able to make sail again and bear away eastwards, rounding the Cape two days afterwards, our fifty-sixth from England, in 37 degrees south latitude—the meridian of the "Flying Dutchman's fortress," as Table Mountain has been termed by those who once believed in the Vanderdecken legend, being a little over 18 degrees east longitude.

"Begorra, that's a good job done wid anyhow," said Tim Rooney on "Old Jock" telling us that all danger of weathering the Cape was past and that we were well within the limits of the Southern Ocean, whose long roll, however, and the cold breath of the Antarctic ice-fields had already betrayed this fact to the old hands on board. "I once knocked about in a vessel as were a-tryin' to git round this blissid place for a month av Sundays, an' couldn't."

"And what did you do, measter?" asked Joe Fergusson, who had a great respect for the boatswain and was eyeing him open-mouthed. "What did you do when you couldn't sail round it?"

"Be jabers we wint the other way, av course, ye nanny goat," cried Tim, raising the laugh against Joe. "Any omahdawn would know that, sure!"

The wind hauled round more to the west-sou'-west again when we had passed the Argulhas Bank, reaching down to the southward until we were in latitude 39 degrees South; so, squaring our yards again, we preserved this parallel until we fetched longitude 78 degrees east, just below Saint Paul's Island, a distance of some three thousand miles. We accomplished this in another fortnight after rounding the Cape; and then, steering up the chart again, we shaped our course nor'-east by north, so as to cross the southern tropic in longitude 102 degrees East.

After two or three days, we reached a warmer temperature, when the wind falling light and becoming variable we crossed our topgallant and royal yards again, spreading all the sail we could so as to make the best of the breezes we got. These were now mingled with occasional showers of rain, as is customary with the south-west monsoon in those latitudes at this time of year, it being now well into the month of May.

For weeks past the Silver Queen had delighted the captain, and, indeed, all of us on board, with her sailing powers, averaging over two hundred knots a day, which considering her great bilge was as fast as the most famous clippers; but now that she only logged a paltry hundred or so, going but five or six per hour instead of ten to twelve, "Old Jock" began to grumble, snapping and finding fault with everybody in turns.

The men forward, too, reciprocated very heartily in the grumbling line, there not being so much for them to do as of late; and, the great marmalade question again cropping up, things became very unpleasant in the ship.

One day I really thought there was going to be a mutiny.

John Conroy Hutcheson

The men came in a body aft, headed by the carpenter, whom the captain had been rather rough on ever since he found him that morning we were off Tristan da Cunha aiding and abetting Ching Wang in his cruel cock-fighting propensities; although, strange to say, "Old Jock" seemed to condone the action of the chief offender, never having a hard word for the Chinee albeit plenty for Gregory, the carpenter.

On this eventful occasion Captain Gillespie was seated on the poop in an American rocking-chair which he had brought up from his cabin, enjoying the warm weather and wrinkling his nose over the almost motionless sails hanging down limply from the yards; and he did not disturb himself in anywise when Gregory and the others advanced from forward, stepping aft along the main-deck one by one to the number of a round dozen or more, the crowd halting and forming themselves into a ring under the poop ladder, above which the captain had fixed his chair, looking as if they "meant business."

"Hullo!" cried "Old Jock" rousing himself up, rather surprised at the demonstration. "What are you fellows doing below there?"

"We wants meat," replied the carpenter, taking off his straw hat and giving a scrape back with his left foot, so as to begin politely at any rate. "We aren't got enough to eat in the fo'c's'le, sir, an' we wants our proper 'lowance o' meat, instead of a lot of rotten kickshaw marmalade!"

"Wh-a-at—what the dickens d'ye mean?" roared out "Old Jock," touched on his tenderest point, the word "marmalade" to him having the same effect as a red rag on a bull. "Didn't I tell ye if ye'd any complaints to make, to come aft singly and I'd attend to 'em, but that if ye ever came to me in a body I'd not listen to ye?"

"Aye, aye," said Gregory, "but—"

"Avast there!" shouted the captain interrupting him. "When I say a thing I mean a thing; and so ye'd better go forrud again as quick as ye can, or I'll come down and make ye!"

An indignant groan burst from the men at this; while "Jock" danced about the poop brandishing a marlinespike he had clutched hold of, in a mighty rage, storming away until the hands had all, very reluctantly, withdrawn grumbling to the forecastle.

In the afternoon, they refused to turn out for duty; when, after a terrible long palaver, in which Mr Mackay managed to smooth down matters, the controversy was settled by all the men having half their meat ration restored to them, and being obliged only to accept a half-pound tin of marmalade in lieu of a larger quantity as previously. Both sides consequently gained a sort of victory, the only person discontented at this termination of the affair being the steward, Pedro, who took a malicious pleasure in serving out the marmalade each day. I often caught sight of him watching with a sort of fiendish glee the disappointed faces of the hands as they looked at the open casks of pork and beef, which he somewhat ostentatiously displayed before them, as if to make them long all the more for such substantial fare.

I knew the Portuguese was upset at the amicable end of the difficulty between the captain and crew, for I saw him stealthily awaiting the result, peeping from underneath the break of the poop; and, when the hands raised a cheer in token of their satisfaction at the settlement, he immediately went and locked himself in his pantry, where he began kicking the despised marmalade tins about as if twenty riveters and boiler-makers and hammermen were below!

John Conroy Hutcheson

It was very nearly a mutiny, though.

A westerly current being against us as well as the winds light, it took us nearly a week to get up to the thirty-third parallel of latitude, during which time this little unpleasantness occurred; but then, picking up the south-east trades off the Australian coast, we went bowling along steadily again northward for the Straits of Sunda, making for the westwards of the passage so as to be to windward of a strong easterly current that runs through the strait.

I was the first on board to see Java Head, a bluff promontory stretching out into the sea that marks the entrance to Sunda. This was how it was: we'd got more to the north of the captain's reckoning, and while up in the mizzen cross-trees, in the afternoon of our eighty-fifth day out from land to land, I clearly distinguished the headland far-away in the distance, over our starboard quarter.

"Land ho!" I sang out; "land ho!"

"Are you sure?" cried Captain Gillespie from the deck below looking up at me, when his long nose, being foreshortened, seemed to run into his mouth, giving him the most peculiar appearance. "Where away?"

"Astern now, sir," I answered. "South-east by south, and nearly off the weather topsail."

"I think I'd better have a look myself," said "Old Jock," clambering up the mizzen-shrouds and soon getting aloft beside me; adding as he caught sight of the object I pointed out—"by Jingo, you're right, boy! It's Java Head, sure enough."

He then scuttled down the ratlines like winking.

"Haul in to leeward!" he shouted. "Brace round the yards! Down with your helm!"

"Port it is," said the boatman.

"Steady then, so!" yelled "Old Jock," conning the ship towards the mouth of the straits. "Keep her east-nor'-east as nearly as you can, giving her a point if she falls off!"

By and by, we entered the Straits of Sunda; and then, keeping the Java shore on board, we steered so as to avoid the Friar's Rock in the middle of the channel, making for Prince's Island.

The wind and current being both in our favour, and the moon rising soon after sunset, we were able to fetch Anjer Point in the middle watch and got well within Java Sea by morning. Next day we passed through Banca Strait by the Lucepara Channel, keeping to the Sumatra coast to avoid the dangerous reefs and rocks on the east side, until we sighted the Parmesang Hills. After that we steered north by east, by the Seven Islands into the China Sea.

So far no incident had happened on our nearing land, which all of us were glad enough to see again, as may be imagined, after our now nearly three months confinement on board without an opportunity of stretching our legs ashore, the only terra firma we had sighted since leaving England having been Madeira, the Peak of Teneriffe, and the rocks of Martin Vas; but now, as we glided along past the lovely islets of the Indian Archipelago, radiant in the glowing sunshine, and their atmosphere fragrant with spices and other sweet odours that concealed the deadly malaria of the climate, a new sensation of peril added piquancy to the zest of our voyage.

On passing the westernmost point of Banca, as the channel

we had to pursue trended to the north-east, we came up to the wind and then paid off on the port tack; when, just as we cleared the group of islands lying at the mouth of the Straits of Malacca to windward, we saw a large proa bearing down in our direction, coming out from behind a projecting point of land that had previously prevented us from noticing her.

"Hullo!" I exclaimed to Mr Mackay whom I had accompanied from aft when he went forward on the forecastle to direct the conning of the ship, motioning now and again with his arms this way and that how the helmsman was to steer. "What a funny-looking vessel, sir. What is it?"

"That's a Malay proa," replied he. "They're generally ticklish craft to deal with; though, I don't suppose this beggar means any harm to us in such a waterway as this, where we meet other vessels every hour or so."

"Do you think it's a pirate ship?" I asked eagerly, "I should like to see one so much."

"More than I should," said he with a laugh; "but I don't suppose this chap's up to any game like that, though, I think, all the Malays are pirates at heart. He's most likely on a trading voyage like ourselves, only he's going amongst the islands while we're bound north."

However the proa did not bear away, either to port or starboard, nor did it make for any of the clusters of islands on either hand; and, although it was barely noon when we had first noticed her, as night came on, by which time we were well on our way towards Pulo Sapata, running up to the northwards fast before the land breeze that blew off shore after sunset, there was the proa still behind us!

It was very strange, to say the least of it.

Nor was I the only one to think so; for the hands forward, and among them Tim Rooney, the boatswain, had also observed the mysterious vessel, as well as taken count of her apparent desire to accompany us.

"Bedad she ain't our frind, or, sure, she'd have come up an' spoke us dacintly, loike a jintleman," I heard Tim say to the sailmaker, outside the door of his cabin in the deck-house. "She's oop to no good anyhow, bad cess to the ould thafe, as sure as eggs is mate; an' may I niver ate a pratie ag'in if I'm tellin' a lie sure, for I misthrusts them Malay raskils jist as the divil hates howly wather!"

John Conroy Hutcheson

CHAPTER THIRTEEN

THE TAIL-END OF A TYPHOON

"But I allers heard them Malay chaps are awful cowards," said Adams, continuing the conversation. "You never sees 'em singly, their pirate proas, or junks, allers a sailing with a consort. I ought ter know; 'cause, 'fore I ever jined Cap'en Gillespie, I wer in a Hongkong trader; and many's the time we've been chased by a whole shoal of 'em when going to Singapore or along the coast."

"The divil ye have," interposed Tim. "Ye niver tould me that afore, Sails, how's that?"

"I didn't recomember at the time, bo; but now, as that feller is a follering us astern, in course, I thinks on it. There're a lot of them piratical rascals in these waters; but you should go to the back of Hainan to see 'em in their glory, the little creeks and bays there fairly swarms with 'em!"

"Adams!" called out Mr Mackay at this juncture; "Adams!"

"Aye, aye, sir," quickly responded the sailmaker, stopping his talk with Tim Rooney and walking up nearer to Mr Mackay. "Here, sir."

"I want you to go in the chains with the lead," said the other, turning round and speaking confidentially to old "Sails," as Adams was generally termed by his intimates amongst the crew. "There's no man in the ship I can trust to for sounding like you; and it's necessary for us to know what sort of water we're in till we clear all these islands and get into the open sea."

"Aye, aye, sir," answered the sailmaker, who, besides his more distinctive calling, was an experienced seaman, proud of being selected from the rest for such a duty, disagreeable and monotonous though it was. "I'm quite ready, sir."

Thereupon, going back to the boatswain's cabin, where he was provided by Tim with the lead-line and a broad canvas belt, he proceeded to climb over the bulwarks into the fore-chains, fastening himself to the rigging by placing the belt round his waist and hooking it on to the lower part of the shrouds—this arrangement holding him against the side of the vessel securely and at the same time enabling him to have his arms free to use for any other purpose.

Adam's next operation was to swing the lead-line with the weight attached backwards and forwards, like a pendulum, until it had gained sufficient momentum, when he slung it as far forwards as he could, letting the coil of the line which he had over his arm run out until the way of the ship brought it perpendicularly under him; when, hauling it up quickly, and noticing how many fathoms had run out before the lead touched the bottom, he called out in a deep sort of sepulchral chant, "And a half-five!"

"Ha!" exclaimed Mr Mackay, "I thought we were shoaling. Keep it going, Adams."

"Aye, aye, sir," replied the other, swinging the lead as before when he had coiled up the slack and preparing for another throw; adding presently as he had gauged the depth again, "By the mark seven!"

"That's better," cried Mr Mackay; calling out at the same time to the helmsman as we nearly ran over a small native boat crossing our track, "starboard—hard a starboard!"

Adams, however, went on sounding mechanically, not minding the movements of the ship, his sing-song chant varying almost at every throw; and, "By the deep nine" being succeeded by, "And a quarter ten," until the full length of the lead-line, twenty fathoms, was let out without finding bottom.

"That will do now, you can come in," cried Mr Mackay on learning this—"we're now all right and out of danger. Aft, there, steer east-nor'-east and keep a steady helm, we're now in open water and all's plain sailing!"

It took us three days to pilot up to the Natuna Islands, only some three hundred and fifty miles north of Banca, the south-westerly wind which we had with us generally falling slack in the middle of the day, and the land breeze of a night giving us the greater help; but, still, all the while, the suspicious proa never deserted us, following in our track like a sleuth-hound—keeping off at a good distance though when the sun was shining and only creeping up closer at dark, so as not to lose sight of us, and sheering off in the morning till hull down nearly on the horizon.

We had got almost accustomed to the craft by this time and used to cut jokes about it; for, as we were continually passing other vessels bound through the straits, it was obvious that even had the intentions of the proa been hostile it would not have dared to attack us at sea with such a lot of company about.

However, on our getting abreast of Saddle Island, to the north-west of the Natuna group, behold the proa was joined by a companion, two of them now being in our wake when morning dawned and we were better able to see around us. We noticed, too, that this second craft was built more in junk fashion with large lateen sails, and it seemed to be of about five hundred piculs burthen, Mr Mackay said, the size of those craft that are usually employed in the opium trade.

Matters began to look serious, it really appearing as if the beggars were going to follow us all the way up the China Sea until they had an opportunity of attacking us when there was no chance of any other vessel being near!

"Let us stand towards them, Mackay and see what they're made of—eh?" said Captain Gillespie, after squinting away at the two craft behind us. "I'm hanged if I like being dodged in this way."

"With all my heart, sir," replied the other. "But, I'm afraid, as they're well up in the wind's eye they can easily keep out of our reach if they don't want us to approach too near them."

"We'll try it at any rate," grunted out "Old Jock," sniffing and snorting, as he always did when vexed or put out. "Stand by to 'bout ship!"

The watch at once ran to their respective stations, Tom Jerrold and I with a couple of others attending to the cross-jack yard.

"All ready forrud?"

"Aye, aye, sorr," shouted back Tim Rooney from the

forecastle, "all ready forrud."

"Helms a-lee!"

The head sheets were let go as the captain roared out this order, the jib flattening as the vessel went into stays.

"Raise tacks and sheets!" cried Captain Gillespie, when the foretack and main-sheets were cast off just as his next command came—"Main-sail haul!"

Then the weather main-brace was hauled taut and the heavy yard swung round, the Silver Queen coming up to the wind with a sort of shiver, as if she did not like turning back and retracing her course.

However, so "Old Jock" willed it, and she must!

"Brace round your head yards!" he now sung out; and the foretack was boarded while the main-sheet was hauled aft, we on the poop swinging the cross-jack yard at the same time, the captain then calling out to the helmsman sharply, "Luff, you beggar, luff, can't ye!"

And now, hauled up as close as we could be, the ship headed towards the strangers; steering back in the direction of Banca again as near to windward as she could forereach.

It was "like trying to catch a weasel asleep and shave his whiskers," however, to use Tom Jerrold's words; for the moment the proa and her consort observed our manoeuvre and saw that we were making for them, round they went too like tops, and sailing right up in the wind's eye, all idea of pursuit on our part was put entirely out of question within the short space of five minutes or so—the Malay craft showing that they had the power when they chose to exercise it of going two knots to our one.

"Begorra, I'd loike to have a slap at 'em with a long thirty-two, or aven a blissid noine-pounder Armstrong," cried Tim Rooney, as vexed as "Old Jock" was at the result of this testing of the Silver Queen with her lighter heeled rivals to windward. "I'd soon knock 'em into shavin's, by the howly poker, I wud!"

"It's no good, as you said," sniffed out the captain, with a sigh to Mr Mackay, evidently cordially echoing the boatswain's wish, which he must have heard as well as I did, for he stood just to leeward of him. "Ready about again, stand by, men!"

And then, our previous movement was repeated and the ship brought round once more on the port tack, heading for Pulo Sapata to the northwards—the name of this place, I may say, is derived from two Malay words, the one pulo meaning "island" and the other sapatu "shoe," and the entire compound word, consequently, "Shoe Island," or the island of the shape of one.

We did not see anything more of the suspicious craft that day; so we all believed that our feint of overhauling them had effectually scared them away, Tom Jerrold and I especially being impressed with this idea, attaching a good deal of importance to the talk we had overheard between Rooney and Adams, Tom being in his bunk close by the boatswain's cabin at the time when I was outside listening to the two old tars as they confabbed together.

Weeks, though, was of a contrary opinion, and Master Sammy could be very dogged if he pleased on any point.

"I'll tell you what, my boys," said he, with some trace of

John Conroy Hutcheson

excitement in his mottled face, which generally was as expressionless as a vegetable-marrow, "we haven't seen the last of them yet."

"Much you know of it, little un," sneered Tom Jerrold in all the pride of his longer experience of the sea. "Why this is only the second voyage you've ever taken out here, or indeed been in a ship at all; and on our last trip we never tumbled across anything of this sort."

"That may be," argued Weeks; "but if I am a green hand, as you make out, like Graham here, my father was in a China clipper for years, and he has told me more than you'll ever learn in all your life, Mister Jerrold, I tell you. Why, he was once chased all the way from Hainan to Swatow by pirates."

"Was he?" I cried, excited too at this. "Do tell us, Weeks, all about it."

"There ain't anything to tell," said he nonchalantly, but pleased, I could see, at putting Tom Jerrold into the shade for the moment; "only, that they beat 'em off as they were trying to board father's ship off Swatow, when a vessel of war, that was just then coming down from Formosa, caught the beggars in the very act of piracy, before they could run ashore and escape up the hills—as they always do, my dad said, whenever our blue-jackets are after them."

"And then—" I asked, on his pausing at this interesting point, after rousing Jerrold's and my interest in that way, a thing which was quite in keeping with Sam Weeks' character, his disposition being naturally an exasperating one, to other people, that is,—"what happened then?"

"Oh, nothing," he replied coolly; adding after another tanta- lising pause, "I recollect, though, now, dad said as how the beggars were all taken to Canton and given over to the mandarins for trial."

"Yes," said I, "and—"

"Well, some of 'em were tortured in bamboo cages, he told me, and he said, too, that they made awful faces in their agony," Weeks continued, his face looking as if he enjoyed the reminiscence; "while the others, twenty in number, were all put up in a row kneeling on the ground, with their pigtails tied up over their heads so as to leave their necks bare, and the executioner who had a double-bladed sword like a butcher's cleaver, sliced off their heads as if they were so many carrots. It must have been jolly to see 'em rolling on the ground."

"You cold-blooded brute!" exclaimed Tom Jerrold; but I only shuddered and said nothing. "You seem to revel in it!"

"If you'd heard all my dad told me of what those beggars do to the people they capture, sometimes making them walk the plank and shutting them up in the hold of their own ship and burning them in a lump, you'd be glad of their being punished when caught! I only hope they won't seize our vessel; but, I tell you what, I'm certain we haven't seen the last of those two craft yet. They'll come back after us at nightfall, just you see!"

"By Jove, I hope not!" said Tom, impressed by Weeks' communication all the more from the fact of his not being generally talkative, always "keeping himself to himself" as the saying goes. "I hope you won't prove a true prophet, Sammy, most devoutly."

I could see, also, from Mr Mackay's anxious manner and that of the captain, though neither said anything further about the

John Conroy Hutcheson

matter, that their fears were not allayed. There was no doubt that they shared the same impression as that of Sam Weeks; for as we bore away now nor'-nor'-west, with the south-west wind on our quarter, more sail was made on the ship, and a strong current running in the same direction helping us on, we were found to be going over eight knots when the log was hove at six bells, just before dinner-time.

"Old Jock" beamed again at this, walking up and down the poop and rubbing his hands and sniffing with his long nose in the air to catch the breeze, as was his wont when the Silver Queen was travelling through the water.

"By Jingo, we'll weather 'em yet!" he said to Mr Mackay, who also seemed more relieved in his mind; "we'll weather 'em yet."

"Yes, I think so, too," said the latter, scanning the horizon with the big telescope away to windward. "There isn't a trace of them anywhere out there now, and there are no islands for them to hide behind where we last sighted them; so, if we can only carry-on like this, perhaps we'll be able to give them the slip—eh?"

"Humph!" grumbled the other, "so I told you, Mackay; and, you know, when I say a thing I always mean a thing!"

The afternoon passed without any further appearance of the proa or junk, and then the evening came on, the wind veering round to our beam at sunset, making us brace up more sharply. We looked about us pretty keenly now, as might be imagined, but still nothing was to be seen of our whilom pursuers; and so all on board turned in that night much more comfortably than on the preceding one, when the danger appeared more immediate.

The morning, however, told a different tale.

At the early dawn, when I was with Mr Mackay on the poop, the port watch coming on deck just then in their turn of duty, we could see nothing of the suspicious strangers; however as the sun rose higher up, his rays lit a more extended range of sea, and then, far-away off on the horizon to windward, could be seen two tiny white sails in the distance dead astern of us.

"Sail ho!" shouted I from the mizzen cross-trees, where I had gone to look out, Tom Jerrold being sent up aloft forward for the same purpose. "Sail ho!"

"Where away?" cried Mr Mackay, clutching the glass and climbing up into the rigging as he spoke, being as spry as a cat. "What do you make out?"

"Two of them, sir," said I; "and I believe it's these pirates, sir, again. They're on our weather quarter, hull down to windward."

"Right you are, my boy!" cried he presently after a careful inspection of the objects I had pointed out from the top, though he did not come up aloft any higher, his telescope under his arm being rather awkward to carry. "They are the same craft, sure enough. It is most vexatious!"

He went down below to tell the captain, and, of course, the news soon spread through the ship, all hands turning out and coming on deck to have a look at these bloodhounds of the deep, that seemed bent on pursuing us to the death.

They did not close on us, though, keeping the same distance off, some ten miles or so, till sundown, when they approached a little nearer and could be seen astern of us, through

John Conroy Hutcheson

the middle watch, by the aid of the night-glass; but they sheered off again at the breaking of this third day, by which time we could see Pulo Sapata right ahead, a most uninviting spot apparently, consisting of nothing but one big bare rock.

Here, hauling round on the starboard tack, we shaped our course east-nor'-east, to pass over the Macclesfield Bank, in a straight line almost for Formosa Strait, our most direct route to Shanghai, the proa and the junk still keeping after us at a safe distance off.

"By Jingo, I'll tire 'em out yet!" cried "Old Jock" savagely, when, on our getting abreast of the Paracels, although far off to leeward, he saw the beastly things still in our wake as he came on deck in the morning. "I'll tire 'em out before I've done with 'em."

But, now, all at once, we had something more important to think of than even the supposed pirates.

The wind had freshened during the morning, blowing as usual from the south-west and west, and towards noon it slackened again; but no importance was attached to this circumstance, at first, by the captain and Mr Mackay, although, when presently the water became thick and a deep irregular swell set in, they both grew rather uneasy.

"It looks uncommon like a typhoon, sir," said the first mate to "Old Jock," after looking out both to windward and leeward. "There is some change coming."

"I think so, too," said the other. "Go down, Mackay, and have a look at the barometer. It was all right when I came up, but it may have fallen since then; if it has, that will make our doubt a certainty."

"Aye, aye, sir," replied the first mate hurrying down the companion. He wasn't long absent, returning the next moment with the information: "It has gone down from 29.80 to 29.60."

"That means a typhoon, then," said Captain Gillespie; "so the sooner we're prepared for it the better. All hands take in sail!"

The men tumbled up with a will, the sheets all flying as the halliards we're let go and all hands on the yard like bees; and, as soon as the topgallants had been clewed up, these sails were furled and lashed, as well as having the sea-gaskets put on, so as to make them all the more secure.

The topsails followed suit, and then the courses; the ship's head being brought round to the nor'-west, from which quarter the storm was expected, as typhoons always blow eight points to the right of the regular wind, which with us, at the time these precautions were taken, was from the south-east.

The Silver Queen now lay-to, motionless in the water, with only her main trysail and a storm staysail forward set.

"What is a typhoon?" I asked Mr Mackay, when I got down on deck again after helping to hand the mizzen-topsail, the last job we had to do on our mast. "What does it mean?"

"It's the Chinese word for a 'big wind,' my boy," said he kindly; but looking very grave. "You'll soon be able to see what it's like for yourself."

The opportunity he spoke of was not long delayed.

By the time the sails had been taken in and all our

John Conroy Hutcheson

preparations made for the reception of our expected but unwelcome visitor, everything being lashed down that was likely to get blown away, and life-lines rove along the deck fore and aft, the same as when we were making ready to weather the Cape of Good Hope, it was late in the afternoon.

At four o'clock, the commencement of the first dog-watch, the barometer had fallen further down the scale to 29.46; while, an hour later, it was down to 28.96, the wind increasing in force almost every minute and the sea growing in proportion, until the very height of the cyclone was attained.

The dinghy, which was lashed inboard behind the wheel-house, was blown bodily away to leeward, the ropes holding it parting as if they had been pack-thread, heavy squalls, accompanied with heavy rain all the time beating on us like hail, and bursting over the ship in rapid succession; but the old barquey bravely stood it, bending to the blast when it came, and then buoyantly rising the next moment and breasting it like the good sea-boat she was.

At "six bells" the barometer fell to its lowest point, 28.60, when the violence of the wind was something fearful, although after this there was a slight rise in the glass. During the next half-hour, however, the mizzen-topsail, which Tom Jerrold and I, with Gregory to help us, had fastened as we thought so firmly to the yard, was blown to ribbons, the spanker getting adrift shortly afterwards and being torn away from its lacing to the luff rope, scrap by scrap.

The main trysail, also, although only very little of it was shown when set, now blew away too, making a great report no doubt; but the shrieking of the wind was such that we couldn't hear anything else but its howling through the rigging, the captain's voice close alongside of me, as I sheltered under the hood of the companion, sounding actually only like a faint whisper.

The typhoon now shifted from the north-west to the westwards, and the barometer, rising shortly afterwards to 29.20, jumped up thence another twenty points in the next hour.

"It's passing off now," said Captain Gillespie, when he could make himself heard between the squalls, which now came with a longer interval between them. "Those typhoons always work against the sun, and we've now experienced the worst of it. There goes our last sail, though, and we'll have to run for it now."

As he said the words the storm staysail forward was carried away with a distinct bang, hearing which showed that the wind was not so powerful quite as just now—when one, really, couldn't have heard a thirty-five ton gun fired forwards.

On losing this her only scrap of canvas left, the ship half broached to.

Joe Fergusson, however, came to the rescue, no doubt from hearing something the boatswain had said, for the gale was blowing so furiously that the captain would not have thought of ordering a man aloft; for, whether through catching Tim Rooney's remark or from some sailor-like intuition, the ex-bricklayer in the very nick of time voluntarily clambered up the rigging forwards and loosened the weather clew of the foresail.

Mr Mackay who was aft, seeing his purpose, at once told the men at the wheel to put the helm up; when, the Silver Queen's head paying off, she lifted out of the trough of the heavy rolling sea and scudded away nor'-eastwards right

John Conroy Hutcheson

before the wind, which had now got back to the normal point of the "trade" we had been sailing with previous to the storm—when, as this new south-westerly gale was blowing with more than twenty times the force of our original monsoon from the same quarter, the ship, although with only this tiny scrap of her foresail set, was soon driving through the water at over twelve knots the hour, in the very direction, too, we wanted her to go, to fetch our port.

"This is what I call turning the tables," yelled the captain, putting both his hands to his mouth for a sort of speaking trumpet as he roared out the words to Mr Mackay at the wheel. "By Jingo, it's turning the tail of a typhoon into a fair wind!"

CHAPTER FOURTEEN

ATTACKED BY THE PIRATES

It was "the tail of a typhoon" with a vengeance; for as we raced onwards through the boiling sea, now lit up by a very watery moon, lots of broken spars and timbers could be seen, as well as several junks floating bottom upwards, thus showing what the fury of the storm had been and the damage done by its ravages.

Mr Mackay noticed these bits of wrecks and wreckage as the captain spoke; and, mingled with a feeling of pity for those who had perished in the tornado, came a satisfactory thought to his mind.

"Yes, sir," said he in reply to Captain Gillespie's observation, "we're making a fair wind out of a foul one; but, besides that, sir, we've got something else to thank the typhoon for, under Providence. It has probably settled the hash of those piratical rascals that were chasing us!"

"Humph! I forgot all about 'em," snorted out "Old Jock," equally pleased at this idea. "No doubt they've gone to the bottom, and good luck to 'em too. One can't feel sorry for such vermin as those that are prowling after honest craft, and who'd cut one's throat for a dollar."

John Conroy Hutcheson

"We mustn't be too sure, though, sir," continued the first mate, as if he had been turning the matter over in his mind. "We've managed to weather the gale so far, and so might they. Those fellows are accustomed to these seas and can smell a typhoon coming; so, if they ran to windward in time, instead of lying-to and waiting for it, as we did, they might have got out of it altogether by keeping ahead of it."

"Pooh!" ejaculated "Old Jock" contemptuously—"I've no fear of being troubled by them again. They're all down in Davy Jones' locker by this; and may joy go with them, as I said before!"

"Well, sir," said Mr Mackay, not pursuing his theory any further, and desirous of turning the conversation, if conversation it can be called when both were holding on still to the life-lines and shouting at each other more than speaking, "what are we to do now?"

"Carry-on, of course," replied "Old Jock," with a squint up at the watery moon and the flying clouds that ever and anon obscured its pale gleams, making everything look black around the moment it was hidden, "There's nothing else to be done but to let her scud before it until the gale has spent its force. I wish we could get up some more sail, though."

"Would it be safe, sir?"

"Safe!" snorted "Old Jock," sniffing with his nose up directly. "Why, what the dickens have you got to be afraid of, man? We're now in the open sea, with nothing in the shape of land near us for a hundred miles or more anywhere you chose to cast the lead."

"But, you forget, sir," suggested the other good-humouredly, so as not to anger the "old man," who was especially touchy about his navigation; "you forget the rate the ship's going—over twelve knots?"

"No, I don't forget, Mister Mackay; and, if we were going twenty it wouldn't make the slightest difference," retorted the captain, who was thoroughly roused now, as the first mate could tell by his addressing him as "Mister," which he never did unless pretty well worked up and in a general state of temper. "I'd have you to know I'm captain of my own ship; and when I say a thing I mean a thing! Call up the hands to try and get some more sail on her; for I'm going to make the best of this typhoon now, as it has made the best it could of me—one good turn deserves another."

Of course there was no arguing with him after this; so all Mr Mackay could do was to pass the word forward for Tim Rooney, and tell him what Captain Gillespie's orders were—there was no good attempting to hail the boatswain, for not a word shouted could be heard beyond the poop.

"Begorra, it's a risky game, puttin' sail on her, sorr," said Tim meeting Mr Mackay half-way on the main-deck; "but we moight thry lettin' out a schrap more av the fores'le, if the houl lot don't fetch away."

"We must try it," returned Mr Mackay. "He will have it so."

"All right, sorr, I'm agreeayble, as the man aid whin he wor agoin' to be hung," said Tim Rooney grinning, never taking anything serious for very long; "faix I'll go up mesilf if I can't get none av the hands to volunteer. I couldn't order 'em yet, sorr, for it's more'n a man's loife is worth to get on a yard with this wind."

"Very good, Rooney, do your best," replied Mr Mackay. "Only don't run into any danger. We can't afford to loose you, bo'sun."

"Troth I'll take care av that same, sorr," returned Tim with a laugh. "I wants another jollification ashore afore I'd be after losin' the noomber av me mess."

I had come down from off the poop with Mr Mackay, and now, standing by his side, watched with anxiety Tim's movements.

He had no lack of volunteers, however, for the ticklish work of laying out on the yard, Joe Fergusson's previous example having inspired whatever pluck was previously wanting; and, almost as soon as he got forward we saw several of the hands mounting the fore rigging on the starboard side—this being the least dangerous, as there was no chance of their being blown into the sea against the wind.

But Tim Rooney would not suffer them to go aloft alone, his stalwart figure being the first to be seen leading the way up the shrouds, with Joe Fergusson close behind, not satisfied apparently with his previous attempt; and both, I noticed in the moonlight, which just then streamed out full for a few minutes, had their jack-knives between their teeth, ready for any emergency, as well as to cut away the double lashings of the foresail, "sea-gaskets" having been laced over the regular ones so as to bind the sail tighter to the yard.

As they went up, the crew were flattened like pancakes against the ratlines; and Mr Mackay and I held our breath when they got on the foot-rope from the shrouds, holding on to the yard and jack-stay, with the wind swaying them to and fro in the most perilous manner. Tim Rooney especially seemed in the most dangerous position, as he made for the lee earing, whence he might be swept off in an instant into the foaming waves that spurted up from the chains as if clutching at him, while Joe Fergusson worked his way out to the end of the weather yard-arm, fighting the fierce gusts at every sliding step he took.

Then, when all were at their posts, Tim gave some sort of signal to the four others whom he allowed to go up with him, and at the same instant the gaskets were severed, parties of men below slacking off the clewlines and pulling on the sheets by degrees. By this means the foresail, having been double-reefed fortunately before being furled, was set satisfactorily, without a split as all of us below expected, the hands getting down from the yards while we were yet hauling the tack aboard.

The effect of this additional sail power on the ship was magical, lifting her bows out of the water and making her plunge madly through the billowy ocean, now all covered with foam and spume, like a maddened horse taking the bit between his teeth and bolting.

"She wants some after sail to steady her," roared the captain bending over the poop rail, although he held on tightly enough to it the while, and calling out to Mr Mackay, who remained with me just below him on the main-deck. "We must try and get some sort of rag up."

Mr Mackay made a motion up at the fragments of the main trysail, which, it may be remembered, had been carried away by the first blast of the typhoon.

"Aye," roared back "Old Jock," understanding him, and knowing that if the first mate had spoken he couldn't have heard a word he said, from the fact of the wind blowing forward. "I know it's gone, but try a staysail."

"Bedad, he bates Bannagher!" said Tim Rooney, who had

returned aft and joined Mr Mackay and I under the break of the poop, where we were sheltered more from the force of the gale. "I niver did say sich a chap for carryin' on, fair weather an' foul, loike 'Ould Jock Sayins an' Mayins.' Sure, he wants to be there afore himsilf!"

"We must rig up a storm staysail, I suppose," replied Mr Mackay, smiling at the other's remark. "Try one on the mizzen staysail—the smallest you've got. Ask Adams, he'll soon find one; and, mind you, send it up 'wift' fashion, so as to lessen the risk of its getting blown away, bosun."

"Aye, aye, sorr," said Tim, opening his eyes at this expedient of hoisting a sail like a pilot's signal, and starting to work his way forward again along the weather side of the deck. "Begorra, you're the boy, sure, Misther Mackay, for sayin' through a stone hidge as well as most folk!"

But the dodge succeeded all the same, and likewise had the advantage of steadying the vessel, which did not roll nearly so much when the after sail was hoisted, with the sheet hauled in to leeward; although, the Silver Queen bent over when she felt it, as if running on a bowline, notwithstanding that the wind was almost dead aft and she spurring on before it.

As the night came on it darkened more, the moon disappearing altogether and the sky becoming completely covered with black angry clouds; while heavy showers of cold rain pelted down on us at intervals from midnight till "four bells" in the middle watch.

Then the rain ceased and the heavens cleared a bit, a few stars peeping out; and the phosphorescent light from the sea enabled us to have a good view of the boiling waves around us, still heaving and tossing as far as the eye could reach, although the wind was perceptibly lessening.

An hour later its force had fallen to that of a strong breeze, and the captain had the topsails and mizzen-topgallant set, carrying on still full pitch to the north-east, notwithstanding that just before dawn it became pitch dark again and we couldn't see a cable's length ahead.

The starboard watch had been relieved shortly before this, but Mr Saunders remained up, as indeed had most of us since the previous afternoon; while Captain Gillespie, indeed, never left the deck once since the first suspicion of the typhoon.

He now yawned, however, the long strain and fatigue beginning to tell on him.

"I think I'll go below," he said; and, turning to Mr Mackay, all amiable again, especially at having carried his point of "carrying on" successfully in spite of the first mate's caution, he remarked with a sniff, "You see, Mackay, we've gone on all right and met no dangers, and it'll puzzle those blessed pirates, if they're yet in the land of the living, to find us at daybreak!"

Just as he uttered these words, however, there was a tremendous shock forwards that threw us all off our feet, succeeded by a peculiar grating feeling under the ship's keel, after which, her heaving and rolling ceased as if she had suddenly sailed from amidst the waves into the calm water of some sheltered harbour. A second shock followed soon, but not so violent as the first; and then, all motion ceased.

"By Jingo, she's aground!" snorted out "Old Jock," scrambling to his feet by the assistance of Mr Saunders' outstretched hand. "Where on earth can we've got to? there's no land here."

Mr Mackay said nothing, although he had his suspicions, which indeed had led in the original instance to his remonstrance against the captain's allowing the ship to rush on madly in the dark; but, presently, as the light of morning illumined the eastern sky and we were able to see the ship's position, a sudden cry of alarm and recognition burst from both—

"The Pratas shoal!"

This was their joint exclamation; and, on the sun rising a little later on, when the whole scene and all our surroundings could be better observed, the wonder was that the Silver Queen was not in pieces and every soul on board her drowned!

To explain our miraculous escape, I may mention that this shoal, which Captain Gillespie and Mr Mackay so quickly named beyond question, was a circular coral reef almost in the centre of the China Sea, and about a hundred and thirty miles distant from Hongkong, absolutely in the very highway of vessels trading east and west.

Breakers encircled it, showing their white crests on every side, the sharp points of the coral composing the reef almost coming to the surface of the water, while at some spots it was raised above it. In these latter places it was covered with rank grass, exhibiting incipient signs of vegetation; and, within the reef, inclosed by a lagoon some three miles wide that went completely round it, lay a small island, on which were several shrubs and a prominent tree on a slight elevation, which will in process of time become a hill, whereon stood also the remains of a pagoda, or Chinese temple, while pieces of wreck and bleached bones were scattered over the shores. Of course we did not notice all these things at first, but such was the result of our subsequent observations and investigations.

As wild, desolate, and dreary a spot it was as ever anchorite imagined or poet pictured; such, at all events, we all thought on looking at it and realising the providential way in which our safety had been effected.

It happened in this wise.

There were one or two breaks in the reef surrounding this desert isle, as we could see from a link missing here and there in the chain of breakers. This was especially noticeable towards the south-western portion of the rampart the indefatigable coral insect had thrown up, where an opening about double the width of the Silver Queen's beam was plainly discernible. Through this fissure in the reef, piloted by that power which had watched over us throughout all the perils of our voyage, the ship had been driven; and she had beached herself gradually on the shore of the little island, as her way was eased by the placid lagoon into which she entered from the troubled sea without the natural breakwater. Here she was now fixed hard and fast forward, with her forefoot high and dry, although there was deep water under her stern aft.

"Thank God for his mercy!" exclaimed Mr Mackay fervently; and I'm sure I echoed this recognition of the loving care that had so wonderfully preserved us. "We couldn't have got in here without striking on the reef, if we had seen the entrance before our eyes and tried our very best; not, at all events, with that gale shoving us on and in such a sea as is running—only look at it now!"

"Oh, aye," agreed Captain Gillespie, gazing out as we all did

John Conroy Hutcheson

at the creamy line of foaming breakers all round, that sent showers of surfy spray over the coral ledge into the placid lagoon, which was calm and still in comparison, like a mountain tarn, albeit filled with brackish sea-water all the same. "Oh, aye, it's wonderful enough our getting here; but how are we going to get out—eh?"

"No doubt we'll find a way," said the other, who had bared his head when giving thanksgiving where it was due; and whose noble, intelligent face, I thought, as I looked at him admiringly, seemed capable of anything, he spoke so cheer-fully, his courage not daunted but increased, it seemed, all the more by what had happened—"No doubt we'll find a way, sir."

But "Old Jock" wouldn't be comforted.

Obstinately insisting before, against Mr Mackays advice, that we were going on all right, he was even more dogmatically certain now that we were all wrong; saying that, as far as he could see, the ship and her cargo and every one of the thirty-one souls she had on board were doomed!

"I can't see how it's going to be managed, Mackay," he replied despondingly to the other's cheery words, even his nose drooping with dismay at the prospect, superstition coming to aid his despairing conviction. "I knew there was something uncanny when those pigs jumped overboard that evening, and I told you so, if you recollect, Saunders; and you know, when I say a thing, I mean a thing."

"Aye, aye," said the second mate, thus appealed to; and who being a shallow-pated man with little feeling for anything save the indulgence of his appetite, thought there was some connection, now the captain put it so, between the loss of the porkers and the ship's being castaway, he not having been let into the secret of the reason for the strange behaviour of the pigs on the occasion referred to. "Aye, aye, cap'en, I remember your saying so quite well."

Mr Mackay couldn't stand this, and he walked down the poop ladder to conceal his amusement; and I followed him when I found him bent on consulting Tim Rooney as to what was to be done, the captain being hopeless at present.

"Be jabers, we're in a pritty kittle av fish an' no mistake!" said Tim when asked his opinion about the situation. "We might be able to kedge her off, sorr, an' thin ag'in we moightn't; but the foorst thing to say, sorr, is whither she's all roight below."

"A good suggestion," answered Mr Mackay. "Tell the carpenter to sound the well at once."

"That'd be no good at all, sorr," interposed the other, "for the poor craythur's got her bows hoigh an' dhry, while she's down by the starn. The bist thing as I'd advise, sorr, excusin' the liberty, is to get down alongside an' say if she's started anythin'. That big scrape she got as she came over the rafe, I'm afeard, took off a bit av her kale, sorr."

"Right you are, Rooney, sensible as ever," said Mr Mackay. "We'll have a boat over the side at once and see to it."

This, however, was a work of time, for the jolly-boat, which was the only one of moderate size we had left, since the dinghy had been carried away in the typhoon, was stowed inside the long-boat; and so purchases had to be rigged to the fore and main yards before it could be raised from its berth and hoisted over the ship's bulwarks.

But, all hands helping, the job was done at last; when Mr

John Conroy Hutcheson

Mackay descended the side-ladder into the boat along with the boatswain and a couple of men to pull round the ship, so as to ascertain what, if any, damage she might have received. I could not help noticing, though, that the captain did not exhibit the slightest interest when the first mate submitted what he was about to do and asked his permission—only telling him that he might go if he liked, but he thought it of little use!

I should have liked to have gone with them too, and I mentioned this to Tom Jerrold, as he and I leant over the bows and watched the jolly-boat and those in her below us; for although Tim Rooney had spoken of the ship being "high and dry" she was still in shallow water forward, the shelly bottom being to be seen at the depth of two or three feet or so, the beach shelving abruptly.

While the two of us were looking at the boat, though, and the island in front spread out before us, with its solitary tree, ruined Chinese pagoda and all, which Ching Wang was also inspecting with much interest from the forecastle, we were suddenly startled by a shout aft from Captain Gillespie, who still remained on the poop.

"Hi, Mackay," he cried, "come back. Here is that blessed proa and junk, and a whole fleet of pirates after us!"

This made both Tom and I turn pale, although Ching Wang betrayed no expression of alarm when we explained the captain's hail to him, only his little beady eyes twinkling.

"You fightee number one chop, tyfong makee scarcee chop chop, Sabby? No goodee when sailor-mannee fightee!"

When we got aft, where we were soon joined by Mr Mackay, who had instantly obeyed the captain's order of recall, and said, by the way, that they could not discover much injury to the ship forward save that a portion of her false keel had been torn off, "Old Jock" pointed out some specks on the horizon to windward. These, on being scrutinised through the glass by the first mate, were declared to be the now familiar proa and her consort, a fact which I corroborated with my naked eye from the mizzen cross-trees whither I at once ascended.

The sea, I noticed too, had calmed down considerably outside the reef, which the pirate junks gained later on in the afternoon, coming through the opening we had observed to the south and west one by one, in single file, and then advancing towards the Silver Queen in line.

Presently, when about half a mile off, they stopped on a flag being hoisted by the leading proa, which appeared to command the expedition; and then, amidst the hideous din of a lot of tin-kettly drums and gongs, the pirates, for such they now showed themselves to be without doubt, opened fire on the ship with cannon and jingals—the balls from the former soon singing in the air as they passed over our masts, their aim, however, being rather high and eccentric, although the first that whistled past made me duck my head in fright, thinking it was coming towards me.

"Oh!" I cried; but I may say without any exaggeration or desire to brag, that I did not flinch again, nor did I utter another "Oh!"

John Conroy Hutcheson

CHAPTER FIFTEEN

CHING WANG AND I ESCAPE
IN THE SAMPAN

It must not be thought, though, that we were inactive all the time the pirates were coming nearer after the first warning of their unexpected approach.

No, on the contrary, we made every preparation, with the means at our disposal, to receive them with proper respect.

"Begorra, if they'd ownly tould us afore we lift the ould country we'd a had some big guns, too," said Tim Rooney as he blazed away at a chap with a red sash on in the prow of the proa, taking aim at him with one of the Martini-Henry rifles that had been brought up by the captain from his cabin. "So, me hearties, ye'll have to take the will for the dade, an' this little lidden messenger, avic, to show as how we aren't onmindful av ye, sure, an' that there's no ill falin' atwane us!"

Yes, we had made every preparation.

The moment Captain Gillespie was assured that the the pirates—towards whom he had conceived a deadly hatred, although believing them lost in the storm that had caught us—were coming again in chase of our unfortunate ship, he woke up once more into his old animated self, his nose twisting this way and that as he sniffed and snorted, full of warlike energy.

"I'll soon teach 'em a lesson," he cried cheerily to Mr Mackay. "When they tackle Jock Gillespie, they'll find their match; and, ye know, when I say a thing I mean a thing!"

Thereupon he bounced down the companion, telling Jerrold and me to follow him; which, as may be supposed, we did with the greatest alacrity, "Old Jock" not often inviting us to his sanctum.

"Here, lads," he said, emptying out an old arm-chest which was stowed under his bunk on to the floor, "lend a hand, will ye?"

Of course we did "lend the hand" he requested thus politely in a tone of command, only too glad to overhaul the stock of weapons tumbled out all together from the chest.

There were a couple of Martini-Henry rifles, sighted for long ranges; three old Enfields of the pattern the volunteers used to be supplied with some years ago; a large bore shot-gun; and a few revolvers of various sorts—one of the latter making my eyes glisten at the sight of it, for it was just suited to me, I thought.

The captain seemed to anticipate my wish, even before I could give it utterance.

"Do ye know how to fire a pistol?" he asked Jerrold and me, looking from one to the other of us, with a profound sniff of interrogation. "Have either of ye handled ere a one before?"

"Oh, yes, sir," said I; while Tom Jerrold laughed.

John Conroy Hutcheson

"Don't you remember, cap'en," he cried, "giving me that fat one there, the Colt revolver, last voyage when you thought there was going to be a mutiny; and how you instructed me how to use it?"

"Oh, aye, I remember. I clean forgot, lad; this bother about the ship has turned my head, I think," snorted he, not a bit angrily though. "Well, take the same weapon again now, lad, as you're familiar with it; and you, youngster, have you got any choice?"

"I'd like this one, sir," I replied, fixing on my original selection, as he turned to me and asked this question, "if you'll let me have it. I won't hurt it."

"No, I don't fancy ye will," he said, sniffing and chuckling and twitching his nose. "I hope ye'll hurt some of those rascally pirates with it, though."

The captain then opened another chest, a smaller iron one, which he also dragged out from under his bunk, unlocking it with a heavy key he took off a bunch which was hanging up on a nail over his writing-desk and throwing back the lid.

This second receptacle, we soon discovered, contained a lot of cartridges for the rifles, there being a hundred or more of various sorts, some for the breech-loaders and some for the Enfields of the old-fashioned regulation size. There were also a variety of smaller cartridges for the revolvers, and "Old Jock" gave Tom and I each a package of these latter for our weapons.

In the chest, likewise, were two or three large flasks of powder and a lot of bullets loose, which the captain crammed into a leathern bag and told us to take on the poop with the rifles, Tom and I carrying up a couple each with the bag of bullets and powder-flasks and then returning for the rest.

In our absence "Old Jock" had ferreted out from some other hiding-place of his a couple of swords and a number of cutlasses, which he likewise directed us to take up the companion, he assisting us; until, presently, we had the whole armoury arranged on the top of the cabin skylight.

"Now, Mackay," said Captain Gillespie, blowing like a grampus after his exertions, "take y'r choice, but I think that the two best shots in the ship ought to have the Martini rifles; and if I were picking out the picked marksmen—he! he! that's a joke, 'picking' and 'picked,' didn't intend it though— I'd have chosen y'rself and the bosun!"

Of course we all laughed at his joke, as he had taken such pains to point it out; and he was so pleased with it himself that it was some time before he could speak again, he sniffed and snorted so much.

"Not bad that, Mackay," he said; "not bad—eh? But which of these things would ye like best—eh?"

"I think I'll take the breech-loader, sir," replied the other, suiting the action to the word and proceeding to examine the lock of one of the Martini-Henrys, which seemed to be an old acquaintance of his, for he loaded the chamber much quicker than I could manage my new acquisition; "and I don't believe you could do better than hand the other to Rooney, as you suggested. He's the best shot in the ship, I'm certain."

"Y'rself excepted," interposed the captain wonderfully politely for him; singing out loudly at the same time, "Bosun!"

"Here, sorr," cried Tim, who had been waiting below close to the poop ladder, expecting the summons, and who was all agog at the prospect of a fight. "Here I am, sorr."

"Well, bosun," said Captain Gillespie, "it looks as if we'll have to fight those rascals coming up astern and making for us. The cowards! They didn't dare attack the old barquey when she was all ataunto in the open sea; and only now rely on their numbers and the fact of our being in limbo here. However, if they do attack us, we shall have a fight for it."

"Bully for ye, sorr!" cried Tim enraptured. "It's mesilf as loikes a fight, sure. I'm niver at pace barrin' whin I'm in a row, sure, sorr!"

"Then you'll be soon in your element," retorted Jock grimly. "Call the hands aft."

"Aye, aye, sorr," answered Tim; and going up to the rail he shouted out in his ringing voice, "All ha-a-nds aft!"

"Now, my men," said "Old Jock," leaning over the poop and addressing them as they stood below on the main-deck— "we've got a batch of rascally pirates coming up after us astern; and, as you know, we can't run away from 'em. What will ye do—cave in to 'em or fight 'em?"

The crew broke into a rousing cheer.

"Ye'll fight 'em, then?"

"Aye, aye, fight 'em till we make 'em sick!" shouted one of the hands speaking for the rest, who endorsed his answer on their behalf with a "Hip, hip, hooray!"

"And one for the skipper," shouted Joe Fergusson, who was a

sailor of sailors by this time and had learnt all their ways and talk, dropping out of his old provincialisms. "Hip, hip, hooray!"

"And another for Mr Mackay," cried a voice that sounded like that of Adams, causing the hooraying to start again with fresh force, this cheer being much heartier than the first.

"Now, men," said Captain Gillespie, "as ye've let off all your gas, let me see what ye can do in action. Bosun, serve out the cutlasses and distribute the rest of the guns."

This being done and all of the men armed in one way or another, the deficiencies of the captain's armoury being made good by the aid of handspikes which Mr Mackay had thoughtfully ordered to be brought aft while we were taking up the rifles and other things from the cabin. Even Billy, the ship's boy, got hold of an old bayonet, which he brandished about near Pedro Carvalho the steward, who had come out of his pantry to see what all the noise was about, which gesture on his part almost frightening the Portuguese, who, as I've related before, was an innate coward, into a fit. At all events, it made him turn of a yellowish pallor that did not improve his complexion.

"Carramba!" he exclaimed, as he retreated back within his pantry. "Fora, maldito!"

When offered a weapon, Ching Wang only smiled that innocent bland smile of his, producing his own long knife, that had a blade like an American bowie, being over a foot long and with a double edge.

"Me one piecee in tyfong tummee tummee, chop chop, pijjin!" he said, brandishing the awful blade in a way that I'm sure the "kyfongs," the Chinese term for pirates, would not relish, especially in such friendly relation with their "tummee tummees."

All the crew being now armed, the captain and Mr Mackay disposed them in parties about the deck and forecastle to windward, so as best to oppose the pirates' attack; while the men provided with the Enfield rifles were placed in the tops, with the bullets and powder for ammunition when their cartridges ran short. Tim Rooney took his station with Mr Mackay on the poop, from which the advancing pirates could best be picked off, and where also were gathered the captain, as a matter of course; Mr Saunders, who carried an old single-barrel pistol with a heavy lock, which the second mate intended to make more use of as a club than to shoot with; and Tom Jerrold and Sam Weeks, as well as myself—Sam being sadly jealous of Tom and I from the fact of our having revolvers, while he, coming too late after they'd all been distributed, had to be contented with a marlin-spike—poor Sammy!

It was thus that we all awaited the attack, every man Jack of us being at his specially appointed post and on the alert; when the pirates—after pounding away at us a long time at a distance, with the result of neither wounding a soul on board nor damaging the ship very materially, none of the shot penetrating her hull between wind and water, the only thing we had to fear—at length mustered up courage enough to give up their rather unremunerative game of "long bowls" and come to close quarters.

I had got quite accustomed now to the rushing sound of round shot in the air and the waspish phit phitting of rifle bullets past my head; and I was filled with a wild excitement that made my heart pant, as I stood on the poop between Mr Mackay and Tim Rooney.

These two were peppering away at the leading proa and the junks, as they paddled in hastily towards the ship with their long double-banked sweeps, anxious to get in close alongside and so to be sheltered by our hull from the murderous and rapid fire which the wielders of the Martini-Henrys rained on them.

But every bullet found a billet in some pirate breast sooner or later, one of the villainous desperadoes falling over his oar here and another dropping down on the bamboo deck of a junk there; while, occasionally, some wretch would tumble overboard with a wild yell, in answer to the ping of the rifle, shot through the heart as dead as a herring, and going down to his grave amongst the fishes in Neptune's coral caverns below!

"There's that scoundrel of a fellow in the red sash again," cried Mr Mackay, when the Malay proa, which still led the van, was only about half a cable's length off. "There he is, Rooney,—do you see him?"

"Aye, bad cess to the black divil, I say him well enough, sorr," returned Tim, carefully putting a fresh cartridge into the chamber of his weapon. "Begorra, I thought I'd kilt the beggar a dozen toimes alriddy; but he's got the luck of ould Nick, an' sames to save his skin somehow or ither. Here goes for him ag'in—take that now, ye ould thaife!"

"Ping!"

But the pirate captain, as the tall dark man in the stern of the proa seemed to be, only let fall the long crease which he had held in his right hand brandishing at us, the bullet from Tim's rifle having broken his arm, that also dropped powerless by his side.

"You nearly had him there," cried Mr Mackay, now taking a shot. "I hope I'll have better luck though."

"I hope ye will, sorr," heartily echoed Tim. "I mint to riddle his carkiss an ownly winged him. The ugly black divil sames to kape a charmed loife, an' I dare say his ould frind below helps him, the nayghur!"

Mr Mackay, however, was equally unsuccessful; for, as luck would have it, another of the pirates jumping up in front of the chief received the bullet intended for him.

The scoundrel who got killed was, certainly, one off the list; still, the small fry did not count like their leader, the loss of whom all of us thought might have paralysed the enemy's advance.

It really seemed, however, as if the gigantic villain, who towered over his men, bore a charmed life; for, although our fellows in the tops with the Ennelds, as well the first mate and boatswain, aimed at him, while, now that the proa was within revolver range, the captain and Tom Jerrold, and even I, with my little weapon, pelted bullet after bullet in his direction, all of us missed hitting the swarthy scoundrel. We noticed, too, on seeing him closer, that he appeared to be more of Pedro Carvalho's nationality than belonging to the Malay race, his features and shape of head being altogether different; albeit, he was fully as ugly as his rascally comrades in the proa and following junks—a hybrid lot of Javanese and Chinese and all the vile scourings of the Straits Settlements; long-haired heavy-eyed and sullen-looking most of them, with narrow retreating foreheads, and evidently of the lowest type of humanity.

As they got closer and closer to the ship, too, we noticed that several had red sashes round their blue frocks, into which were stuck fearful curved knives and the butt-ends of pistols; and so, with "so many Richmonds in the field," it was not to be wondered that Tim Rooney and Mr Mackay had previously missed their mark—albeit now that the proa was near, it was strange that they could not pick off the pirate leader, who, as the proa sheered up alongside the Silver Queen, looked up at us astern and grinned a horrible sardonic grin, drawing the while his solitary left hand across his bare tawny throat with a most unmistakable gesture.

"Ping!—ping!" came from Mr Mackay's and the boatswain's rifles again in quick succession.

And yet again, marvellous as it may seem, they both missed. There was no longer time, though, for any more pot shots; for, with a wild savage howl and the beating of drums and gongs again, mingled with a shower of jingal balls over the ship, the proa struck against the fore-chains on our starboard bow, one of the junks steering to our port side at the same time, while another remained across our stern and raked us fore and aft with round shot, there being a couple of hundred at least of the bloodthirsty demons in the three craft assailing us. There were probably as many more, too, in the junks astern, which were coming up more leisurely, leaving their comrades in the van to bear the brunt of the fray.

"Now, men!" shouted "Old Jock," who I must say came out like a brave man and a hero on the occasion, losing all his peculiarities and littlenesses of manner and behaviour—at least we did not notice them. "Now, men, we've got to fight for our lives! We must first try and prevent the pirates getting aboard; and, when we can't do that any longer and they gain the decks, we'll retreat into the cabin and barricade ourselves, and fight 'em again there."

"Hooray!" cried the men. "Hooray!"

John Conroy Hutcheson

"And when we can't hold the cabin any longer," continued Old Jock, who seemed to be in a punning vein this afternoon, "we'll go below to the hold, and hold that as long as we can!"

"Hooray!" shouted the hands again, full of the fire of battle now and spurred on by his words. "We'll fight, old man, never fear!"

"And when we can't fight 'em any longer, my lads," cried Captain Gillespie, looking round at us all with an expression of determination that I had never seen in his face before, "we'll blow up the ship sooner than surrender to this villainous gang!"

The cheer that followed this ending of his speech was so loud and genuine, so full of British pluck, so hearty, that the pirates absolutely quailed at the sound of it, holding back a second or two before they sheered up alongside with the intention of boarding us.

They only made a short delay, though, during which we were not idle with our guns and revolvers; for, the next moment, with another yell of defiance, the pirate craft flung their grapnels in our rigging and climbed up on both sides of the ship simultaneously.

"Come down out of the tops!" shouted Mr Mackay to the hands aloft. "Come down at once, we want all of your aid with cold steel now!"

These soon joined us, and then followed a series of shouts and cries and shots and groans which it makes me dizzy even now to think of; until, after losing three of our number, amongst them being poor Mr Saunders, whom we dragged in mortally wounded with us, we all retreated to the cabin, barricading ourselves there with all sorts of bales and boxes, and bracing up the saloon table, which we had previously unloosed from its lashings, to act as a shield under the skylight.

The pirates made a rush after us, but we were too quick for them; so then, leaving us alone for awhile, they proceeded to rummage the ship forward, where, from the noise they made hacking and hewing at the deck, they were evidently trying to break open the hold so as to get at the cargo. But the hatchways being constructed of iron beneath the wood their battering away at them did not bother us much for the moment, as we knew they would find their work cut out for them and the job a long one.

Meanwhile, poor Mr Saunders lay dying on the cabin floor, bleeding from a wound in his breast. The captain said there was no hope for him, for he had been shot through the lungs; and as I bent over him with a glass of water I had got from the pantry, he murmured something that sounded like Ching Wang.

"By Jove!" exclaimed Mr Mackay. "Where is the Chinaman?"

Nobody knew; and although Mr Saunders had been the first to miss him, he could not say anything else about him, or tell us what had become of the poor fellow. We were all, therefore, giving him up for lost, when, suddenly Pedro Carvalho, who, it may be remembered, bore no friendly feeling towards the cook, called out from the pantry window whence, through the jalousies, or open shutters, he could survey a portion of the main-deck.

"Diante de Deos!" he exclaimed, "dere is dat raskil Ching Wang yondare, chummy chumming and chin chinning does peerats. Yase, yase, dere he is! I see him! I see him! Carajo!

Cozenheiro maldito!"

This news came upon us like a thunderbolt, but none of us would believe it until we had been absolutely convinced of the truth of what the steward had stated by seeing for ourselves. Yet, there was no mistake; for sure enough we could presently see with our own eyes, Ching Wang on the friendliest terms, apparently, with a lot of the yellow pirate rascals, who were of his own celestial nationality, away forward, the cook showing them all that was to be seen and grinning and gesticulating away finely!

Still, even then we could hardly believe in his treachery.

Somehow or other, too, whether through Ching Wang's offices or not, of course, we could not say, the pirates did not bother us much during the day, only coming up to the skylight occasionally and firing down on us as well as they could with their clumsy muskets and pistols—a fire which we just as promptly returned, aiming wherever we saw a flash. They once pitched in one of their terrible fire balls or "stink-pots" of fulminating stuff to asphyxiate us with its beastly smell; but Tim Rooney, taking hold of it and plunging the obnoxious thing in a bucket of water, rid us at once of the poisonous fumes.

In the evening, when it was growing dark, a tapping was heard at one of the ports in the captain's cabin; and both Tim and I were just on the point of firing, when, to our great surprise Ching Wang's well-known voice was heard.

"Chin, chin lilly pijjin! Comee one chop quick, me wantee talkee talkee. Lis'en me, an' you lickee kyfong number one go!"

"I thought he'd never turn traitor," cried Captain Gillespie emphatically; Tim Rooney adding with equal warmth, "Nor I, sorr. I've allers found the Chinee chap a good Oirishman ivery day he's bin' aboord!"

The upshot of Ching Wang's communication was, that the pirates were anxious to get all they could out of the ship and clear off; and, believing that he had joined them, they had sent him to negotiate terms with the captain, the pirate chief saying that he would spare all our lives if we would let him have what dollars there was on board and a ransom for the ship, on account, of course, of their not being able to get at the cargo.

Before Captain Gillespie could indignantly refuse making any terms with the rascals, Ching Wang proceeded to say that he had overheard the pirates saying that the reason for their violent hurry was that an English gunboat had been seen in the distance cruising off the mouth of the Canton river.

"Me gottee sampan," continued Ching Wang, declaring now his real motive. "Lilly pijjin squeezee one port, me go along findee gunboat an' catchee kyfong chop chop!"

"First rate," cried Mr Mackay, who acted as general inter- preter, knowing the Chinaman's lingo well, explaining that the reason why Ching Wang had not gone off by himself in the sampan was that he did not know the right course to steer for the Canton river in the first place; and, secondly, he was afraid that the officers of the gunboat might not believe his story about the Silver Queen being assailed by pirates unless some European belonging to her accompanied him. "Nothing could have been more sensible, you see, cap'en; and Ching Wang's got his head screwed on straight."

"And where is this boat ye're going in?"

John Conroy Hutcheson

"Sampan, go long now," returned Ching Wang, motioning with his hand to the water below the stern. "Go long chop chop, soon lilly pijjin come down topside."

His selection of me, though apparently a very flattering one, was due to the fact of my being the only one capable of squeezing through the port, Weeks, who had grown awfully fat on the voyage, being incapable of accomplishing the feat, while all the rest of us were far too big.

"How will ye be able to steer for Canton?" asked Captain Gillespie sniffing—"even if ye know all about managing the boat?"

"Oh, sir," cried I, quite joyous at the idea of starting off on such an expedition and coming with a British gunboat to take the pirates by surprise and give them a licking, "Ching Wang'll see to the sampan, as he calls it, and I will steer, sir, if you give me the course, sir. I've got a little compass here on my watch chain."

"Humph!" he ejaculated; "I think ye'll do, boy. Ye're smart enough at any rate for the job; and, besides, there's no one else that can get through the port. Ye can go!"

"Thank you, sir," said I, grateful for even this semi-reluctant concession, being afraid he might refuse; and then, squeezing gingerly through the port and carefully lowering myself down by a rope which Tim Rooney hitched round the captain's bunk, I landed on the bottom boards of the boat that old Ching Wang had ready below.

I recollect well Tim's whispering softly as I let go my hold of the port sill, "Sure, now, take care av y'rsilf, Misther Gray-ham, sorr, an' don't forgit what the skipper's tould you about your coorse whin ye gits outsoide the rafe; ye're to steer nor'-nor'-west, wid a little more west in it, an' kape a good look-out for the blissid gunboat—an'—an' God bliss ye me bhoy, an' that's Tim Rooney's dyin' wish if ye niver say him ag'in!"

John Conroy Hutcheson

CHAPTER SIXTEEN

THE "BLAZER" TO THE RESCUE

"Hist!" whispered Ching Wang softly, catching hold of my legs as I came down the rope to prevent my feet making a noise on touching the bottom of the sampan; while he carefully guided me into a seat in the stern-sheets. "Makee quiet, tyfong watchee. If catchee no go, all up topside!"

I hardly needed this caution; although, after receiving it I was as still as any mouse suddenly finding itself in the company of a cat unsuspicious of its presence could possibly be.

It was quite dark now, the hull of the ship looming faintly above us, a big black shadow, and the water was without a glimmer near, save where, just ahead, the light of a flare-up, which the pirates had kindled on the forecastle, shone out over the sea there, besides illuminating the island beach— where a number of black figures could be seen moving about opening some casks, which, Ching Wang explained to me, he had assisted in getting up from the forehold, so as to distract their attention from us for awhile; for, knowing that these casks contained salt pork, and being acquainted with the predilections of his countrymen for this dainty, he was certain they would have an orgy before proceeding to further hostilities.

This impression of the Chinaman proved to be quite correct; for not only did the pirates rout out the salt pork, but they immediately proceeded to cook it in Ching Wang's coppers, which were full of boiling water which he had got ready in the first instance for the purpose of throwing over the gentlemen as they boarded the ship. He had, however, subsequently changed his mind on this point, thinking that by adopting the guileless subtlety of his race and pretending to side with our enemies he might in the end be of more effectual service to us.

Of course the Chinaman did not mention to his new allies the original use for which the coppers were intended, as such candour on his part might have led to his getting into "hot water" and so spoilt his little plot, the complete success of which was further assured by his purloining Tim Rooney's private bottle of rum from his cabin in the deck-house, and bestowing it with his benediction on the stalwart Portuguese captain of the pirates. This gentleman, being partial to the liquor, enjoyed himself to such an extent over the unexpected treasure-trove, keeping it selfishly for his own gratification, that he was more than "half-seas-over" ere his rascally fellow cut-throats had begun their pork feast; so, he was equally disinclined with them for further active operations against the ship, the captain and crew of which he regarded for the moment in a most benevolent spirit on account of their having saved him the trouble of making them captive, probably at the expense of several lives on his side, by locking themselves in the cabin below of their own accord!

I got out all this by degrees from Ching Wang, as, paddling in the most noiseless fashion across the lagoon where it was darkest, and carefully avoiding the other junks anchored out

John Conroy Hutcheson

in the middle, he directed the course of the sampan towards the opening in the reef. This became all the more distinct as we got near its edge from the phosphorescent glitter of the surf breaking over the coral ledge, excepting at the place where the Silver Queen had steered through the rocks and breakers and entered the calm sheet of water within.

The pirates ashore on the island and on board the junks were all too busy to notice us, and indeed their eyes must have been wonderfully acute to have done so through the darkness that enveloped sky and sea alike, swallowing our little barque up in its folds; so, when we got well outside the reef and beyond the line of breakers Ching Wang put up a small sprit-sail, which he had been thoughtful enough to take out of the long-boat when he had secured the sampan, rigging it on top of one of his oars, and stepping it forward like a lug.

We then kept the wind which we knew was south-west on our port hand and pretty well abeam, steering as nearly as we could guess to the northward and westward, according to Captain Gillespie's directions to me; for there was not light sufficient yet to see my little pocket-compass so as to take the proper bearings for making a straight course to fetch the mouth of the Canton river.

When daylight came, fortunately, not a trace of the reef or the ship and pirate craft could be seen, though Ching Wang peered over our starboard quarter, where we ought to have sighted any trace of them, while I shinned up the little mast too for a better look-out.

Nothing was to be seen, not even a passing sail—only the rolling sea far and wide as far as the eye could reach, now lit up by the early dawn and rose-coloured in the east, where the sun, just rising above the horizon, was flooding the heavens with crimson tints, that presently changed to gold and then gave place to their normal hue of azure. This the ocean reflected with a glorious blue, seeming to be but one huge sapphire, except where crystal foam flecked it here and there from the topping of some impatient wavelet not content to roll along in peace till it reached the shore.

I could, of course, look at my compass now, and I noticed that by keeping the wind abeam we had been working in the right direction during the night, the head of the sampan now facing pretty nearly nor'-nor'-west, "and a little westerly too," as Tim Rooney enjoined on me at parting.

Ching Wang told me in his pigeon English that we must have already run from thirty to forty miles—"one hunled li," he said; so, we had therefore accomplished a quarter of our journey towards the coast.

The sun rose higher and higher, until it was almost over our heads at noon, when the wind dropping I found it very hot. Besides the discomfort of this the fact of our not getting on so fast as previously made me anxious about those we had left behind, although the Chinaman told me the pirates would not be likely to start fighting again until it was getting towards evening, which was their favourite time for attack, as they always kept quiet in the day.

They would, he said, be especially afraid now of making a row in the day more than at any other time, for fear of the sound of the fray being heard by the gunboat, which they knew was cruising about near.

"I only wish we could see it now, Ching Wang," I cried, thinking that before we got to the Canton river and returned with the man-of-war, all our shipmates might be murdered and the poor Silver Queen set fire to by the ruffians after pillaging her, as they would be certain to do when Captain

Gillespie and the brave fellows with him could hold out no longer. "I only wish we could sight her now."

"You waitee, lilly pijjin," said he. "Bimeby soon comee."

It was dreary work, though, waiting, for we were going along very slowly on the torpid sea, which seemed to swelter in the heat as the breeze fell; but about two o'clock in the afternoon the south-west wind springing up again, we once more began dancing on through the water at a quicker rate, the sampan making better progress by putting her right before wind and slacking off the sheet of our transformed sprit-sail. An hour later, Ching Wang, who had gone into the bows to look out, leaving me at the tiller, suddenly called out:

"Hi, lilly pijjin!" he shouted, gesticulating and showing more excitement than he had ever displayed before, his disposition generally being phlegmatic in the extreme. "One big smokee go long. Me see three piecee bamboo walkee, chop chop!"

I rose up in the stern-sheets equally excited; and there, to my joy, I saw right ahead and crossing our beam, a small three-masted vessel, showing the white ensign and blood cross of Saint George, the most beautiful flag in the world, I thought.

It was the gunboat, without doubt.

She had sighted us long before we noticed her; and seeing from our altering our course now that we desired to speak her, she downed her helm and was soon alongside the sampan.

Breathless, I clambered on board, a smart blue-jacket with "HMS Blazer" printed in gold letters on the ribbon of his straw hat, handing me the sidelines of the accommodation ladder, which reached far enough down for me to step on to it from the gunwale of the sampan; and when the lieutenant in command of the gunboat, a handsome fellow like Mr Mackay, addressed me, I could not at first speak from emotion.

But my mission was too important to be delayed, and I soon found my voice; a very few words being sufficient to explain all the circumstances of the case to the lieutenant.

"Full speed ahead!" he called out to the officer on the bridge, as soon as he had heard me out, directing also the blue-jacket who had received me at the entry port to pass the word down that he wanted to speak to the gunner; while Ching Wang was invited to come on board and the sampan veered astern by its painter and taken in tow.

The lieutenant turned to me when these orders had been given, although he did not keep me half a minute waiting; and, calling me by my name, which I had told him, said, "We shall be up to the pirates before nightfall, Mr Graham, for the old Blazer can go ten knots on an emergency like this. I've no doubt we'll be in plenty of time to rescue your shipmates before they have another brush with the pirates."

He then invited me to go below and have some refreshment; but I was too anxious about those on board the poor Silver Queen to care about eating then. However, I took a nice long drink of some delicious lemonade with pleasure, for I was so thirsty that my tongue had swollen to the roof of my mouth; while Ching Wang, who had recovered his usual placid and imperturbable demeanour, accepted the hospitalities of the crew with great complacency, his emotion not affecting his appetite at any rate.

If I did not care about eating, though, I was highly interested in the preparation of the Blazer presently for action, her

John Conroy Hutcheson

five-inch breech-loaders being loaded with Palliser shell and the hoppers of her machine-guns filled; while the crew with rifles in their hands and cutlasses by their side mustered at quarters.

"I think, Mr Graham," said the lieutenant, noticing my admiring gaze, "we'll be able to teach your Malay friends something of a lesson—eh?"

"I hope so, sir," I replied. "I don't think there's much thinking about it, though. I'm only afraid they'll run away before we can reach them."

"No fear of that," said he laughing. "The Blazer, as I've told you, can travel fast when we want her; and if she's not fast enough, why, that gun there on the sponson forrud can send a speedier messenger in advance of her, to tell the pirates she's coming!"

"Will it reach them inside the reef, sir?"

"Reach them inside the reef!" he repeated after me in a quizzing sort of way. "Of course it will, my lad, and further too. That gun will carry seven miles at an elevation of less than forty-five degrees!"

"Oh, crickey!" I exclaimed; whereat he and the other officers laughed at my astonishment, which my face betrayed, of course, as usual. The crew, though, who were near were too well trained to laugh, except according to orders. Being men-o'-war's men, they only smiled at my ejaculation.

It was getting on for sunset when we sighted the Pratas shoal, the masts of the Silver Queen being seen much further off than the reef, although I forgot to mention that her sails of course had been furled after she grounded; and, as we got nearer and nearer, we did not hear any noise of rifle shots, or the junks' matchlocks, as would have been the case if they had been fighting again—my comrades I was certain would die dearly.

I hoped that they had not begun yet; for I could not bear to think that their fate might have been sealed in my absence, and all those brave fellows, perhaps, been butchered by the pirates!

Closing in upon the reef and making for the entrance on the south-west side, we noticed that boats were passing to and fro between the junks and the ship.

Just then a puff of smoke came from the stern of the ship, followed by the sound of a rifle shot in the distance, after which followed a regular fusillade of musketry fire.

The lieutenant had meanwhile not been idle, the man-of-war's launch and pinnace having been lowered with their nine-pounders in the bows, all primed and loaded; and, on my getting after him in the pinnace, he gave the order to pull in towards the scene of action, the gunboat meanwhile bringing her big Armstrongs to bear on the fleet of junks in the middle of the lagoon, only waiting until we got well up to the ship before firing so as to take the pirates by surprise.

I cannot describe the feeling I had as we dashed forward, the thought of checkmating the bloodthirsty scoundrels and saving my shipmates being too great to be expressed by words.

Ching Wang, whom the lieutenant allowed to come in the pinnace with me, also looked wonderfully excited again, for one generally so phlegmatic:—he seemed really to turn his back on the traditions of his race.

John Conroy Hutcheson

We, though, rushed forwards; and, when close to the Silver Queen, the lieutenant ordered the captain of the gun in the bows to "fire!" into a junk that was coming round under her stern.

"Bang!" and a shell burst right in the centre of the junk's bamboo deck, sending forty of the villains at least to Hades, for she was crowded with men. A wild yell of surprise came from the pirates at the report of the gun, succeeded by a faint hurrah from those on board the Silver Queen. This told us that Captain Gillespie and the rest now knew, from the second report caused by the bursting of the shell, that their rescuers had at last arrived, in the very nick of time.

Then a big boom rolled in from seaward as the gunboat opened fire with her five-inch Armstrong, shell and shot being pitched into the group of junks as fast as those on board the Blazer could load; the launch and pinnace, with Ching Wang and myself in the latter, pulling to the ship and boarding her on both sides at the same time.

Captain Gillespie and all the hands who had been intrenched in the cabin, now burst out of their prison; and after this, those pirates who were not cut down by the men's cutlasses or shot, surrendered at discretion, as did also their brother scoundrels on the island and in the junks, who were all caught completely in a trap, there being no creeks here for them to smuggle their boats into, nor mountain fastnesses to retreat to, the gunboat commanding the only way of escape open to them, and her launch and pinnace within the lagoon having them at their mercy.

"Begorra I am plaized to say you ag'in, Misther Gray-ham, sorr!" cried Tim Rooney, wringing my hand again and again as Mr Mackay released it—all the poor fellows who had been relieved from almost instant death by the coming of the gunboat seeming to think that I had brought about their rescue, whereas, of course it was Ching Wang who ought to be thanked, if anybody had to be praised, beyond Him above who had sent us on our mission and brought the Blazer up in time. Tim, too, was even more absurd about the whole matter than any of the rest.—"Bedad, you've saved us all, sorr," said he again and again; and I could only get him off this unpleasant tack by asking what further damage the pirates had done after I left.

They had not done much, he said, their leader having only just succeeded in breaking open the main-hold, and just beginning another attack on the cabin, when the report of the shell from the Blazer's pinnace as it burst made the pirates scramble overboard for their lives.

"But, sure, I caught that chafe villain av theirs, at last, Misther Gray-ham."

"Oh, did you!" I cried. "That chap in the red sash?"

"Aye, I kilt him as de'd as mutton jist now by the dor av me cabin in the deck-house, where, would ye belaive me, sorr, the thaife wor drainin' the last dhrop av grog out av me rhum bottle!"

"He didn't steal it though," said I, telling him all about Ching Wang's plot for making the rascal drunk; whereat Tim was highly delighted, patting the Chinaman on the back as the latter blandly smiled and beamed upon him, not understanding a word he said. After this matter was settled I bethought me of my bird "Dick."—"And how about the starling?"

"Oh, that's all roight," said Tim. "He scramed out 'Bad cess to ye' whin he saw the ugly pirate cap'en fall, an' sure, that

John Conroy Hutcheson

wor as sinsible as a Christian."

Everybody had got off pretty well, the majority only having a few slight scratches and flesh wounds; all, save, of course. the three of the hands who had been killed on deck in the first attack, and poor Mr Saunders, who, Tim said, was sinking fast.

He did not die yet awhile, though, having a wonderful constitution and persisting in eating and living where another man would have expired long since.

And the ship? She wasn't lost after all, as might have been thought, albeit ashore there on Prata Island and inside the reef. Oh, no. Mr Mackay managed it all, and surprised everybody by the way he did it—making even Lieutenant Toplift of the Blazer open his eyes.

I'll tell you what he did.—Our chief mate battened down two of the pirate junks, making them water-tight, and then, weighting them with heavy ballast till their decks were almost flush with the water, he made them fast under the bows of the ship.

The ballast was then taken out of them, when, of course, as they floated higher they lifted the Silver Queen; and a stream anchor being then got out astern she was floated out into the lagoon, where on subsequent examination she was found pretty water-tight below and staunch and sound all round.

To get her out of the lagoon, the passage through the reef was well buoyed and the ship lightened of her cargo, a large portion of which was taken out of her and stowed in the junks.

She was then kedged over the reef, as Tim Rooney had

suggested to Mr Mackay in the first instance as the best plan; the Blazer's officers and crew helping us to get her outside, and afterwards assisting us in loading her up again.

Then, our dear old barquey sailed for Hongkong, where she put in for temporary repair so as to be able to prosecute the remainder of her voyage, and here poor Mr Saunders died at last, and was laid to rest in "Happy Valley," the English burying-place, that has such a poetical name and such sad surroundings!

We were detained nearly a month here docking, and during our stay Captain Gillespie rejoiced all hands by rewarding them for their pluck in fighting and floating the ship again with the present of a month's wages for a spree ashore. "Old Jock" could well afford to be liberal, too; for a native speculator gave him a better price for the balance of his marmalade than he would have realised if he had fed the men on it throughout our home voyage.

Our repairs and refit being at last completed we set sail for Shanghai, casting anchor in the Yang-tse-kiang eight days exactly after our leaving Hongkong.

John Conroy Hutcheson

CHAPTER SEVENTEEN

HOMEWARD BOUND

"Bedad, sorr, it sames I'm dhramin', sure," observed Tim Rooney to Mr Mackay as the two now stood together on the forecastle, looking out over the hows. "It's moighty loike the ould river; an' I'd a'most fancy I wor home ag'in, an' not in Chainee at all at all!"

"You're not far wrong, bosun," replied Mr Mackay, smiling at his remark, or rather at the quaint way in which it was made. "I can fancy the same thing myself, the appearance of the Yang-tse-kiang hereabouts being strangely like that of the Thames just below Greenhithe."

I, overhearing their conversation, thought the same too; for, although, of course, there was no dome of Saint Paul's in the distance, nor forests of masts, nor crowds of steamers passing to and fro, nor all that bustle of business and din and dense black smoke from those innumerable funnels that distinguishes the waterway which forms the great heart artery of London, still there were many points of resemblance between the two—the show of shipping opposite Shanghai, where we lay, being almost as fair as that which is to be seen sometimes at the mouth of the Thames on a fine day, when it blows from the south and there are many wind-bound craft waiting to get down Channel.

The sampans and other native boats, darting about hither and thither in shoals, somewhat made up for the absence of the panting tugs and paddle steamers plying on the former stream, albeit there was no deficiency here either of Fulton's invention, steamers running regularly a distance of more than seven hundred miles up the Yang-tse-kiang; and, as for houses and the signs of a numerous population, there were plenty of these, although different to the bricks and mortar structures of our more accustomed eyes in England, with the peaks of pagodas doing duty for church spires, while the paddy fields planted with rice on either hand offered a very good imitation of the low-lying banks of our great mother river along the Essex shore.

"Aye, it's the very image, an' as loike as two pays," reiterated Tim Rooney on my joining the two. "Don't ye think so, too, Misther Gray-ham?"

"I wish you would leave the 'ham' out of my name!" I replied laughing, but a bit vexed all the same. "I think you might by this time, it's getting quite a stale joke."

"Faix, I dunno what ye manes, sorr," he replied, pretending to be puzzled, but the wink in his eye showing clearly that this density of his mental powers on the point was only assumed. "Sure, an' I can't hilp me brogue, ye know, if ye manes that?"

"Nobody says you can," said I rather shortly; for one or two of the hands by the windlass bitts were grinning, as well as Sam Weeks who was standing by, too, and I did not like being made fun of before them. "No one could mistake you for anything else but a Paddy all the world over!"

John Conroy Hutcheson

"Begorra, an' I'm proud av that very same, Misther Gray-ham," he retorted, not one whit put out by my words, as I imagined he would be. "If other folks had as little to be ashamed av, it's a blissid worrld sure this'd be, an' we'd be all havin' our wings sproutin' an' sailin' aloft, loike the swate little cheroob, they says, looks arter poor Jack!"

A general laugh followed this; and the captain just then coming out of his cabin, where he had been busy getting all his papers and bills of lading together, and ordering the jolly-boat to be lowered to pull him ashore, Tim turned away to see to the job—so, he had the best of me in our little skirmish, albeit we were nevertheless good friends afterwards.

In the afternoon, Captain Gillespie came off to the ship again, with a gang of coolies under a native comprador. These were sent by the consignees to help discharge the cargo into a lot of small junks that they brought alongside; but the Chinamen made a poor show, contrasting their work with that of our stalwart able-bodied tars, one of whom thought nothing of handling a big crate as it was hoisted out of the hold which it took ten of the others merely to look at.

Fortunately, only a few boxes of the Manchester stuffs that were stowed in our fore compartment were found damaged by the sea, the rest of the goods being in good condition, and the cargo generally as sound as when it came on board in the docks; a result which afforded "Old Jock" much satisfaction, as he had feared the worst. The only loss, therefore, the owners would have to suffer would be the small amount of our freight that had been jettisoned when the ship first went ashore on the Pratas, the cargo that had subsequently been taken out to lighten her before getting her off the shoal having been carefully preserved.

"'All's well that ends well,'" cried he, rubbing his hands and sniffing and snorting, when the people ashore reported this after a systematic examination of all the bales and stuff. "I told ye so, Mackay, I told ye so; and when I say a thing, ye know, I mean a thing."

"I'm sure, I'm only too glad everything has turned out right," replied the first mate, smiling to himself, though, at "Jock's" assertion of having prognosticated this favourable issue, the contrary being the case; for, he'd been grumbling all the way from Hongkong about the salvage to be paid, and compensation to the consignees for deterioration of the cargo, besides perhaps demurrage for late delivery, the ship arriving at Shanghai more than a month beyond her time. "'All's well that ends well,' as you say, sir; and I only hope we'll soon have a freight back which will recoup any loss the owners may have suffered from the mishaps of our voyage out."

But, hoping for a thing, and having it, are two very different things.

It was the middle of July when we finally reached Shanghai, and it took us, with the slow way of going to work of the Chinese coolies and their comprador and the people ashore and all, a good three weeks to unload our cargo; so that, by the time we had the hold swept out and got ready below for the reception of a freight of tea promised the captain, lo and behold we found we were too late, for the consignment intended for us was now well on its way home in another vessel. This latter, however, we were told in excuse for our disappointment, had been waiting longer for a cargo than us, having been lying in the river since May, and only starting off as we commenced discharging.

We were cheered up, though, by the hope of having a cargo of the second season tea, which the shore folk said was expected in the town from up country shortly; which "shortly" proved to be of the most elastic properties, it being September before we received authoritative information of our expected freight being at last at Shanghai and ready for shipment.

When it came, though, we did not lose much time in getting it on board and stowed, even Tom Jerrold and I working under hatches.

"Begorra, we'll show them poor craythurs," cried Tim Rooney, bracing himself up for the task and baring his sinewy arms with much gusto as he buckled to the job, setting the hands a worthy example to follow. "Aye, we'll jist show them what we calls worruk in our counthry, me darlints. Won't we, boys?"

"Aye, aye," roared out the men, all anxious to set sail and see Old England again; sailors being generally the most restless mortals under the sun, and never satisfied at being long in one place. "Aye, aye, bo, we will!"

And they did, too, "Old Jock" rubbing his hands and snorting and sniffing in fine glee as the tea-chests were rattled up out of the junks alongside and lowered into the hold, where they underwent even a greater amount of squeezing and jamming together than our original cargo out, the process of compression being helped on by the aid of the jack-screws and the port watch under Mr Mackay—who now superintended the stowage of the cargo, in place of poor Mr Saunders. No one, apparently, save the faithful Tim Rooney, gave a thought to the latter, now resting in his quiet tomb in Happy Valley!

"Bedad, we miss our ould sickond mate, sorr," I heard him say to Mr Mackay, who was a little strange to the job, having had nothing to do in the stowing line for some time, his duties as first mate being more connected with the navigation of the ship. "He wor a powerful man to ate, sure; but he knew his way about the howld av a vissil, sorr, that same."

"That means, I suppose, bosun," replied Mr Mackay laughing and coughing as the tea-dust caught his breath, "that I don't—eh?"

"Be jabers, no, sorr," protested Tim; "I niver maned to say that, sorr, aven if I thought it. But poor ould Misther Saunders samed, sorr, to take koindly to this sort av worruk, betther nor navigatin'; which he weren't a patch on alongside av you, sorr, as ivery hand aboard knows."

"Get out with your blarney," said Mr Mackay good-humouredly, urging the crew on to fresh exertions by way of changing the topic. "If we stop jawing here long we'll never sail from Shanghai before next year. Put your hearts in it, men, and let us get all stowed and be done with it."

"Look aloive," yelled the boatswain, following suit; "an' hurry up wid thim chistesses—one'd think ye wor goin' to make the job last a month av Sundays, sore!"

They "hurried up" with a vengeance; so that, before the week was out, the tea was all stowed and the hatches battened down, with the ship quite ready to sail as soon as Captain Gillespie got all his permits and papers from the shore—of which latter, by the way, I may confess, Tom Jerrold and I got tired at last.

I had received no less than three letters from home, all in a batch, when we got to Shanghai, one also coming after we arrived, telling me about father and them all; and it seemed, as I read of their doings at the vicarage and what went on at

John Conroy Hutcheson

Westham, as if it had been years since I left England, instead of only six months or so passing by; the change of life and all that had happened making me feel ever so much older.

However, reading these dear home letters made me long all the more to get back and see them again; and, in anticipation of this, you may be certain I did not forget to make a good collection of nice things for mother and my sister Nellie, as well as some "curios" for father, such as he had promised in my name when the letter came which made my mother grieve so, telling that all the arrangements had been completed for my going to sea,—do you recollect?

Yes; and besides the curios I myself bought ashore, I had one given me, at the very last moment before we left the Yang-tse-kiang, by Ching Wang, who, much to the surprise of all, said he wasn't going back in the Silver Queen—not, at all events, this voyage, he made the captain understand, being desirous of remaining at Shanghai until the next year.

"Me likee lilly gal, she likee me," he explained with his bland vacuous smile and his little beady eyes twinkling. "Me wifoo get chop chop. Two men not stop one placee—no go ship and 'top shore too."

"You rascal!" shouted "Old Jock" in a rage, "you served me just the same trick the voyage before last. You'd better come with us now, for I'm hanged if I give you the chance again."

"No, cap'en," grinned the imperturbable Chinaman, "no can do."

So, amidst the chaff of the men, who asserted that Ching Wang must have about fifty wives by this time at various ports, considering the number of times he had contracted matrimonial engagements, he went over the side into a sampan he had waiting for him, smiling blandly to the last, and giving me as a parting present the little brass figure of Buddha which he worshipped as his deity. This was a sure token of the strong affection he entertained for me, his "lilly pijjin," as he always called me from the time that Tim Rooney had commended me to his good graces.

"He'll come back with us next trip," said Mr Mackay, as he with all of us gave Ching Wang a parting "chin chin" on the celestial cook being presently rowed ashore in great state, sitting in the stern-sheets of his sampan and beaming on us with his bland smile as long as his round face could be distinguished, dwindling away in the distance till it finally disappeared. "I'm sorry to lose him, though, sir, for he was a capital cook, besides being a plucky fellow. Recollect how he helped to save all our lives the other day, as well as the ship and cargo."

"Humph!" grunted "Old Jock," who appeared to have forgotten this. "He's served us a shabby trick now, by going off like that at the last moment, and I've half a mind not to have any truck with him again."

"Ha, ha, cap'en," laughed Mr Mackay, "you said so last time, don't you remember? Yet, you brought him aboard again with the other hands before we started from Gravesend this trip. You're too good-natured to bear in mind all the hard things you say sometimes."

"Perhaps I am, Mackay, perhaps I am," sniggered and snorted "Old Jock," thinking this a high compliment. "Though, when I say a thing, I mean a thing, you know."

Ching Wang, when he got ashore, did not forget his old friends and leave us altogether in the lurch; for he sent off a black cook, a native of Jamaica, one Tippoo by name, to take his place; and as a messenger from the brokers on shore came off at the same time with the ship's papers, nothing now delayed our departure from Shanghai.

Then was heard Tim Rooney's piercing whistle once more on board, and the welcome—thrice welcome cry:

"All ha-a-nds make sail!"

The topsails were soon loosed by one watch, while the other hove up the anchor in fine style to the chorus of "Down in the lowlands, oh!"

"Up and down!" cried Matthews on the forecastle, taking poor Saunders' place here, for he was now doing duty as second mate, although he had not yet passed the Trinity House examination for the post. "Anchor's up and down, sir!"

"Then heave and paul!" answered Mr Mackay from the poop, calling out at the same time to the men standing by the halliards: "Sheet home and hoist away!"

In another minute, the topsails were dropped and the yards hoisted, the jib run up and the spanker set; when, as our anchor cleared the ground, soon peeping over our bows and being catted and fished in the old fashion, the Silver Queen's canvas filled and she bade adieu to China with a graceful curtsy, making her way down the Yang-tse-kiang at a rate that showed she was as glad as those on board her to lose sight of its yellow waters at last!

It was the 14th September when we sailed; and, although it was rather early in the year for it, the nor'-east monsoon had already begun to blow, fine and dry and cold, bowling us down through the Formosa Channel and into the China Sea beyond, "as if ould Nick war arter us," as Tim Rooney said.

In our progress past the same latitudes in which we had previously encountered such perils, we now met with nothing of interest; steering south by the Strait of Gaspar—to the other side of the island of Banca, instead of by our former route when coming up—we navigated Sunda the same day, getting out into the Indian Ocean at the beginning of October.

Shaping a course from here to pass about a hundred miles to the southward of Madagascar, our nor'-east wind changing to a nor'-westward in 15 degrees south latitude, which was all the more favourable for us, we were able to fetch the Cape of Good Hope in forty-three days from our start. Our passage round the stormy headland was now comparatively easy, being aided by the strong current that comes down the African coast through the Mozambique, and so did not cost us any bother at all, as we had fine weather all the time until we turned into the Atlantic.

From the Cape to the Channel we made a splendid passage, sighting the Lizard on the 20th December and getting into dock on the afternoon of the 22nd of the month. Strange to say, too, we were towed up from the Downs by our old friend the Arrow, just as we were towed down the river at starting on our eventful voyage.

Captain Gillespie gave me leave to go home the next day, telling me he would write when the ship would be ready again for another trip early in the following year; and so, bidding my mess-mates a cordial farewell, I was soon in a train on my way to Westham once more, with "Dick" the starling in a bran new wicker cage I had bought for him at Shanghai, as well as my sea-chest packed full of presents for the home-folk and everybody.

John Conroy Hutcheson

It was late in the afternoon of Christmas-eve when I reached the old well-known little station, which seemed to look ever so much smaller than when I left; and the very first person I saw whom I knew—none of my people coming to meet me, as they did not know when I would arrive, not expecting me indeed until the next morning—was Lawyer Sharpe, as ferrety-looking as ever!

He gave me a hearty greeting, however, saying he was glad to see me back again, and to have "ocular demonstration," as he expressed it, that I had not been lost at sea as was reported; so, I recalled what father had said when I had turned up my nose at the legal profession, and thought Mr Sharpe no doubt was misjudged by a good many, and might not be altogether such a tricky customer as the Westham folks made out.

Leaving my traps at the station to be sent on by a porter, only taking Dick's cage with me, I was soon trotting along through the village, passing old Doctor Jollop on my way. He, too, was the very same as ever, without the slightest alteration, muddy boots and all; for, although there was a little sprinkling of snow on the ground, as befitted the season, it had thawed in the streets of Westham, and as a matter of course the doctor, who always appeared to choose the very muddiest of places to tramp in, had managed to collect as much of the mire as he could on his boots and legs.

But, mud or no mud, he was a jolly kind old fellow, and more really pleased again to see me than—even with the most charitable feelings I must say it—Lawyer Sharpe pretended to be.

"Just back in time, Allan, for the plum-pudding," he called out on seeing me. "Eh, my boy, eh?"

"Yes, sir," said I, laughing as I shook hands with him. "Just in time for it."

"And the pills, too," he added, chuckling as he went into a cottage close by. "And the pills, too; you mustn't forget them."

Nasty old fellow, as if I wished to be reminded of anything so disagreeable at such a moment!

The next instant, however, I was at the vicarage gate, when Nellie, who was on the watch, although as I've said I was not expected till next day, flew out of the porch and had her arms round my neck, with my mother after her and father and my brother Tom, too—the latter bringing up the rear, his dignity not allowing him to hurry himself too much; and what with meeting and greeting these all thoughts of Doctor Jollop and his pills and everything else were banished from my mind—everything, save the delicious feeling of being at home again.

"And what have you here, Allan?" inquired sister Nellie when all the kissing and hugging was over, and I'd asked and answered at least a thousand questions. "A bird?"

"Yes, a starling," said I, introducing Dick and telling them his history as we all went back into the house, keeping this a surprise and not mentioning about the little beggar in my letter from Shanghai. "I've brought him home for you, Nellie."

"Oh, thank you, Allan," she cried, hugging me again. "What a dear little fellow!"

"Ah, wait till you hear him talk," said I, speaking to Dick and giving him my old whistle, "Dick, Dick!"

"Hullo!" cracked the starling, so comically, in Tim Rooney's voice that they all burst out laughing, "here's a jolly row!"

Dick then whistled a couple of bars, which was all he could accomplish, of "Tom Bowling," after which he ejaculated his favourite expression, "Bad cess to ye!" in such a faithful imitation of my friend the boatswain's manner that father smiled with the rest; although he said drily, "Your bird, Nellie, I hope will learn better language when he has been amongst us a bit longer!"

My chest arriving presently from the station, I had the happiness of showing them all that I had forgotten none when away; for I had got a Mandarin hat for Tom, and two old china jars I had brought for mother delighting her heart, while Ching Wang's idol which I gave father especially pleased him. He became, too, I may add, all the more deeply interested in this little idol when I told him all the circumstances connected with it, and the impression the Chinaman's devotion to his god had made on me.

I have little further to say, having now given a full, true, and faithful account of my first voyage; although I might point out to you that I was no longer a "green" apprentice, but now able to "reef, hand, and steer," as "Old Jock," or rather Captain Gillespie to speak more respectfully of him, said when I was leaving the ship, expressing the hope of having me with him on his next trip out, as I "had the makings of a sailor" in me, and was "beginning to be worth my salt."

I had told father, though, so much about Tim Rooney, recounting all his kindness to me on board the Silver Queen from almost the first moment I saw him—almost, but not quite, the commencement of our first interview having been rather alarming to me—that nothing would suit him but my friend Tim's coming down to Westham for a short visit, if only for a day.

Of course, I wrote to him, inclosing a letter father sent inviting him, and Tim came next day prompt as usual in his sailor fashion, winning all the hearts at the vicarage before he had been an hour in the place.

Father naturally thanked him for all that he had done for me, which made the bashful boatswain blush, while he deprecated all mention of his care of me.

"Bedad, sorr," said he to father in his raciest brogue, and with that suspicion of mirth which seemed always to hover about his left eye, "it wor quite a plisure, sure, to sarve him; for he's the foorst lad I iver came across as took so koindly to the thrade. 'Dade an' sure, sorr, I belaive he don't think none the worse av it now, by the same token; an' would give the same anser, sorr, to what I've axed him more nor once since he foorst came aboord us. Faix, I'll ax him now, your riverince. Ain't ye sorry, Misther Gray-ham, as how ye iver wint to say, now?"

"No, not a bit of it," replied I sturdily, in the same way as I had always done to his stereotyped inquiry. "And I'll go again cheerfully as soon as the Silver Queen is ready again for her next voyage."

"There ye are, sorr!" cried Tim admiringly. "He's a raal broth av a boy entoirely. Sure, he'll be a man afore his mother yit, sorr!"

Choose from Thousands of 1stWorldLibrary Classics By

A. M. Barnard
Ada Leverson
Adolphus William Ward
Aesop
Agatha Christie
Alexander Aaronsohn
Alexander Kielland
Alexandre Dumas
Alfred Gatty
Alfred Ollivant
Alice Duer Miller
Alice Turner Curtis
Alice Dunbar
Allen Chapman
Alleyne Ireland
Ambrose Bierce
Amelia E. Barr
Amory H. Bradford
Andrew Lang
Andrew McFarland Davis
Andy Adams
Angela Brazil
Anna Alice Chapin
Anna Sewell
Annie Besant
Annie Hamilton Donnell
Annie Payson Call
Annie Roe Carr
Annonaymous
Anton Chekhov
Archibald Lee Fletcher
Arnold Bennett
Arthur C. Benson
Arthur Conan Doyle
Arthur M. Winfield
Arthur Ransome
Arthur Schnitzler
Arthur Train
Atticus
B.H. Baden-Powell
B. M. Bower
B. C. Chatterjee
Baroness Emmuska Orczy
Baroness Orczy
Basil King
Bayard Taylor
Ben Macomber
Bertha Muzzy Bower
Bjornstjerne Bjornson

Booth Tarkington
Boyd Cable
Bram Stoker
C. Collodi
C. E. Orr
C. M. Ingleby
Carolyn Wells
Catherine Parr Traill
Charles A. Eastman
Charles Amory Beach
Charles Dickens
Charles Dudley Warner
Charles Farrar Browne
Charles Ives
Charles Kingsley
Charles Klein
Charles Hanson Towne
Charles Lathrop Pack
Charles Romyn Dake
Charles Whibley
Charles Willing Beale
Charlotte M. Braeme
Charlotte M. Yonge
Charlotte Perkins Stetson
Clair W. Hayes
Clarence Day Jr.
Clarence E. Mulford
Clemence Housman
Confucius
Coningsby Dawson
Cornel.s DeWitt Wilcox
Cyril Burleigh
D. H. Lawrence
Daniel Defoe
David Garnett
Dinah Craik
Don Carlos Janes
Donald Keyhoe
Dorothy Kilner
Dougan Clark
Douglas Fairbanks
E. Nesbit
E. P. Roe
E. Phillips Oppenheim
E. S. Brooks
Earl Barnes
Edgar Rice Burroughs
Edith Van Dyne
Edith Wharton

Edward Everett Hale
Edward J. O'Biren
Edward S. Ellis
Edwin L. Arnold
Eleanor Atkins
Eleanor Hallowell Abbott
Eliot Gregory
Elizabeth Gaskell
Elizabeth McCracken
Elizabeth Von Arnim
Ellem Key
Emerson Hough
Emilie F. Carlen
Emily Bronte
Emily Dickinson
Enid Bagnold
Enilor Macartney Lane
Erasmus W. Jones
Ernie Howard Pie
Ethel May Dell
Ethel Turner
Ethel Watts Mumford
Eugene Sue
Eugenie Foa
Eugene Wood
Eustace Hale Ball
Evelyn Everett-green
Everard Cotes
F. H. Cheley
F. J. Cross
F. Marion Crawford
Fannie E. Newberry
Federick Austin Ogg
Ferdinand Ossendowski
Fergus Hume
Florence A. Kilpatrick
Fremont B. Deering
Francis Bacon
Francis Darwin
Frances Hodgson Burnett
Frances Parkinson Keyes
Frank Gee Patchin
Frank Harris
Frank Jewett Mather
Frank L. Packard
Frank V. Webster
Frederic Stewart Isham
Frederick Trevor Hill
Frederick Winslow Taylor

Friedrich Kerst
Friedrich Nietzsche
Fyodor Dostoyevsky
G.A. Henty
G.K. Chesterton
Gabrielle E. Jackson
Garrett P. Serviss
Gaston Leroux
George A. Warren
George Ade
Geroge Bernard Shaw
George Cary Eggleston
George Durston
George Ebers
George Eliot
George Gissing
George MacDonald
George Meredith
George Orwell
George Sylvester Viereck
George Tucker
George W. Cable
George Wharton James
Gertrude Atherton
Gordon Casserly
Grace E. King
Grace Gallatin
Grace Greenwood
Grant Allen
Guillermo A. Sherwell
Gulielma Zollinger
Gustav Flaubert
H. A. Cody
H. B. Irving
H.C. Bailey
H. G. Wells
H. H. Munro
H. Irving Hancock
H. R. Naylor
H. Rider Haggard
H. W. C. Davis
Haldeman Julius
Hall Caine
Hamilton Wright Mabie
Hans Christian Andersen
Harold Avery
Harold McGrath
Harriet Beecher Stowe
Harry Castlemon
Harry Coghill
Harry Houidini

Hayden Carruth
Helent Hunt Jackson
Helen Nicolay
Hendrik Conscience
Hendy David Thoreau
Henri Barbusse
Henrik Ibsen
Henry Adams
Henry Ford
Henry Frost
Henry James
Henry Jones Ford
Henry Seton Merriman
Henry W Longfellow
Herbert A. Giles
Herbert Carter
Herbert N. Casson
Herman Hesse
Hildegard G. Frey
Homer
Honore De Balzac
Horace B. Day
Horace Walpole
Horatio Alger Jr.
Howard Pyle
Howard R. Garis
Hugh Lofting
Hugh Walpole
Humphry Ward
Ian Maclaren
Inez Haynes Gillmore
Irving Bacheller
Isabel Cecilia Williams
Isabel Hornibrook
Israel Abrahams
Ivan Turgenev
J.G.Austin
J. Henri Fabre
J. M. Barrie
J. M. Walsh
J. Macdonald Oxley
J. R. Miller
J. S. Fletcher
J. S. Knowles
J. Storer Clouston
J. W. Duffield
Jack London
Jacob Abbott
James Allen
James Andrews
James Baldwin

James Branch Cabell
James DeMille
James Joyce
James Lane Allen
James Lane Allen
James Oliver Curwood
James Oppenheim
James Otis
James R. Driscoll
Jane Abbott
Jane Austen
Jane L. Stewart
Janet Aldridge
Jens Peter Jacobsen
Jerome K. Jerome
Jessie Graham Flower
John Buchan
John Burroughs
John Cournos
John F. Kennedy
John Gay
John Glasworthy
John Habberton
John Joy Bell
John Kendrick Bangs
John Milton
John Philip Sousa
John Taintor Foote
Jonas Lauritz Idemil Lie
Jonathan Swift
Joseph A. Altsheler
Joseph Carey
Joseph Conrad
Joseph E. Badger Jr
Joseph Hergesheimer
Joseph Jacobs
Jules Vernes
Julian Hawthrone
Julie A Lippmann
Justin Huntly McCarthy
Kakuzo Okakura
Karle Wilson Baker
Kate Chopin
Kenneth Grahame
Kenneth McGaffey
Kate Langley Bosher
Kate Langley Bosher
Katherine Cecil Thurston
Katherine Stokes
L. A. Abbot
L. T. Meade

L. Frank Baum
Latta Griswold
Laura Dent Crane
Laura Lee Hope
Laurence Housman
Lawrence Beasley
Leo Tolstoy
Leonid Andreyev
Lewis Carroll
Lewis Sperry Chafer
Lilian Bell
Lloyd Osbourne
Louis Hughes
Louis Joseph Vance
Louis Tracy
Louisa May Alcott
Lucy Fitch Perkins
Lucy Maud Montgomery
Luther Benson
Lydia Miller Middleton
Lyndon Orr
M. Corvus
M. H. Adams
Margaret E. Sangster
Margret Howth
Margaret Vandercook
Margaret W. Hungerford
Margret Penrose
Maria Edgeworth
Maria Thompson Daviess
Mariano Azuela
Marion Polk Angellotti
Mark Overton
Mark Twain
Mary Austin
Mary Catherine Crowley
Mary Cole
Mary Hastings Bradley
Mary Roberts Rinehart
Mary Rowlandson
M. Wollstonecraft Shelley
Maud Lindsay
Max Beerbohm
Myra Kelly
Nathaniel Hawthrone
Nicolo Machiavelli
O. F. Walton
Oscar Wilde

Owen Johnson
P.G. Wodehouse
Paul and Mabel Thorne
Paul G. Tomlinson
Paul Severing
Percy Brebner
Percy Keese Fitzhugh
Peter B. Kyne
Plato
Quincy Allen
R. Derby Holmes
R. L. Stevenson
R. S. Ball
Rabindranath Tagore
Rahul Alvares
Ralph Bonehill
Ralph Henry Barbour
Ralph Victor
Ralph Waldo Emmerson
Rene Descartes
Ray Cummings
Rex Beach
Rex E. Beach
Richard Harding Davis
Richard Jefferies
Richard Le Gallienne
Robert Barr
Robert Frost
Robert Gordon Anderson
Robert L. Drake
Robert Lansing
Robert Lynd
Robert Michael Ballantyne
Robert W. Chambers
Rosa Nouchette Carey
Rudyard Kipling
Saint Augustine
Samuel B. Allison
Samuel Hopkins Adams
Sarah Bernhardt
Sarah C. Hallowell
Selma Lagerlof
Sherwood Anderson
Sigmund Freud
Standish O'Grady
Stanley Weyman
Stella Benson
Stella M. Francis

Stephen Crane
Stewart Edward White
Stijn Streuvels
Swami Abhedananda
Swami Parmananda
T. S. Ackland
T. S. Arthur
The Princess Der Ling
Thomas A. Janvier
Thomas A Kempis
Thomas Anderton
Thomas Bailey Aldrich
Thomas Bulfinch
Thomas De Quincey
Thomas Dixon
Thomas H. Huxley
Thomas Hardy
Thomas More
Thornton W. Burgess
U. S. Grant
Upton Sinclair
Valentine Williams
Various Authors
Vaughan Kester
Victor Appleton
Victor G. Durham
Victoria Cross
Virginia Woolf
Wadsworth Camp
Walter Camp
Walter Scott
Washington Irving
Wilbur Lawton
Wilkie Collins
Willa Cather
Willard F. Baker
William Dean Howells
William le Queux
W. Makepeace Thackeray
William W. Walter
William Shakespeare
Winston Churchill
Yei Theodora Ozaki
Yogi Ramacharaka
Young E. Allison
Zane Grey